MAD
WORLD

AN ORAL HISTORY OF
NEW WAVE ARTISTS
AND SONGS THAT DEFINED
THE 1980s

LORI MAJEWSKI / JONATHAN BERNSTEIN
FOREWORD BY NICK RHODES
AFTERWORD BY MOBY

ABRAMS IMAGE, NEW YORK

Editor: DAVID CASHION
Designer: EVAN GAFNEY
Managing Editor: DAVID BLATTY
Production Manager: ERIN VANDEVEER
Photo Research: MEG HANDLER

Library of Congress Control Number: 2013945690

ISBN: 978-1-4197-1097-1

Photo credits: Page 7: courtesy of John Taylor; p. 14: Allan Ballard/Scopefeatures; p. 19: (l) REX USA, (r) Richard Young/REX USA; p. 25: Charles Charas; p. 26: Associated Newspapers/Associated Newspapers/ REX USA; p. 32: Charles Charas; pp. 34–35: Paul Edmond; p. 40: EMI; p. 45: Paul Edmond; p. 46: Kevin Cummins/Getty Images; p. 53: Courtesy of Peter Hook Archives; p. 55: ABC Photo Archives/Getty; p. 61: Kevin Cummins/Getty Images; pp. 84–85: Elisa Leoneli/REX USA; p. 70: Warner Bros.; pp. 74–75: Kevin Cummins/Getty Images; p. 79: Charles Charas; p. 81: Warner Bros.; p. 82: Virginia Turbett/Getty ; p. 92: Ray Stevenson/REX USA; p: 98: Virginia Turbett/Getty; p. 105: Ilpo Musto/REX USA; p. 107: EMI; p. 108: Adrian Boot/Urbanimage; p. 114: Courtesy of Annabella Lwin; p. 120: poprockphotos.com; p. 124: Adrian Boot/Urbanimage; pp. 130, 134: Mute; p. 136: Keystone Colour/Getty Images; p. 140: L. J. van Houten/REX USA; p. 143: courtesy of Kim Wilde; p. 147: David Corio/Getty; pp. 152–53: 1980 © Laura Levine; pp. 158–59: poprockphotos.com; p. 185: Virginia Turbett/Getty; p. 186: Adrian Boot/Urbanimage; p. 173: ITV/REX USA; p. 174: Denis O'Regan/Getty; p. 181: Courtesy of Kim Wilder; p.183: poprockphotos.com; pp. 188–89, 191, 194: Courtesy Terri Nunn; pp. 196–97, 200: Fin Costello/Getty; pp.204–5: courtesy of Robbie Grey; p. 209: Sire; pp. 210–11: Fin Costello/Getty; p. 215: Eugene Adebari/REX USA; pp. 218–19: Gunter W. Kienitz/REX USA; p. 225: Eugene Adebari/REX USA; p. 226: Kevin Cummins/Getty; p. 230: Harry Goodwin/REX USA; p. 233: Warner Bros.; p. 234: Stephen Wright/Getty; p. 288: Kevin Cummins/Getty; pp. 242–43, 252: Universal Archives; p. 254: Mike Prior/Getty; p. 265: Kevin Cummins/Getty; p. 266: Hulton Archive/Getty; p. 272: PHOTOREPORTERS INC/REX USA; pp. 274–75: Rob Verhost/Getty; p. 283: courtesy of INXS; p. 284: Mike Prior/Getty; p. 292–93: Virginia Turbett/Redferns/Getty; pp. 300–301: courtesy of Bill Wadhams; p. 309: Michael Ochs Archives/ Getty Images; pp. 310–11: Retna; p. 315: Larry Ellis/Express Newspapers/Getty Images; p. 317: Columbia Records; p. 319: Courtesy of Moby; p. 320: (top) Julie Spinoso, (bottom) courtesy of Beatrice Colin.

Printed and bound in the United States
10 9 8 7 6 5 4 3

THE ART OF BOOKS SINCE 1949

115 West 18th Street
New York, NY 10011
www.abramsbooks.com

To John: "Your love is life, for love is land" (LM)

To Julius Bernstein, 1931–2013 (JB)

CONTENTS

he seventies were a remarkable time for modern music, producing an enormous diversity of artists across multiple genres. Rock was split into subcategories: progressive, glam, heavy metal, hard rock, and art rock. During the decade, strangely, these sounds co-habited the same airwaves alongside disco, reggae, electro, funk, and punk. By the late seventies, hip-hop and rap had begun to emerge. There were no rules, but somehow, having a unique identity was a requirement, and even the performers following a trend invariably carved out their own personalities. Everything was handmade: analog, no computers, and no digital vocal tuning.

My favored stick of rock was glam, where Bowie, T. Rex, Roxy Music, Sparks, and Cockney Rebel provided the soundtrack to my youth. Each had an individually captivating sound, and together they told the story I wanted to hear through those times in Britain. Other kids at school were lost in a haze of Pink Floyd and Genesis, or were queuing endlessly to secure Led Zeppelin tickets. We were all members of different factions, but wherever you belonged, the music was inspirational. It was an important voice in our culture, a way for our generation to express its singularity.

In 1976, suddenly everything else seemed "last summer." Punk exploded, blazing through much of the musical landscape that had come beforehand. It transformed the way we were. It was a revelation, an unprecedented surge of energy, but it also burned out fast. It was from these ashes that the music of the next decade was to rise. Bands like the Police, the Cure, and Siouxsie and the Banshees had already established their own sound and were able to drive smoothly into the eighties. Adam and the Ants remodeled and made the transition. Generation X did not—though Billy Idol had resurfaced as a solo artist by 1981.

In the afterglow of punk, there were unexpected outcomes. Being in a band now seemed startlingly possible; the obstacles had been removed. Everything was more accessible. Indie record labels were thriving. Small venues were springing up in every town. The music press was actively searching for the next sound. There were even opportunities to get played on late-night radio. Attitude and ideas had overthrown musical virtuosity. Just a few years earlier, when superstars were untouchable, none of this would have been attainable.

Technology was advancing fast, and the synthesizer was finally affordable, resulting in a stream of artists who integrated electronics into their organic sound. Gary Numan, Ultravox, and Japan were among those bridging the decades. The Human League became one of Britain's first purely electronic acts, and Joy Division fused punk, synths, and beats to pioneer the way for all that was to follow. Through the blurred edges of this period, a new wave of bands had been gestating and plotting their grand entrance. Those who materialized included U2, Depeche Mode, Spandau Ballet, Culture Club, Tears for Fears, the Smiths, and Duran Duran. While we each had entirely distinctive sounds and outlooks, there was a common thread: We had all experienced the U.K. during the seventies, under the same gray skies, enduring political turbulence and social unrest. We were different reflections of similar views, reactionaries to our surroundings. Some chose to express the darkness, others looked toward the light. In Duran Duran's case, we attempted to strike a balance between the two. We wanted to lift people's spirits, rather than fight misery with misery. If you limit yourself to grainy black

and white, you can create some beautiful imagery, but sometimes we simply wanted to use full, widescreen technicolor.

Although for a period of two years I was principally transfixed by punk, it was in 1977 that I properly discovered electronic music via Kraftwerk, who proved to be a lasting inspiration. Later that year, I also heard the song "I Feel Love," by Donna Summer, and this had a profound influence on how I perceived music from that point on. Additionally, it led me toward a greater appreciation of disco; Chic were now filed next to the Clash in my album collection. These elements, merged with many other stylistic references, formed the basic blueprint for Duran Duran: the raw energy of punk, disco rhythms, electro pulses, and the panache of glam rock, which was already deeply embedded in our consciousness. It was a band's manifesto that ultimately defined their characteristics and set them apart from their contemporaries. Broadly speaking, the artists who came up through this period took their influences from the same pool of musical predecessors. Yet there is no doubt that if all the members of those bands gathered together, opinions about the merits of those performers would vary enormously. That said, I am supremely confident that there would be one exception: We would unanimously agree upon David Bowie being the common pivotal influence on all of our collective musical styles.

Elsewhere in the world, Australia spawned INXS, who could have comfortably fit in with the British bands. However, in the United States, the musical DNA had metamorphosed in different ways. The Velvet Underground arguably invented alternative music. The Stooges and New York Dolls sowed the early seeds for a new wave. Patti Smith, the Ramones, Richard Hell and the Voidoids, the B-52s, Television, Blondie, and Talking Heads were seminal artists evolving through the mid-seventies CBGB scene, the latter two acts going on to produce some of the most significant albums of the early eighties.

Despite inroads made by the New York scene and a few other isolated bands, such as Devo, America still had a national propensity to gravitate toward traditional rock music. It looked unlikely that any international artists were going to break the radio blockade in the eighties, but change was on its way over the airwaves. Several alternative stations began to surface, WLIR in Long Island and KROQ in Los Angeles being among the first. They developed a contemporary audio language in stark contrast to the old guard, showcasing the brave and the new. This provided a platform for aspiring U.K. bands who had ventured to U.S. shores for the first time with a dream to break it big. As the radio format grew exponentially, a second transmutation occurred, this time within cable television: the launch of MTV, a 24-hour music-television channel. These factors greatly contributed to a seismic change. A second British Invasion was well underway in America, and the combined force of its new sounds broke down the doors.

In today's music world, there are very different factors crafting the careers of aspiring musicians. These are a reflection of our times and social attitudes. If there were no reality TV, and the Internet had not become a central portal in our lives, then music would have advanced in different ways. In my opinion, while reality TV creates opportunities for some, it takes away chances from others. Commercial radio has increasingly narrow playlists, and what is broadcast to the listening audience is in many ways more conservative and formulaic. The few remaining major record labels now spend markedly less time and money on artist development. Through massive exposure on TV, acts are rapidly thrust into the spotlight, frequently unprepared, and then usually exploited to within a breath of survival. The fallout of this evolution has established a culture wherein the public has a short attention span, with artists becoming more ephemeral, finding it harder to sustain a career.

But the way we consume music now is probably the greatest change of all. Everything is available everywhere, 24 hours a day, online. There are ceaseless choices, from every conceivable period and genre. The difficulty becomes making a decision . . .

Of course, there have been some other spectacular developments too, like the ability to create a song in your bedroom with a basic computer program, then instantly broadcast it online to a potentially immense audience. This kind of freedom opened a Pandora's box for the digital generation and has undoubtedly produced some notable artists pushing musical boundaries, particularly within the urban and electronic dance-music genres.

Personally, I always embrace progress and have little time for nostalgia, but it is important to put everything in context and to appreciate the best things that every period has to offer. Each band has their own story. We were lucky enough to grow up during an era when invention, experimentation, style, and innovation were applauded. It was a culture where the predilection was for standing out from the crowd rather than fitting in. Artists were musically adventurous, less driven by commerce, and their main objective was to create extraordinary music. If you happened upon commercial success, fame was a byproduct, rather than a priority. Idiosyncratic and eccentric songs often mingled in the mainstream charts. The public was open-minded, and there was a true appreciation for the currency of ideas and imagination.

One thing that remains as true today as it was in the eighties: While those in their teens and early 20s have a limited musical vocabulary, they remain the key source for change in music. Possibly it's a youthful energy, a swagger, a blinkered belief that they are right. Or perhaps it's something truly intuitive that they have learned from closely studying a microcosm of eclectic songs from the past and present. For us, when we started Duran Duran, we were absolutely convinced we were right. Our sound was going to be the future. Maybe that is true of all young artists. If you don't believe in yourself, nobody else will.

NR, London, 2013

**"New York to East California,
there's a new wave coming I warn you"**

Kim Wilde, "Kids in America"

"Just don't call it 'new wave.'"

Mute Records supremo Daniel Miller to this book's authors

WHAT IS NEW WAVE?
In the U.K., home to the majority of the artists featured in this book, new wave was initially code adopted by journalists and disc jockeys eager to be perceived as cool but too nervous to actually use the word "punk" with all its threatening implications.

In America, new wave was an umbrella the size of a circus tent. It covered synth pop, ska, goth, alternative rock, bubblegum, Eurodance, industrial, new romantic, blue-eyed U.K. soul, and electronic dance music. It was a Tower of Babel populated by American bands who wanted to be British, British bands who wanted to be German, and German bands who wanted to be robots. It was an insane asylum whose patients were predominantly ambiguous, untouchable males with sucked-in cheeks, 3-D makeup, and wedding-cake hair.

Perhaps America was overzealous in applying the term to anyone who didn't look or sound like George Thorogood and the Destroyers, but one thing united these two great nations: the shared understanding that the music produced between 1978 and 1985 marked the last golden age of pop.

This wasn't the first time that music was changed by maverick interlopers from another genre. David Bowie and Marc Bolan had both shrugged off the grubby vestiges of hippiedom and tumbled headfirst into glam. But it was the last time it would happen on a scale this massive and this weird. The biggest names who made the greatest hits were a generation of punks who turned themselves into international pop stars.

There are many compelling reasons why the punk proletariat seized the means of production and began poufing up their hair and slapping on the mascara. Here are a few:

1. Boredom and snobbery Once the initial shock value wore off, punk quickly decayed into a shout-y, guitar-banging dead end for its original practitioners. While there was an up-and-coming generation of bands in love with the prospect of forever being stuck in a shout-y, guitar-banging dead end (here's to you, Sham 69 and U.K. Subs), the first batch of British punks, most of whom were affiliated with London art schools, wanted to do everything they could to disassociate themselves with that unwashed mob.

2. Disco didn't suck. Not in the U.K., anyway, where black dance music had always been venerated and gay audiences had always been tastemakers. There, the summer of '77 wasn't just "God Save the Queen" and "White Riot," it was "I Feel Love" and "Staying Alive" too. As one-time punk rockers like ABC, Duran Duran, and INXS proved, disco and punk did not make strange bedfellows.

3. The British music papers You know how Fox News keeps its geriatric constituency in a constant state of paranoia and outrage by making sure every single day is the Worst Day Ever? (See: The War on Christmas! The New Black Panther Party! Death Panels!) The British music press operated in a similar manner. Only, to maintain a competitive edge, they went all out to make sure each week was the Best Week Ever. Punk was a massive shot in the arm for these papers; they had a revolution to write about, and all the main parties were easily accessible. Once the bloom faded from that rose, the papers had to find the next big thing. So every week

there'd be a new trend—mod! psychobilly! cowpunk!—and a fresh crop of stars in the making. If this manic approach shone a spotlight on people who had no business listening to music, let alone making it, it also set the stage for 2 Tone, the ascendancy of electronic music, and the rise of Britain's new breed of pop groups. In addition, it created a generation of artists to whom good reviews and music-press credibility still mattered. They wanted to look good, achieve fame, make money, and still be respected. And they saw this as an attainable goal because of . . .

4. Bowie The voice, the hair, the videos, the clothes. The way he cut up words to construct lyrical collages. The way he juggled genres. Pretty much every musician who drew breath in the eighties owes everything to the career blueprint of David Bowie.

5. *Top of the Pops* It was a cheaply made, poorly produced BBC show that had been a staple of British Thursday nights since Beatlemania, and it didn't discriminate. If you had a hit, you got to mime it in front of an audience that, at its eighties peak, grew past the 15-million mark. Spandau Ballet, Human League, OMD: All of them saw their cult followings swell and their chart positions soar because of *TOTP*. And most of them got so big that they could restrict their appearances and rely instead on . . .

6. Music videos and MTV MTV was originally conceived as a radio station with pictures—a network that sounded like American radio at the start of the eighties. The British bands who fled punk, embraced Bowie and disco, and who were hailed by the music press and appeared on *Top of the Pops* had no place on such a station. They were unknowns. They did not have significant live followings. The majority of them did not even have U.S. record deals. But the executives behind MTV were in such a mad scramble to get their new cable channel up and running that it never occurred to them to question whether there were sufficient videos by Journey, Loverboy, and Rod Stewart to fill out 24 hours of airtime. As it happened, there were not, which is why the network was forced to shift its gaze to Europe, where weirdly attired groups with indecipherable accents cavorted in overblown mini-movies. City by city, suburb by suburb, adolescent record buyers began pledging allegiance to Duran Duran, Eurythmics, and the Human League. A Flock of Seagulls followed, as did Depeche Mode and Simple Minds.

Were the artists ridiculous? Was the music overproduced? Was the influence of Bowie ubiquitous to the point of being suffocating? Guilty on all counts. But it was also an era of imagination, vaulting ambition, and incredibly memorable songs. The accidental British Invasion of the eighties created a world in which Madonna, Prince, and *Thriller*-era Michael Jackson thrived.

We're not saying great pop songs aren't written anymore. It's just that a decade of TV talent shows has given us a breed of performer whose only personality characteristics are humility, gratitude, and an undying love for their mommies. And when those humble, grateful performers embark on their careers, any remaining traces of their individuality and autonomy are autotuned out of them by superstar producers.

Mock and ridicule the excesses of the eighties if you want, but don't try and deny that the stars of the era had personality. They may have been pretentious, pompous, and absurd, but it was their own pretension, pomposity, and absurdity. They didn't have to bow their heads and nervously wait for the approval of a jaded record executive on a judging panel. Love or hate them, they were their own glorious creations. They were not boy bands. They were not manufactured. They were, for better or worse—worse being Kajagoogoo—the last of the big pop groups.

And their songs are still with us. You might laugh at them. You might yelp your way ironically through them at karaoke (in which case, put this book down. No, don't. Your money's as good as anyone else's. It's just your personality that's lacking). Or you may unabashedly love them. But you never forgot about them.

Neither did we, which is why we wrote this book. We wanted to know the stories behind our favorite songs from our favorite era. To find out, we phoned, Skyped and met up with some of our favorite acts, and we ended up reminiscing about a whole lot more: the good times, the bad times, the hits, the flops, the money, the madness, the fights and, of course . . . the hair.

Here's what this book isn't: a definitive oral history of the new wave era deserving of its own floor in the Smithsonian. Here's what it is: a random sampling of the decade, a bunch of snapshots summing up songs and artists embedded in our hearts. Your favorite eighties anthem might not be here; some obscure oddity might be in its place. But then, there might be something you haven't thought about in years and can't believe we were smart and resourceful enough to include, i.e., not "The Safety Dance."

Here's how it works: Each chapter begins with an introductory paragraph that puts the artist and song into a broader context—where and how they fit in with the culture, their enduring influence, and so on. Following that, we, the brilliant authors, provide individual commentary. *Who are we, and what makes us think our opinions matter?* Good question! We are Lori Majewski: American, obsessed past the point of sanity with Duran, Depeche, the Smiths, New Order and . . . you get the idea. She loves it all, uncon-ditionally, wholeheartedly, and hysterically. We are also Jonathan Bernstein: Scottish, sour by nature, too uptight and suspicious of emotion to declare himself a fan of anybody, but a staunch supporter of the sheer oddball nature of the era. Next, the artists recall their songs, careers, regrets, memories, and journeys. Although we conducted these interviews in time-honored Q&A style, we run the answers as edited monologues. All of the interviews were conducted individually. Finally, each chapter concludes with a "mixtape" in which we recommend similarly themed songs by other artists.

We're all too familiar with the strikes against the eighties: It was the video decade; the visuals took precedence over the music; it was all style over substance. The prosecution rests. We can't refute any of these charges. However, no music video, no matter how gargantuan the budget or drug-crazed the director, can salvage a dud song. And none of the 36 songs in this book are duds! These are the new classics: 36 songs that still have life left in them, that don't sound like relics, and that continue to get airplay and show up on soundtracks, compilations, and reissues. We fought over these 36 songs. We fought even harder over the other 36 we had to leave off the list. And there's another, other 36 we're still grumbling about having had to jettison. Toni Basil, your day will come! **JB/LM**

ADAM
AND THE
ANTS

"KINGS OF THE WILD FRONTIER"

Adam Ant was the male Siouxsie Sioux. Like the Banshees, the Ants were among the last of the original U.K. punk bands to sign a record deal. Like Siouxsie, Ant cultivated a darkly sexual, proto-goth persona, enjoyed a voluble, devoted following, and refused to skimp on the eyeliner. Unlike Siouxsie, Ant got no respect. In the late 1970s, Britain was able to sustain four weekly music papers, all of which wielded a degree of influence and regarded Adam and the Ants as a lamentable vehicle for a narcissistic phony. They labeled Ant an inauthentic buffoon, an art student dabbling in S&M imagery. The Adam and the Ants responsible for the likes of "Whip in My Valise," "Red Scab," and "Deutscher Girls" deserved most of the derision they received. But the Adam and the Ants who recorded the likes of "Kings of the Wild Frontier," "Dog Eat Dog," and "Antmusic"? They're a principal reason this book exists. When Ant decided to retire the empty shock value of his previous incarnation, to recruit co-conspirator, guitarist, and former Banshee Marco Pirroni and to launch an all-out assault on the mainstream, he did it in the weirdest way possible. None of the musical and visual elements Ant plundered for his reinvention pointed to his subsequent ascendance to teen idol status, but the totality of his image, his theatricality, and the sense of community in his calls-to-arms struck a massive chord. Refusing to settle for life as a stalwart of the independent circuit unshackled Ant's imagination and his ambition. He went from a punch line in bondage pants to the man who would be king.

JB: Forget the white stripe and the line "I feel beneath the white, there is a redskin suffering from centuries of taming." The only tormented minority Adam Ant truly identified with was the Entertainer. Adam and the Ants may have rebooted themselves with a chaotic new look and a vibrant new sound, but the dismissive treatment the old Ants had received at the hands of the media still rankled. "Kings of the Wild Frontier" is a squeal of outrage from a flamboyant, full-color performer freeing himself from a tawdry, foul-smelling, monochromatic post-punk universe. Ant basically had one theme:

 The artifice of show business was infinitely preferable to the music press–mandated notion of credibility. He rehashed that sentiment in "Prince Charming," "Stand and Deliver," and "Goody Two Shoes." But he never sounded so alive, so energized, and so hell-bent on writing his own legend as he did in "Kings of the Wild Frontier." It was a combination of the liberation he felt about throwing off his old (white) skin and the fact that no one had any expectations of him. It was the lingering resentment over the devious way momentary Svengali Malcolm McLaren made off with three of his Ants to form Bow Wow Wow. (For more on this sordid tale, see our Bow Wow Wow chapter on page 114.) It was the way Marco Pirroni's guitar twanged over the drumming duo's thundering Burundi beat. It was the way Ant announced his second act with the declaration "A new royal family! A wild nobility! We are the family!"

LM: There were two singers who shook me up in the way I imagine Elvis Presley did my late-1950s teenage counterparts: Michael Hutchence and Adam Ant. Neither was textbook handsome like, say, John Taylor or Rick Springfield. And while both were usually bare-chested under their tough-looking leather jackets, neither was what you'd call buff. Still, the way they moved onstage and made eye contact with the camera suggested they were sex incarnate. Watching these two, I was never so sure of my heterosexuality. But while Hutchence's deep, conversational singing voice always sounded bedroom-ready, Ant was capable of screams and yelps that suggested you caught him in the middle of the act. That has to be why Sofia Coppola chose "Kings of the Wild Frontier" for the scene in *Marie Antoinette* in which the queen finally finds coital satisfaction while cheating with the studly Count Fersen. When I met Ant for our interview, he made his entrance wearing eyeliner and eyeliner-drawn sideburns, and a pencil mustache that was more Captain Jack Sparrow than Prince Charming. Still, I couldn't help staring into his blue eyes and thinking, *Don't you ever stop being dandy, showing me you're handsome.*

ADAM ANT: I was doing graphic design at Hornsey College of Art. I started up a college band called Bazooka Joe. I was playing bass and writing and singing. Bazooka Joe did their debut in London at St. Martin's College of Art in November 1975. That was the night I saw the Sex Pistols—they were the support act. They looked great, dressed in really great clothes. They played very simple songs: Small Faces and Who covers and a few of their own. It wasn't screaming, 15-minute guitar solos in denim-clad outfits; it was, like, 10-second guitar solos. They were really tight. And they had a complete disregard and contempt for the audience that I'd never seen before and quite liked.

That was the catalyst. I thought, *Something's happening here, and it's not that difficult.* There were very few people who were interested in the Pistols at the start. Bazooka Joe were too set in their ways—they were a rock band and didn't like punk. So I left the band that night and formed the Ants, and that was the start of the career. That was the sort of influence the Pistols had on people. Most of the people in that room went on to form their own bands.

The early Adam and the Ants got a lot of criticism from the media, so much so that we didn't get signed. We had a large following, but they didn't care about that. They just didn't like the idea of signing me. Our first big single, "Dog Eat Dog," was more or less a general assault on the public. I thought our music was better than everyone else's, as every band does, and I put it lyrically. "Only idiots ignore the truth" was a result of being ignored for three years.

In 1979 Malcolm McLaren approached me at a party, and I was quite surprised, really. I think he'd been watching what we were doing and certainly liked the following. After the Pistols, I think he wanted that following. I enjoyed my time with Malcolm. I learned a lot—his theories became very useful to me in my dealings after that time. He stripped it down to a realistic approach to the music industry: simple things like don't be so esoteric; if you want a hit record, put your face on the cover; the structure of a good hit single. He was a great historian of music, which you wouldn't have thought. He came across as an anti-music person, but he actually knew a hell of a lot. And he became a friend, so it was a great loss when he died a few years back.

It wasn't exactly as Zen as that, though. I think he had the idea for Bow Wow Wow before he met me. It seemed like a mutiny at the time. But if it had to happen, it was the right time to happen. And no one can force you to do that. The other three saw a better opportunity to work in their own setup, so they did. I could never have worked for Malcolm. Bow Wow Wow was pretty much

Malcolm plus them backing his musical ideas. But they went off and did Bow Wow Wow, and I thought they did some good work. It also gave me an object of competition. I had my eye on them, and we had to blow them out of the water, and I think we did.✱ Annabella [Lwin, former Bow Wow Wow lead singer] is actually a friend of mine.

My songs tend to be a travelogue of my life. Every album has a different look, a different sound, different lyrical content. The hard, simple punk stuff of the first few singles was completely different from the first album, *Dirk Wears White Sox*, which was quite a weird record. It certainly wasn't a punk record. Then *Kings of the Wild Frontier* and *Prince Charming*—every album's been different from the one before.

I liked Lenny Bruce a lot. I'd been listening to him a lot in the late seventies, and Jackie Mason too. And during an art history course, I'd tapped into the Futurists, who were doing some amazing work in sculpture. They all basically got killed in the First World War, so there was only a tiny body of

work. I didn't particularly like their politics, but I thought their art was fantastic, marvelous. They were like the punk rockers of the art world, doing weird stuff, ballets and musicals where none of them could play at all. They'd just be blowing trumpets and beating each other up.

What I tapped into then and still do is history. I'm well up on the Regency dandy period. I love certain parts of military history: Napoleonic history, the Charge of the Light Brigade. I took all of these images that I'd grown up with and made a mutant, a hybrid. Punk got really dark by about '79—really druggie, really political, very gray, very nasty. I hated it. So I wanted to do something that was the reverse: colorful, heroic. Pirates and Native Americans were, in their pure essence, quite heroic themes. I'd done my homework on them, then blended them into this idea, and the music matched.

"Kings of the Wild Frontier" is really a mark on all sorts of colors and societies where you feel held back. The lyrics "I feel beneath the white, there is a redskin

---

✱ **LEIGH GORMAN, Bow Wow Wow, formerly of Adam and the Ants:** I remember Adam came on *Top of the Pops* with "Dog Eat Dog" with his white line on his face. I thought, *That's it. He's done it*. We'd just put out "C30, C60, C90, Go." The guy at the record label called up Malcolm and said, "These sales figures don't match your chart position. You guys should be at number 14 or 12 right now, and you should be going on *Top of the Pops*, but they've held you back." So we went over to EMI and trashed the place. I think we threw Cliff Richard [gold] records out the window. Malcolm was trying to create a stunt like the Pistols. It completely backfired: They didn't promote the single. And Adam comes along with his image, his better-sounding production, and his more innocuous lyrical subject, goes on *Top of the Pops*, and everyone goes nuts.

STYLE COUNCIL

"[Michael Jackson] phoned me up and asked where I got the jacket from." Ant says, "I told him where to go, and he went and got it. It's a hussar jacket, a theatrical costume from Bermans in London. I sent him down to my friend who worked there. He said, 'I want an Adam Ant jacket,' and they gave him one."

suffering from centuries of taming"—it's not just the color of your skin; it's the class you're born into. If you're born poor, if your parents don't have any money, it's quite a hard life for you. The Apache war stripe was a declaration of war, as I saw it, on the [record] industry I was up against. They were the enemy. But it was also quite a spiritual thing. I gained a great deal of comfort from studying their ways and philosophies.

When I came to the USA in 1981, I had a complaint from a Native American society in New York City, and I had to meet with them about it. They were concerned that I was using the stripe. They thought it was just me stereotyping Indians—I don't use the word "Indians"; it's "Native Americans." So I went to see them, I spent the day, and I said, "Look, come and see the show, and if you think I'm using it in a derogatory way, I'll take it off." They came to see it, loved it, and it was

all right. I got the go-ahead. I wouldn't have felt comfortable if I thought I was offending people for no just reason, the fact you just don't know your subject. My father was a Romani Gypsy, so I'm very up on the way the Gypsy society is portrayed. They're quite dismissive—they say "Gyppo," which is a slur. It's not nice. So having dealt with that in my family, you respect other people.

I write songs for me. I don't write songs for other people. As far as "Prince Charming" is concerned, I was addressing myself. I wanted to present myself in a good way. My granddad may not have had a lot of money, he may have been born in a caravan, but he looked very smart, very clean, and that stayed with me. That was part of the "Prince Charming" idea. "Ridicule is nothing to be scared of" was a line I felt was quite apt, certainly being in the pop business.

"Goody Two Shoes" was a manifesto

about what was happening at that point. "You don't drink, don't smoke"—purely because I didn't drink or smoke, people made assumptions. I thought that was quite a good lyric. And it worked. That certainly broke me in the States. "Two weeks and you're an all-time legend / I think the games have gone much too far," that was almost like saying, "Look, I've had enough of this," and I took all the makeup off.

When video came along, right there, there was a revolution that I was able to embrace. I had a film school training, so I storyboarded them myself, and I could co-direct them. The video became as important as, if not more important than, the music. It didn't hurt that I had had a video go out to homes in the USA before I arrived. When I did my first American tour, our record company commissioned a pirate ship to sail us up the Hudson River to our New York concert. They'd seen what was going on on MTV. People were dressing up like me before I even got here. That wouldn't have happened before video, because I would have had to go out and do the tours first. But those music videos . . . you can't put that on the radio.

In '81, I did a royal variety show. It was great playing for the queen, marvelous. It's very popular now—the pop world seems to fraternize a lot with the royals. But back then I got a lot of stick for doing it. They thought I'd sold out: "Oh, you've gone very straight." It was a very traditional thing for me to do. But the queen's very hip, as she proved with the [2012] Olympics. And she was then. I remember watching the Rolling Stones and the Beatles meeting the queen, so I thought it can be no bad thing.

MARCO PIRRONI: Adam and the Ants were basically the group I would dream about back in school. This wild, glam-rock, mishmash, looking-weird thing. I didn't have the pirates worked out, but I wanted everyone in the playground talking about us the next day. Like seeing Roxy doing "Virginia Plain" or Bowie doing "Starman" on *Top of the Pops*—as soon as you saw that, you couldn't watch the rest of the show. You couldn't sleep because you were so excited.

I was completely done with punk by the end of '77. It became an excuse to be stupid. It lost style; it lost subversiveness; it got really conformist. I thought the early punk thing was that old Oscar Wilde thing: "We're all in the gutter, but some of us are looking at the stars." Well, the second generation was basically just "We're all in the gutter." They never moved on. A lot of them still haven't.

I was sitting around waiting for another band to join when I got a call from Adam, which was a surprise. I knew him very vaguely. I'd seen all the incarnations of the Ants, and I thought they were really good.

They had some great songs but, me being me, I was always like, "I could do better."

It's really strange, because the only two bands I really liked were the Ants and the Banshees, and I got to join both. But journalists loved the Banshees and hated the Ants. I didn't think the Banshees were that great, to be honest. I thought the Ants were better. I didn't understand why there was this constant slagging. It felt like every review was bad. But then, you know what journalists are like, especially back in the day. They were powerful—talk about make-or-break. But "Kings of the Wild Frontier" did get good reviews. They were like, "You are a genius now."

When I started working with Adam, he'd just been thrown out of his band. It must have been a right kick in the bollocks. He called me up the day after and said, "Look, I've been thrown out of the Ants." I said, "Eh? How could you be thrown out of the Ants? Adam and the Ants!" I don't think the band was particularly happy. They weren't going anywhere. They got Malcolm in as a

last-ditch attempt, and Malcolm had other ideas. He had the Bow Wow Wow project. He thought, *I can use these three guys, but I can't use Adam—he won't do as he's told. He's going to be trouble.* I think Adam was curled up in the fetal position for at least an hour. I'm sure there were some tears. It was like, "Someone stole my girl! Fucking bitch, I'll show her!" Quite a normal reaction.

Malcolm had come up with all these ideas about the tribal drumming, and in my head, it was very much *The Good, the Bad and the Ugly.* There was a stage show called *Ipi Tombi* that was all African drummers, and Adam was like, "We should get these guys from *Ipi Tombi* down." I was terrified: "I don't know anything about African drummers, or how to get them, or what I'm supposed to do with them." Bow Wow Wow also used African drummers, but we went about it in a completely different way. I didn't see them as rivals as much as Adam did, because he obviously had personal issues. It did turn it into a bit of a race. Until we actually heard them. Once our album was number one,

MIXTAPE: 5 More Acts of Culture Plunder 1. "Buffalo Gals," Malcolm McLaren 2. "Rapture," Blondie 3. "Aie A Mwana," Bananarama 4. "John Wayne Is Big Leggy," Haysi Fantayzee 5. "Tantalize," Jimmy the Hoover

Adam wasn't feeling any need for revenge.

"Kings of the Wild Frontier" was the first song we wrote together. It was just two guitars. We didn't have any recording equipment. There was no way of recording it. We didn't even have a Dictaphone. We had to remember it every time we did it. It wasn't a fully formed concept at all. I had no clue about songwriting. If it was now, we could just get the records we want to sound like and sample them. But back then it was like we were working on this formless thing that didn't exist: African drumming plus twangy guitar. It was just a thing in our heads. It took fucking ages. We were in my house, this little flat in Earl's Court. We worked a few hours a day—you can't do more than that because then your mind starts going.

"None of us were averse to wearing makeup. Being glam rockers, Bowie and Roxy fanatics, we had no problem with it.... I'm still the world's greatest glam-rock obsessive."

You start forgetting everything. When we recorded it with the band, it was the first time it sounded like an actual song. But we always had the title. It was from *Davy Crockett*, which I used to love as a kid.

My guitar sound wasn't so much Duane Eddy; it's more James Bond. It also comes from Phil Manzanera's solo in the middle of "Needles in the Camel's Eye" [from Brian Eno's *Here Come the Warm Jets*]. There's a twangy guitar solo on *For Your Pleasure*. It was more John Barry and Ennio Morricone than Duane Eddy. That's the way I work: My mind is full of old records. It was also glam rock and Mick Ronson—he was my big guitar hero.

None of us were averse to wearing makeup. Being glam rockers, Bowie and Roxy fanatics, we had no problem with it. Having two drummers was totally Glitter Band–inspired. It also looked great. I'm still the world's greatest glam-rock obsessive. Totally pathetic. All my favorite records were made in 1972. *For Your Pleasure*, *Transformer*, *Electric Warrior* —that's what I still listen to. It's amazing I still find things to steal.

The record company left us alone. There were these A&R men—I don't know how old they were; they seemed ancient to me, [though they were] probably 24 or 26. They just took everything from the *NME*. When we said, "Look, we want to be this pop band with two drummers and lots of makeup," they were baffled. We said, "Let us try and explain. You know pop stars, right? You know how they go on telly, and they like guitars and girls and money?" "That's what you want to do?!" 'Cause that was the uncool thing. But we said, "Yeah!"

We weren't marketed. We were just left to our own devices. I didn't know that musicians were interfered with by A&R men. I didn't know what an A&R man did. We never went through the traditional routes—we never had art direction, we didn't go to budget meetings. We only did what we wanted. When we did "Prince Charming," it was like, "We're known for records with lots of drums on them—let's do a record with just one drum."

THAT WAS THEN *BUT THIS IS NOW*

Ant and Pirroni's hit-making partnership continued through the eighties and into the nineties with Ant solo singles "Goody Two Shoes" and "Wonderful." Pirroni went on to work with Sinéad O'Connor on her acclaimed albums *The Lion and the Cobra* and *I Do Not Want What I Haven't Got*. Meanwhile, Ant dabbled in stage and TV acting and moved to Tennessee to raise a daughter.

In the early 2000s, he was plagued by a well-publicized series of mental problems that saw him institutionalized on several occasions, including following a 2002 incident in which he threw a car alternator through a pub window. In 2011, he started playing live again with his new band, which he took to America in 2012 for his first tour of the States in 17 years to support his album,

Adam Ant is the Blueblack Hussar in Marrying the Gunner's Daughter.

ANT: I went to see *This Is It* after Michael Jackson passed away. I sat there and I thought, *A lot of the performers are going*. Poly Styrene had passed away, and a number of other musicians, and there is only a certain time in your life when you can physically keep doing this. I'm pretty fit, so I thought, *Now's a great time to get back on board*.

In 2013 [I released] a new album. It may have been 16 years between albums, but it's hopefully worth the wait. If I wanted to just do it for the money—and money's not a bad thing when you've got a family, you've got expenses—then I would've just done those eighties-hits tours where you get paid a lot to go out and sing your hits amongst other

"Not taking any time off for 20 years, it's hardly surprising I'd succumbed to [mental breakdowns]."

people from that generation. Once you do that, you can't really go back to being taken seriously as a competitive, contemporary artist. Fortunately, I've managed to steer clear of that.

It's very tempting because I was offered the O2 Arena. Take Spandau Ballet. I was offered that kind of situation where you hire a massive venue, like the O2, with 10,000 to 15,000 seats; they spend a year promoting it, and that's it. You've made your comeback. Where do you go from there?

Not taking any time off for 20 years, it's hardly surprising I'd succumbed to [mental breakdowns]. The main thing with mental health is to realize the alarm bells

and the triggers that cause it. In my case, it's primarily due to overwork. Anybody who's been through any kind of mental illness will tell you that you have to be very careful and live each day as it goes. I've learned to just say no. That was not the case before, where it was all, "Just do another few gigs," and "We've got to have the record out next Thursday." It was a [hamster] wheel. You've got to know how to get off. When I'm on tour, I'm really celebrating for myself. This is me having fun; this is me surviving. This is growing older with grace. There's still lead in the pencil.

PIRRONI: We were arrogant back then. We thought everyone else was shit. Looking back, they weren't all shit. That attitude was a reaction against bands like New Order,✳✳ which we hated. They were coming from exactly the same place we were. They had exactly the same records. But at the time, I hated all that gray, grim Northern bollocks. But now I can see it's just all *Low* and *Heroes*.

As far as working with Adam again, it would be nice one day, but I don't see it happening. We'd have to speak to each other to find that out, wouldn't we?

✳✳ **PETER HOOK, New Order:** Musically, I love Adam and the Ants. They're one of my favorite groups. But it was very difficult for me as a Northern male to relate to the dandy look. We would've been laughed out of Manchester had we even considered it. Bernard [Sumner] and I used to go out in London with all them lot—Siouxsie and the Banshees to the Embassy Club, Rusty Egan when he used to run the Blitz. We looked like working-class yobs, and everyone else was dressed up as a pirate. Leigh Bowery had a candle melted all over his head, and there's me and Barney in our motorbike jackets looking like greasers.

he late 1970s were teeming with highly regarded synthesizer acts of which great things were expected. The original, enigmatic incarnation of the Human League had a ton of U.K. music-press credibility and a fan following that included the godfather of new wave himself. "Listening to the Human League is like listening to 1980," Bowie said—in 1979. Meanwhile, Orchestral Manoeuvres in the Dark's debut single on Factory, "Electricity," put them near the top of most major labels' sign-them-now lists, and Ultravox received raves for their album *Systems of Romance*, which saw the group jettison their glam-punk origins and embrace the Teutonic android within. No one expected anything from Gary Numan. You could read your way through a small forest of British pop papers and magazines and never see his name. You could listen to months of late-night radio shows and never hear one of his songs. But Numan was the first and, albeit briefly, the biggest star produced by Britain's burgeoning electronic music scene. In 1979, less than a year after he made his recording debut, he had two consecutive number-one singles and albums in Britain, and by 1980 "Cars" hit the Top 10 in the United States. He was soon overtaken by the better-known electronic acts he had originally surpassed but, for one shining moment, Numan's out-of-nowhere success was like discovering an alien among us.

GARY NUMAN

"CARS"

JB: In 1972, David Bowie made his debut on *Top of the Pops* performing "Starman." The next day, legend has it, hardened British soccer thugs were slathering on nail polish and eyeliner. I was too young and clueless to have any lasting memory of that phenomenon. In 1978, Gary Numan, then the 20-year-old leader and focal point of synth act Tubeway Army, appeared on both *TOTP* and boring elder-sibling *The Old Grey Whistle Test* in the same week, performing "Are 'Friends' Electric?" While Numan didn't have quite the seismic generational impact that Bowie did, that one-two TV punch sired a vast cult of British Numanoids almost overnight—and that phenomenon, I was absolutely around for. Numan's glowering mass of worshipers, with their black hair, black suits, red ties, and mad, staring eyes, made quite the picture. Their idol may have lacked Bowie's performance skills, fluid sexuality, and unique vision, yet there was something about his chalky pallor, panicked gaze, and strangled yelp of a voice that made him seem like a genuine man who fell to Earth. Even when he tackled subject matter as universal as automobiles, he still seemed like an alien visitor awkwardly attempting to acclimate himself to human transportation. But whether you were entranced by his otherworldliness or felt outrage at his wholesale pilfering of leftover bits of Bowie, "Cars" is a compelling testimony to Numan's ability to pen a hook sturdy enough to last a lifetime.

LM: In 1980 I was nine years old, and my favorite group was Air Supply. My favorite album was the *Grease* soundtrack. My father had Warren Zevon's *Excitable Boy* on repeat. I knew nothing of Ziggy Stardust, so when "Cars" came out, I thought Gary Numan was the most original thing ever. He was like a space vampire. "Cars" was my introduction to new wave, and that momentous event occurred while I was simultaneously laying eyes on that space vampire! For me, that was the moment when video plunged a stake through the heart of the radio star. Although I didn't yet know what new wave was, I recognized this Gary Numan guy hailed the arrival of a new sound—music that was dance-y like disco, exciting, and futuristic. Later I found out that everything I thought was new and exciting about him had been ripped off from David Bowie. But I didn't care and still don't.

GARY NUMAN: My introduction to electronic music was by accident. I got signed up by the Beggars Banquet label with my punk band, Tubeway Army, at the end of '78, pretty much as the punk thing had peaked and was on its way out. They sent me to record what had been my live set up to that point, 40 minutes of punk songs. When I got to the studio, there was a Minimoog synthesizer in the corner of the control room waiting to be collected by a hire company, which, luckily for me, never turned up, and I was able to use it for two or three days. I'd never seen one before, and I loved it. It had been left on a setting that sounded amazing, this huge bottom-end, roaring, rumbling sound. I wouldn't have known how to get that sound; I didn't know anything about synthesizers. They were just a bunch of dials to me.

Over the next day or two, I was able to experiment. I developed a massive passion for electronic music practically overnight. I very hastily converted my pure punk songs into electronic songs, and I went back to the record company with a pseudo-electronic punk album. It wasn't what they wanted, it wasn't what they signed me for, and, understandably, they were quite unhappy with it. When we presented the album, it got really silly. One of the directors stood up to fight me—it got that childish. The thing that saved me was the record company had no money whatsoever. Whatever tiny budget they had to put me in the studio, they'd blown it all. They couldn't afford to put me back in to give them the album they really wanted. It was one of the rare occasions that being on a label with no money was actually a good thing.

The album, *Tubeway Army*, went out in 1978, and it didn't set the world on fire, but it didn't go down badly the way they thought it would. So they put me back in the studio to do another one just a few months later, and that one, *Replicas*, went to number one. I had a number-one single ["Are 'Friends' Electric?"] and a number-one album at the same time, so I was vindicated.

Within a few months of "Are 'Friends' Electric?" going to number one in the U.K., "Cars" came out and went to number one. I went from never having seen a synthesizer to having two number-one singles and a number-one album in 12 months. It was pretty meteoric. I was doing interviews with technology magazines about programming synthesizers and didn't have a clue what they were talking about. They were asking me about envelopes and fills and boffin shit. I just blagged and bullshitted my way through it. I pretended I knew what they were talking about, then I'd go home and try to figure it out. It was a really exciting time, but I was hopelessly out of my depth.

I went from being absolutely unknown—I think I'd done one tiny interview with a little local punk fanzine—and then I was number one. There was nothing in between. It was like living in a bipolar world where people you've never met love you all of a sudden, then you walk around a corner and somebody hates the air that you breathe even though you've never met them. And you're suddenly doing TV shows with people you've loved and admired for years, and now you're one of them, but you don't feel like you're one of them—you feel like an intruder that snuck in the back door. I thought that I'd been very lucky to get where I was and that my songwriting needed to be much, much better to justify the amount of success I had. So I actually felt slightly embarrassed and guilty at times about finding myself in the position I was in.

I'm glad it happened, nonetheless. I look back on it now and think I probably could have enjoyed it so much more if I had just been a bit calmer and more worldly and definitely if it had happened a little more slowly. I'd made it on my second album, and I'd made it massive. At one point, in the U.K. alone, I was selling 45,000 singles a day. It was all down to *Top of the Pops*. You got on that program and you pretty much made it overnight. It was very difficult to get on; you had to have at least a small amount of success. Again, with me, I was very lucky.

> **"Was 'Cars' easy to write? Piece of piss, innit? I'd wanted to learn bass guitar better.... The first four notes I played on that guitar, and I thought, *That's all right.*"**

For a month or two, *Top of the Pops* did a thing they called "Bubbling Under," where they would take a song that wasn't on the chart but showed some sort of movement. It was between me and Simple Minds—we both had songs out that got to number 80 or something like that. And they picked me because my band was called Tubeway Army. They thought that was a slightly more interesting name than Simple Minds. Just luck. Suddenly, I was seen by 12 million people, and "Are 'Friends' Electric?" was number one.

After that, as far as I was concerned, Tubeway Army was finished. Tubeway Army was a punk band; this was a completely new thing. I wanted to be on my own. I wanted to be Gary Numan now. If I'd had my way, it would have been Gary Numan from the beginning, but Beggars Banquet said they'd invested money in the Tubeway Army name, and they didn't want to drop it. They made me stick with it through the first two albums. It wasn't until "Are 'Friends' Electric?" and *Replicas* went to number one that I had enough clout to get what I wanted. I was eventually able to become Gary Numan when "Cars" came out.

Was "Cars" easy to write? Piece of piss, innit? I'd wanted to learn bass guitar better; I'd never written a song on the bass. So I went to Shaftesbury Avenue in London and bought myself a cheap bass called a Shergold Modulator. I've still got it—it hangs on a wall in my studio. I took it home, got it out of its case, and the very first thing I played was [sings the first four notes of "Cars"]. That was it. The first four notes I played on that guitar, and I thought, *That's all right*.

Honest to God, "Cars" took me 10 minutes—all the parts, all the arrangements. Another 20, and the lyrics were done. The whole thing took about half an hour, from opening the case to having the finished bass line, arrangement, lyric, and vocal line sorted out. The keyboard line came a bit later when I got to the studio, because I didn't have a synth; I had to rent one. It was the most productive 30 minutes of my life.

Out of all the songs I've written, "Cars" was by far the quickest. I've written 300 or 400 songs—that are available on CD; I've written a lot more than that—and only two on bass, one being "Cars," the other completely forgettable. It's become this electronic anthem, one of the most well-known electronic songs ever, but it was written on a bass.

One of the other things that's weird about it is it's almost an instrumental. It doesn't have a vocal chorus. All the singing happens in the first 60 seconds, then there's another three minutes of instrumental. I had a similar issue with "Are 'Friends' Electric?," but that was the opposite: That was five and a quarter minutes long, you couldn't dance to it, and it had a spoken-word chorus not a sing-along chorus. If you think of all the

MIXTAPE: 5 More Synthetic Songs Filled with Paranoia and Alienation
1. "Airwaves," Thomas Dolby   2. "Ghosts," Japan   3. "Suburbia," Pet Shop Boys   4. "Underpass," John Foxx   5. "Private Plane," Thomas Leer

"I used to think that the car was a tank for the civilian. You could sit inside your car, lock your doors, and it would keep you safe."

boxes you're supposed to tick to have a radio-friendly song, "Are 'Friends' Electric?" didn't tick any of them, and "Cars" didn't do that much better.

The problem I've always had with "Cars" is when I play it live, and especially when I do it on TV, I just stand on the stage, and my bit is over pretty quickly, and then I've got to stand there and try to look interested. I used to think, *What the fuck am I going to do?* I can't dance—I dance like an idiot. When I play it live, even now, I'll often put another keyboard on stage just to give me something to do with my hands. For a few years I stood on the side and had a drink, or I'd go and sit down. I've always had an uncomfortable relationship with the last two or three minutes of the song.

Lyrically, "Cars" came from an incident that happened to me in London. I was in my car and in a bit of traffic, and there were a couple of men in front of me in a white van, and they got out. I'd obviously done something—I must have cut them off a while back. I don't remember. But they were fucking furious, these blokes. They came back at me, shouting. I locked all my doors—I didn't want any trouble. They were kicking my car, banging on the handles, and swearing at me, for fuck's sake! I don't know what I did, but it must have been pretty bad. *Eventually*, I thought, *I'm gonna have to get away from this.* There was enough room for me to get up on the pavement, so I drove up and I went along, with these people chasing me, scattering pedestrians in my wake, shitting my pants. I was really scared. I managed to get away up the high street. It was quite a shocking experience, and that's where the idea for "Cars" came from. In modern society, I used to think that the car was a tank for the civilian. You could sit inside your car, lock your doors, and it would keep you safe. It puts you in a little protective bubble. You can maneuver through the world, but you don't really have to engage. That's how it felt to me, and that's what the song's about.

THAT WAS THEN
BUT THIS IS NOW

Gary Numan continues to tour and record and has released 15 albums since 1980's *Telekon*. His influence has been hailed by musicians like Damon Albarn and the Sugababes and comedians like Noel Fielding. His 1980 Top 10 chart showing with "Cars" marks the beginning and end of his American success, but if fate deigns to allow you only a solitary hit, "Cars" isn't a bad one to have. It single-handedly prepared the United States for the British-led electronic onslaught that was lurking just around the corner. In the ensuing decades, it has been sampled, covered, remixed, and reissued countless times. Long after there are cars, there will be "Cars."

NUMAN: I've got a huge amount of credibility now, strangely enough. I never had it when I was selling number-one albums. It's been a slowly building thing for me. Marilyn Manson did one of my songs. I started to hear interviews with people like Trent Reznor talking about me being an influence on them—people I admired and had no idea they even knew who I was. It's given me a huge boost of confidence, and it's helped a lot of people to reevaluate me, the music press in particular. When my *Pleasure Principle* album came out in '79, it got fucking crucified. It got pretty much slammed into the ground by everyone who reviewed it. Yet, a little while ago, the *NME*—who've been unbelievably hostile toward me over the years—called it one of the groundbreaking electronic records of the last few decades.

There's been a fundamental shift in the way people see me and think of me, but the undeniable fact in the middle of all this is that I only ever had one single that was successful in America. Just the one. Better than none. But I never did better in America when I had that initial opportunity, and I live on in the vague thread of a hope that I might have something there again in the future.

W

hen MTV reluctantly opened the door to British and European acts, the ones that came stumbling through were by and large an odd lot. Some seemed provincial, others awkward; a few were just plain carnival acts (not to speak ill of the dead, but Falco). Duran Duran were none of these things. They were the MTV generation's Rolling Stones. This wasn't a band evolving away from its grubby, indie beginnings—Duran were born to be big. The so-called Fab Five (singer Simon Le Bon, keyboardist Nick Rhodes, bassist John Taylor, and two other unrelated Taylors, drummer Roger and guitarist Andy) broke out of Birmingham, England,

DURAN

then promptly conquered the world. They saw it as their duty to live out the lifestyle they depicted in their wildly overproduced videos. The supermodels they squired, the luxury yachts and private jets, the rock-god decadence and debauchery—they bathed in it, and yet we didn't hate them for it. No band so synonymous with the overindulgent eighties transcended the decade better. They survived the vagaries of fashion, lineup changes, the passing of the years, and the profitable lure of the package-tour nostalgia circuit to become the era's distinguished elder statesmen. And their hair still looks immaculate.

DURAN

LM: Duran Duran chose me — I had no choice in the matter. I still remember, clear as day, the first time I saw the "Hungry Like the Wolf" video. It was like I was being possessed. From then on, everything was different: Everything I thought and felt was in the name of Duran Duran. I traveled to their concerts and waited outside their hotels and recording studios. I ran an internationally known Duranzine before pursuing a career in entertainment journalism just so I could be paid to be near them. I married a man named Simon, only to divorce him for an even hotter guy named John. I have lived for them, lied for them, and questioned my own sanity over them. And I'd do it all again. Don't say a prayer for me now—save it 'til the morning after!

JB: My Five Stages Of Duran Duran:

1. Denial. "Haven't heard them. Not going to waste my time. They'll be gone in five minutes. I don't like their puffy shirts."
2. Anger. "This is shit. It's shit! Why are people so hysterical about them? They're a one-hit, all right, two-hit wonder—at best. In a few years, you're all going to be embarrassed about liking them."
3. Bargaining. "Let me never have to hear their songs or see their videos again, and I swear I'll be a better, less selfish, more thoughtful, and caring person."
4. Depression. "Maybe it's me. Maybe I'm wrong about everything and everyone else is right. Is that possible?"
5. Acceptance. "Fine. They wrote a few good songs. They had staying power. They turned out to be way more consistent than groups I liked a lot better at the time. I have grudging respect for them. Okay?"

JOHN TAYLOR: We were perfect, and very few bands come out of the bag perfectly formed. Whether you liked us or not, that was a question of taste, but we were fully developed. And the moment Simon stepped in, we became the band that made "Girls on Film." The serious press had such a hard time with Duran in the beginning, and one of the reasons is because there was nothing for them to do. A lot of other bands—and I hesitate to say Radiohead, U2, or even the Rolling Stones—it took them three albums to find their thing, and along the way, their journalist friends had become their champions. The press fueled a part of their story, so they could own them. With Duran, they were like, *What are we going to do?*

NICK RHODES: "Girls on Film" originated in 1979 in Birmingham. We had a rehearsal room in a squat where Andy Wickett, our singer at the time, was living. We'd recently parted company with Stephen Duffy. Andy had this phrase "girls in films": "Girls in films look better." John and I decided to change it to "girls on film." It just sounded better. There is a reason why it's been used so often as a phrase since. If you could hit on one of those every day, you would.

TAYLOR: After Andy Wickett left, we said to the next singer [Jeff Thomas], "We've got this chorus, write the verse as you see fit," and he wrote his own. Then we fell out with Jeff. The thing about "Girls on Film" is Nick and I trusted our instincts. We could have cast it away when we fell out with Andy, but Nick and I held on to it. With Simon, again we said, "We've got this chorus—write whatever you want for the verse." And his opening line was absolutely fantastic: "See them walking hand in hand across the bridge at midnight." There are so many little hooks—every line of the verse is a hook, you know? I know, because we play it every night, and I'm singing along, "Lipstick cherry all over the lens as she's falling." It's one long hook, which it needs to be,

because the chorus is so simple. Simon had never even listened to the previous singers' versions. I guess that's testament to the crazy, evocative simplicity of the phrase "girls on film." It's actually mind-racing. It's that suburban view upwards to the catwalk, to the silver screen—to unattainable beauty on that level—that the suburbanite always dreams of.

RHODES: Girls have always been a thing, thankfully, for our species. Simon really did write the master lyric, which was much funnier, more clever, and more ironic than it had been previously. It was about girls in films; it was about exploitation. It was about the old Hollywood clichés of the casting couch but the excitement and the glamour of it, too.

SIMON LE BON: I wanted something that was a bit edgy, because I wanted the band to be edgy—not too soft. So an homage to girls in the movies was not what I was after. I wrote the song as a fantasy. It's a guy watching these models, and they're being exploited for the camera, for the producer, and for the guy who's at home watching them on telly while he's sitting in the bath. He feels that he's got his own special relationship with them, and he realizes that the girls can take him all the way. At the end of the third verse, when it goes, "Give me shudders in a whisper take me up till I'm shooting a star"—that, to me, was an orgasm. That is the guy actually coming, and whenever I sing it, I think about that. And the line "There's a camera rolling on her back, on her back"? He's repeating that line as sexual innuendo— because "on her back" definitely means she's having sex, right? But the song is also about the fact that women have to go through so much to make good photographs. And they're selling a product. "Wider baby smiling, you just made a million"—not a million for her, a million for the guy who's making it! So I wanted the song to be fun but have some substance as well.

RHODES: Simon's got a way of finding words that sound beautiful together. But the songs have always had a meaning—even the more abstract songs like "Union of the Snake" or "The Reflex." That period we certainly got more abstract than the first couple of albums, but they always had a story behind them. I'm all for surrealism in lyrics, but at the same time, if you can find something that truly touches somebody emotionally, that's when you're on the track to writing a good lyric, which often leads to a good song.

When Simon first came to meet us, he had this fabulous little notepad with the words "Rov Ostrov" [the name of his previ-

ous band] written on the front. That book, those lyrics, the name Simon Le Bon—we were thinking, *If only he can sing, it'll be perfect!* Everything from the first album was written in that book, and probably the *Rio* album too. How he never lost it, I don't know. We ought to make a facsimile.

TAYLOR: We were incredibly single-minded: We just wanted to be the best that we could be. I was there to craft the very best bass lines, Simon to craft the very best lyrics. The best bands are the ones where the members hold down their own corners. It's like, you take care of your shit, I'll take care of mine. You can't have any slackers.

LE BON: I spent a whole day and a half trying to come up with a new melody because our managers didn't think it was good enough. Finally I said, "That is the melody, guys." And John, Nick, Roger, and Andy backed me up. Because they understood—we were very natural musicians. We had an instinctive feel for what worked and what didn't. They trusted me and my instincts that much to say, "If he says it's right, it's right."

TAYLOR: It took us a long time to get "Girls on Film" right. We were learning to play at that time. There's a CD box set that has the Air Studios demo, on which we hadn't quite refined it yet. If you listen to what Roger and

I are doing on that compared to the version that made the first album, we're playing much more cleverly on the album version. There's more playing—we'd really found our thing. If I had to encapsulate the best of the first few years of the band, I'd take three tracks: "Rio," "The Chauffeur," and the "Girls on Film" 12-inch.

RHODES: The camera clicking at the beginning was something I wanted to add. It was a 35mm Nikon that was put on motor drive. It was something that identified the song immediately. I've always felt that intros are incredibly important. Some of our songs have pretty elaborate intros, like "A View to a Kill" and "Wild Boys." I'm always taken by the thing that catches my ear that I haven't heard before, and that's what "Girls on Film" has—between the camera, that very distinctive drum beat, and one of John's greatest bass lines.

TAYLOR: I had been listening to a lot of Bowie's band of that period: *Station to Station* and

Low. Side one of *Low*, which is the "Sound and Vision" side, was Roger's and my fantasy. If you listen to "Stay" off *Station to Station*, that would give you an idea of what Roger and I were trying to emulate—the tightness of that rhythm section. Everybody says, "Bowie and Eno, the genius of their ideas!" But underneath you have George Murray and Dennis Davis, the greatest rhythm section of that time. You have Stevie Wonder's rhythm section basically slumming it, but everything that Murray and Davis did was incredibly funky. Chic was the other really important one. Chic turned me on to bass.

LE BON: I was brought up on T. Rex and Bowie, and moved on into Lou Reed, a little bit of Genesis on the way, and I was most definitely deep into punk. Look at the Damned—there's great poetry in some of those lyrics. Leonard Cohen, who is a poet—I was into his lyrics very much. I was a big fan of the Doors and Jim Morrison's lyrics. Then there was the humor of the

MIXTAPE: 5 More Sexy Songs About Sex 1. "Into You Like a Train," Psychedelic Furs 2. "Total Control," The Motels 3. "Kiss Me," Tin Tin 4. "So Alive," Love and Rockets 5. "Master and Servant," Depeche Mode

Kinks. And Patti Smith must be mentioned. She was probably, at that time, the single most influential person upon my lyric writing. Now, you might not see any of Patti Smith in my lyrics, but I do. Actually, Patti could almost have written "Girls on Film," because she had that thing about money and sex and youthfulness, and also that whole sexual climax thing. That's straight out of Patti Smith, that is. If you listen to "Birdland" and "Horses," that sexual dynamic curve to climax is definitely there.

TAYLOR: We knew "Girls on Film" was the strongest track on the album, and we fought with EMI. We said, "This has got to be the second single," and they were like, "No, no, no: 'Careless Memories' is the right second single." I look back now, and

I feel like the guy who was doing that, Rob Warr—he used to run Fast Product with Bob Last, who had the Human League before—I was thinking he was trying to sabotage us. So we released "Careless Memories," and that was the last song we'd put out in a long time that wasn't a Top 30 hit. We forced their hand and put out "Girls on Film" when the album came out.

Then we did that six-minute-long video. The subject matter! Do you know how many guys have come up to me and are like, "I love that video!" I had somebody tell me recently, "In the early eighties, I was a thief. Me and my mate, we used to break into chemists' shops, rip off all the pills, and go back to his flat with these piles of speed and just watch the 'Girls on Film' video over and over and over."

There were not a lot of people doing videos, and we saw that opportunity in the rock clubs in America. We were in Memphis a week or so ago, and the guy who was driving me said, "We used to go to this club called Antenna, and they had this big video screen above the dance floor, and they would show your videos." It was that little window before MTV. There was the Rock America circuit of dance clubs, of which the Ritz in New York was like the flagship. You could fit, like, 1,500, 1,600 people in there. There was a screen above the dance floor, and around the end of the seventies, beginning of the eighties, they started playing music videos. The "Girls on Film" video was laser-guided to reach that audience dancing at one o'clock on a Saturday morning at the Ritz.

Our managers drove the video agenda. We were like, "Oh, man, a video?" They were like, "Chaps, this is something we need to do." The people who were getting MTV going had a meeting with [Duran managers] Paul and Michael Berrow, and they said, "We need content." If there had been videos for "More Than a Feeling" and Journey, for all the music that was on the radio at that point, that's what they would have played. But there wasn't, so they were forced to look to the edge, which was all coming out of London. They had to play the Buggles, Ultravox, Peter Gabriel, Duran Duran, because they were visual. They said to us, "What we really want is something like a James Bond video." That's what put the seed into Paul's mind that we should go to Sri Lanka [to shoot videos for the *Rio* album].

The "Girls on Film" video—Jesus, we did that in one afternoon! Everything was shot on this T-shaped set. There was a catwalk, with the band on a stage at the end and the boxing ring at the other. It was conceived with a combination, I would say, of jocularity and foresight. But I didn't like that day. It was what I imagine it must be

"The 'Girls on Film' video... was conceived with a combination, I would say, of jocularity and foresight.... It was what I imagine it must be like to be on the set of a porno movie."

like to be on the set of a porno movie. It was exciting, on the one hand, having all these beautiful girls walking around without clothes on. But the band, we're tripping out, showing off, and not being ourselves. It wasn't comfortable for us.

RHODES: We wanted to make a sexy video, but we wanted it to be funny as well. It's so ridiculous, the things that are in the video—the mud wrestling, the lifeguard, the [kiddie] pool. Some people may think it's politically incorrect, but it wasn't meant to upset anyone. It was made to make people smile, and there's still something about that that really works.

LE BON: What do I remember most about that day? The one with the dark hair. Some guys like blondes, some guys like dark-haired girls, and I realized absolutely which one I liked and was going for. It was very sexy, and then, watching it back, there was some turn-off as well as turn-on. Like, the sumo wrestler guy—I think that is universally the great turn-off in that video.

RHODES: When it got banned, it didn't do us any harm. When you get something banned, it throws a different light on it—like when the Sex Pistols were banned from everything in the U.K. The video became infamous. Everybody wanted to see it because they couldn't. Eventually we made it available on a videocassette, and to promote it we did a signing in Times Square at a place called Video Shack, where there were riots and police horses. The irony is, a lot of the young girls coming in to buy the video technically weren't allowed to watch it.

TAYLOR: After "Girls on Film" and the *Rio* album, the success was so huge in the early eighties that when we lost that in the second half, we thought, *Oh my God, is that it?* It was pretty terrifying. After Andy and Roger left in 1986, we lost a huge part of our firepower, and we had to try to find ways to get the chemistry back. ✱ It wasn't easy. We took such a bashing in our late 20s from the culture. There was this period where everybody said, "Okay, you're out. Get out!"

✱ **NILE RODGERS, producer:** The only time I ever made an album that took a long time was Duran Duran, *Notorious*. The group had broken up—Andy and Roger had left. I had to figure out a way to keep these guys together. I absolutely loved them like brothers, and I couldn't watch Duran Duran just fade away. It was the only time I ever spent a million dollars making a record—that was almost blasphemous to me. But what we got out of it was one of my favorite records of all time. With *Notorious*, I was able to shift the band from this cute boy-band sort of thing—and those [early albums] were great records, by the way. But I knew that, had they stayed in that area, their life span would be limited. I remember the *NME* review of [*Notorious*], and I never remember reviews. After working on that album and spending that amount of money and seeing how hated they were by the British press in those days, I was so proud. I actually have this memorized: It said, "Just when you thought it was time to count these jerks out, they not only make a record that's good but one that's worthy of respect." Duran Duran are, at their heart, really a band. They really are like the Rolling Stones or U2, guys who struggled to get better at what they did, and they struggled together. That's what makes a band, that sense of us against the world, and they have that.

✱✱ **MARK RONSON, artist, producer, and DJ:** John is quite modest as a musician. They got a lot of stick for being pretty boys—people forget they can really play. That amazing rhythm section being the backbone of "Girls on Film" is square one. Then to have that incredible guitar riff—there's nothing light about it. It's like a fucking Les Paul through a Marshall. It's as Steve Jones as anything, which is such a juxtaposition to the slinky groove. Then you have this incredible wall of synth and [lyrics] that are all about sex—that is the home run. It's not just about sex: The song *is* sex. Obviously, it wasn't premeditated like they're mixing it in a lab. It just magically came out. You just know when you put the record on—when that guitar and groove come in, it's just alchemy.

That's when you need Nick Rhodes. He was like, "I'm not moving!" If it were up to me, I'd be in a hole in the ground somewhere.

RHODES: I don't like giving in. By the early nineties we still had a lot of music left in us, so I wouldn't have seen any reason to bow out. John bought into grunge a lot more than I did. The whole movement left me cold. It looked unattractive and, aside from Nirvana, it sounded like something I'd heard before but not as good.

There was no space for us in the media at that time. A lot of journalists would have very happily locked the door on the eighties and thrown away the key with Duran Duran in the vault. But I knew there would always be space for really good songs. By the time we got to making *The Wedding Album* [a.k.a. the band's second self-titled album, 1993's *Duran Duran*], I remember us sitting down and saying, "Okay, let's write songs just like we used to." So we really went back to basics and wrote "Ordinary World" and "Come Undone."

TAYLOR: That was the turnaround. But by the time *The Wedding Album* came out, I'd really slowed down as a bass player. I remember spending a lot of time in New York, becoming aware of all those session musicians and a little ashamed of my own playing style because I wasn't "the

real thing." It almost made me want to go and hide away. Whereas what you hear on the first few Duran albums—the first two, three—is that I was unashamed. I was like, *This is what I can do! Listen to me!* One of the worst things is when you get self-conscious. It became about playing less and less until my playing practically disappeared. It took somebody I respected, Mark Ronson,✱✱ to say, "Look, nobody does that better than you. The way you played on 'Rio'—that's your thing, JT." I was like, "I don't know.... Can I still do that? We need to fit into the culture." But Mark said, "That's how you fit into the culture."

THAT WAS THEN BUT THIS IS NOW

 The original hit-making, multi-Taylor lineup reunited in 2003 to much fanfare. After shedding guitarist Andy Taylor for the second time, they collaborated with fans Timbaland and Justin Timberlake on 2007's *Red Carpet Massacre*, an album that fans hoped would reignite the classic Duran sound. That didn't happen, but they rebounded spectacularly with 2011's Mark Ronson–produced *All You Need Is Now*. They continue to age gracefully.

"It seems absurd to me that we are now in our fourth decade of Duran Duran. "

TAYLOR: It was a really interesting time when we put the reunion together at the turn of the millennium. Not only were we trying to write songs; we were also trying to reinvent the sound of the band. Since Roger, Andy, Simon, Nick, and I had last played together on "A View to a Kill," we'd had hip-hop, the Chili Peppers, Guns N' Roses, trip-hop. Everybody was super self-conscious. Roger would be the first to admit it: He didn't want to be Roger Taylor when he came back—he wanted to be [Red Hot Chili Peppers drummer] Chad Smith. I'm like, "But you're Roger Taylor! I can't play with Chad Smith!"

Also, we'd had this dark sense of our early years, because the culture, at that point, had not come back around to Duran yet. Nobody was giving us any props in 2000. But then Gwen Stefani came on board and Justin Timberlake. MTV acknowledged us with a lifetime achievement award, and suddenly there was a turn of the tide. Suddenly the *NME* is saying "Hungry like the Wolf" is the most important song ever written.

But the thing is, by the time it changes, it doesn't matter. It's actually not really important to us anymore. All the things that I was desperate to attain I don't care about anymore. We're not desperately trying to seek anything from anybody. We're just doing our jobs as best as we can and trying to have a good time doing it.

LE BON: In the modeling world, ["Girls on Film"] has become Yasmin [Le Bon]'s song. No other catwalk girl could ever lay claim to it in the same way that she could. When we did the Fashion Rocks show in London [in 2003], we played the song, and she's one of the girls on the catwalk, and you can see the sense of ownership that she had. That made me very, very proud.

RHODES: It seems absurd to me that we are now in our fourth decade of Duran Duran. The other day I watched a video of us playing the song "Friends of Mine" dressed in military uniforms, and it was alien to me. I have a very good memory of almost all the things we've done—even small German TV shows—but this I didn't. I thought, *Wow, they were an interesting band. Look at what they were doing then!*

You know how, when you graduated high school and went on to college, you got the chance to totally make yourself over? How you got new clothes, a new personality, and a new hairstyle, and you invented a whole new backstory to win yourself a cool new group of friends to replace all those losers you left behind? That's what happened to the most prominent guttersnipes of British punk when they outgrew spitting and safety pins. PIL were nothing like the Sex Pistols. Big Audio Dynamite were nothing like the Clash. The Style Council were nothing like the Jam. New Order, though, were exactly like Joy Division ... until "Blue Monday." The first few records they made following the 1980 suicide of Ian Curtis sounded like the ghost of their singer was still haunting them. But "Blue Monday" changed everything. It turned New Order into a dance-floor mainstay, gave them a new, worldwide audience and the bestselling 12-inch single of all time, paid for the Haçienda (laying the foundation for their native Manchester to become Madchester), and kept them around for the next 30-something years. It also lit the spark for a simmering feud between creative collaborators Bernard Sumner and Peter Hook that would boil over more than three decades later.

NEW

ORDER

"BLUE MONDAY"

LM: When I saw New Order at Jones Beach on Long Island in the late eighties, it was like that moment in *The Wizard of Oz* when Dorothy sees the real Oz behind the curtain. Unlike the other groups I liked, these guys wore regular-Joe clothes. Sumner was the most nondescript frontman I'd ever seen. *No wonder they don't put their photos on the* *record sleeves*, I thought. Still, there was no denying Hooky's rock-god bass playing. Also, New Order had risen from the ashes of Joy Division, inarguably one of the coolest bands ever. And think about this: The list of musicians who graduated from one successful group to another includes Paul McCartney, Ron Wood, Eric Clapton, and Dave Grohl, yet none of them have been in two consecutive game changers like Sumner, Hook, and drummer Steven Morris.

JB: This isn't in my top-five New Order songs. I'd put it behind "True Faith," "Bizarre Love Triangle," "Subculture," and "Age of Consent." I'd probably put it behind "Regret" too. But that doesn't mean that I don't know what a monster it was or that I underestimate its importance. "Blue Monday" utilized all the traditional components of an electronic-dance record, except it omitted any sense of liberation, any chance of escape. Sounding weary and desolate has always been second nature to Bernard Sumner, but hearing him moan, "How does it feel when your heart grows cold?" accompanied by the remorseless grind of machines was especially chilling. "Blue Monday" was a big black cloud hanging over the dance floor. It was the soundtrack to a bleak, dehumanizing future. And it sounded fantastic.

BERNARD SUMNER: After Ian Curtis died, we were all very upset and depressed and, obviously, in shock. When we started releasing stuff like *Movement*, we got a completely negative response from the press, and that sadness turned into anger. It was like, "Come on, give us a break. Can't you just help us out in our hour of need instead of sticking the knife in?" Because the British press can be pretty sadistic. "Blue Monday" was kind of a response to that. It was like, "Fuck you! Here's what we can do."

"Blue Monday" came out, and the press really stuck the knife in—again! They said it was a pile of shit, and it was rubbish and that no one would buy it. And here we are, all these years later....

When we released "Blue Monday," a lot of people who knew us were like, "That doesn't sound like New Order." But that was the point. It's not really our best song, but it was designed like a machine to make people dance. I felt a bit uncomfortable doing music that was just like Joy Division. And as a singer, I felt uncomfortable stepping into Ian's shoes, because I didn't want to sound like an Ian Curtis impersonator. I think the first New Order album, *Movement*, was kind of pseudo–Joy Division but with a different singer. It didn't feel true to me. I wanted to do something that had a different flavor. It was synergy, really, that electronic music—it wasn't born but it blossomed then.

After the death of Ian, we recorded two New Order tracks, "Ceremony" and "In a Lonely Place," in New Jersey somewhere, then every night we'd drive back into Manhattan and go out to nightclubs. So we were influenced by what we were hearing in New York nightclubs and by what we heard in London. I also had a friend in Germany who was sending me 12-inch singles from there.

And I was technically minded. You couldn't buy computers then, so I built a music sequencer. You could buy a music sequencer, but it'd cost you the same as buying a house. So with the help of a scientist who worked with us, I built this synthesizer and music sequencer on the cheap, and we put the two together. Just at that time, the DMX drum machine came out, so we got the scientist to design us a little box that could make them all speak to each other, and we made "Blue Monday" with it.

"Blue Monday" spread because it's a club record, and it caught DJs' attention. It was at the vanguard of electronic dance music. We were on Factory Records, who had a promotional budget of nothing. Zero. They didn't believe in promotion, we didn't do many interviews about it, and somehow we ended up with this worldwide hit.

In England, it kept going in the charts year after year as it got through to a different crowd. People would come back from their summer holidays, and it had been played in places like Ibiza, and suddenly it'd go back up in the charts again.

PETER HOOK: We find that most people are either Joy Division fans or New Order fans. It's very rare to find one who likes both, because they're quite different. Joy Division and New Order existed during very different periods. When New Order came about, times were more fun—everything lightened up.

New Order's way of coping with the grief of Ian's death was to ignore Joy Division. And you must admit, it worked. New Order became successful all around

"New Order's way of coping with the grief of Ian's death was to ignore Joy Division. And you must admit, it worked."

▮▮▮▮▮▮

the world, if not more successful than Joy Division. The trouble was, because we were so young, we were happy to avoid the grief. Looking back now, as a 56-year-old man, I realize, with all of the people I've lost, that grieving is a very important process.

When we did play the Joy Division stuff, Bernard didn't like it. He felt it was miserable. It's a bit of a crass way of putting it, but I understand what he meant. New Order is much poppier, much lighter, much more optimistic. Joy Division's stuff is very dark—you could say gloomy. Plus, he wrote the New Order stuff, so I suppose that means a lot more to Bernard than the Joy Division stuff did.

"Blue Monday" was an experiment in seeing how much we could get the sequencers to do, and we did get them to do a hell of a lot. The fact that "Blue Monday" still sounds as good now as it did 30 years ago is incredible. I'm going to blow me own trumpet: We certainly have a knack for making fantastic music. Me and Mike Johnson, who was the engineer, worked really, really hard, along with Bernard and Steven, to make "Blue Monday" sonically exciting. Bernard and Steven, in particular, were very interested in experimenting with the new technology. I must admit, I wasn't very interested in it. I preferred to rock out. It was that combination of me wanting to be in a rock band and them wanting to be a disco band that gave us our unique sound. We were listening to Sparks, Giorgio Moroder, Suicide, Kraftwerk. And also, in New York we were taken to many clubs: Tier 3, Hurrah. And you were like, "Wow, this is so different to England," that it had an influence on you.

"Blue Monday" was meant to be an instrumental closer to the show. In the studio we just thought we'd have a go at putting lyrics over it. The lyrics and the vocal were the absolute last things that went on. They were done at four o'clock in the morning, right at the end, when the song was written and nearly produced. The lyrics were very much an afterthought, and I think the reluctance to put them on can be heard. But strangely enough, it works. The deadpan, off-beat delivery actually works great as a contrast with the music: How. Does it. Feel. It's such a juxtaposition, isn't it?

With Ian gone, we all tried to be New Order's singer. Our producer, Martin

Hannett, hated us all—Bernard just had the last go. But realistically, with Bernard adding the guitar after he sang, it managed to give you a new style. So he would sing, Steve and I would play, then, when he'd stop singing, he would play guitar. And that gave it the lift, the up and down, the light and dark, that became the New Order sound.

"Blue Monday" was recorded in conjunction with about 10 other songs: "Temptation," "Everything's Gone Green," "Thieves like Us."... It was competing with many other songs in our hearts, if you like. It was nearly seven and a half minutes long, and we were asked to cut it down, but we just didn't do it. However, we did agree to do a shortened version for *Top of the Pops*. *Top of the Pops* was what you watched as a child, and it was one of the only music programs that was on mainstream TV. Everything was about *Top of the Pops*—it was a religious ceremony. Even though you didn't like the acts on *Top of the Pops* most of the time, you still watched it. It was the only TV program that you could guarantee would annoy your parents, and it would educate you as to what was going on musically. So to get our act on it was an honor, and [editing the song] was something we accommodated for that reason. If you played on *Top of the Pops*, supposedly your single went up 15 places, guaranteed. Because we played live—we didn't mime—and sounded terrible and looked terrible, ours was the only record that went down. We were delighted about that, though. It was punk; it was chaotic; it was wild; it cocked a snoot, as we say in England. We were happy—even when the record went down the charts, we were happy.

I got the title "Blue Monday" from a book. Everybody thinks it's from the Fats Domino song, but it wasn't. It came from a fiction book. I would read voraciously in the studio. There was a sheet on the wall, and everybody would write ideas on it. *Power, Corruption and Lies* came from the back of *1984*. "True Faith" came from a James A. Michener book on Texan Catholicism. The titles had very little to do with the songs.

MIXTAPE: 5 More Dark, Depressing, Doom-Filled Dance-Floor Classics
1. "Dr. Mabuse," Propaganda   2. "I Travel," Simple Minds   3. "Der Mussolini," D.A.F.   4. "Sensoria," Cabaret Voltaire   5. "Living in Oblivion," Anything Box

It was tradition, something we carried on, and a mark of excellence that we got from Joy Division. "Atmosphere," "The Eternal"—these words were never mentioned in the songs either.

It was me and Bernard who wrote the melodies. There's long been a personality conflict there. We certainly were not friendly, shall we say. I think Bernard ever only phoned me once. The only time was to ask for a lift to rehearsals because his car battery was dead. And I must admit, I've never phoned him.

It's also ego. It was always me and him fighting for the limelight, not only on stage but musically. To me, New Order wasn't New Order unless it had the bass guitar on it, and he would go to great lengths to try and mix me out. He started trying to get me out of the music a long, long time ago. If you listen, you can hear the bass getting quieter and quieter in the songs as the struggle evolved between Bernard and me. If you look at songs like "Thieves like Us" and "Blue Monday," the bass is as loud as the vocal. Further on, the bass is not as loud as the vocal; it's disappearing. The notable one was "Bizarre Love Triangle." That was the first stand-up fight we had about how much bass was in the song. Bernard felt that the bass dated it. And actually, it's the other way around now, isn't it? You hear the bass, and it gives it a timeless quality.

We went to do "Here to Stay" with the Chemical Brothers, who were great fans of the group. The way I normally work is this: I put bass through the whole track, and then we leave it to the producer to pick the parts. Well, when we went to listen to what they'd done, Bernard and I sat there and listened with the Chemical Brothers—and they had put every bass part in throughout the whole song. Because they loved it. Bernard went fucking mad! He told me the bass was interfering with the lead vocal. It was at that point that I thought, *Oh my God, this band is finished. It's only time before it goes.* He got his own way, like he always did.

THAT WAS THEN
BUT THIS IS NOW

 New Order's original lineup—which also included Morris's wife, keyboardist Gillian Gilbert—continued until 2007, when a frustrated Hook announced he was quitting. Sumner and Morris soldiered on without Hook and Gilbert, who'd departed to be a full-time mother. But then Sumner and Morris decided to form a new group, Bad Lieutenant. Despite Morris's declaration that "there's no future for New Order," 2011 saw a re-formation with Gilbert but not Hook. The bassist responded with a lawsuit accusing the others of touring and planning to record as New Order without compensating him. Then, in 2013, New Order released the long-delayed album *The Last Sirens*, the final tracks recorded while Hook was still a member. Meanwhile, Hook tours the world with his band the Light, playing Joy Division and New Order albums in their entirety. Talk about confusion!

SUMNER: We knew "Blue Monday" was a good song, but we didn't realize just how potent it was. You're too close to the trees. Go on YouTube and type in "the Jolly Boys, Blue Monday." It's two or three 80-year-old guys doing this weird, Jamaican-music version. It's fantastic.

We just played Mexico, and we had 50,000 people. Sometimes you get really young fans. I've spoken to some of them and said, "How have you heard about New Order?" This girl at the airport the other day must have been, like, 16. And they go, "Oh, my sister played it to me" or "My father played it to me." It's passed down through the family like a gold watch.

We'd been trying to get *The Lost Sirens* out for a long time but that's when we had the falling-out with Peter Hook, and he refused to take part in it. He refused to come to the writing sessions and was busy DJing. So we never finished those songs.

HOOK: One of the main problems toward the end of my time with New Order—not New Odor, as they are now—was that Bernard was managing the band, and if anyone upset him, they were in trouble. He became like a dictator. There's an interview with Bernard where he said that one of the problems with New Order was he wasn't allowed to change the chemistry of it, and that was absolutely correct. The chemistry of it was that I played bass on every track. You're not messing with that. You want to mess with that, go form another band. And that was exactly what he did. They now have a bass player that they can tell what to do, whereas before they had a bass player they could not tell what to do and who did what he wanted. That's what made the band fiery and interesting.

If we had sorted it out before New Order had re-formed, I could have wished them the best, could've wished them well. But because of the way they did it, I could never wish them well. What makes me laugh is when journalists take great delight in asking, "Do you think you'll ever get back with them?" Because of the group that I loved and put 32 years into, I'm fighting them tooth and nail. This is a divorce. You know when you're going through the arguments, the splitting of the CDs, who's getting half the dog, and things like that? For someone to ask me if I'm going to get back with them, it does seem strangely ridiculous at this point in time. But in the future you would hope that you and your ex would get on well, if just for the kids. I hope that we can get on well because our fans, who are our kids, would love it if we did. At the moment, we aren't.

I watched the opening ceremony of the 2012 London Olympics and heard "Blue Monday." It was fantastic, it really was. To be put into that context, part of a country's musical history, that was a fantastic compliment. What makes these arguments that New Order have between us quite stupid is the largeness of the thing we've created.

To my mind, you're ruining it with the petty squabbles that you're having now, which are very, very sad.

If you read [Charlatans' singer] Tim Burgess's book, *Telling Stories*, he spends the whole time, the rest of his career, looking for the dead keyboard player. In a way, both Bernard and I may be looking for someone to replace Ian Curtis. If somebody of that stature came in, then maybe we would have stopped fighting. It's just that it never happened, did it?

> **"I watched the opening ceremony of the 2012 London Olympics and heard 'Blue Monday.'... To be put into that context, part of a country's musical history, that was a fantastic compliment."**

"POISON ARROW"

In 1979, Sheffield was the home of Britain's steel industry. It was also the birthplace of oppressive experimental underground acts like Cabaret Voltaire, Clock DVA, and the early, avant-garde, all-male Human League. Martin Fry, a worker in a baked beans factory by day and fanzine writer by night, went to interview another Sheffield industrial group, Vice Versa, and ended up joining their ranks. Dissatisfied with the music they were making, Fry and new bandmates Mark White and Steve Singleton changed the name of their group to ABC and made it their mission to write songs as slick and polished as their previous output had been clanging and thudding. They were not alone in their ambitions: The streets of the U.K. bustled with bands more than happy to trade their indie credibility for glossy productions and chart success (see Scritti Politti, the Associates, Thompson Twins). But with their first international hit, "Poison Arrow," and their debut album, *The Lexicon of Love*, ABC left their contemporaries twisting in the wind. *Lexicon* was a rich, overstuffed chocolate box of a record. Fry's extravagant wordplay was perfectly complemented by Trevor Horn's opulent, everything-plus-the-kitchen-sink production and his regular arranger Anne Dudley's lush orchestration. *The Lexicon of Love* was the sound of a band reaching out to achieve their ambitions, and surpassing them. Expecting them to ever best such a spectacular debut would have been asking the impossible, but at the height of their powers, ABC appeared so unassailable that asking the impossible seemed appropriate.

ABC

JB: I had ABC's number. Without hearing a note, I knew what they were: another new group who had put in hours practicing moody looks for their glossy spread in the *Face*. Another new group with a loquacious egomaniac frontman who had put in hours practicing self-aggrandizing quotes for his feature in the *NME*. Another new group who specialized in the sort of arthritic British funk that had reached pandemic status since Spandau Ballet drew up the blueprint with "Chant No. 1." ABC's first single, "Tears Are Not Enough," did little to alter my sullen adolescent prejudices. Singer Martin Fry proved, as predicted, considerably more accomplished at posing for artfully constructed photographs and hailing his band's greatness in the pop press than he was convincing as the soulful singer of a band who claimed global success as a birthright. Then they released "Poison Arrow." Everything, you, as a young person, might hope you're going to get in a pop record is right there. Emotion, ambition, humor, drama. A point of view. A sense of the ridiculous. A call-and-response bridge. Even a talky bit in the middle. The Julien Temple–directed music video was every bit the record's melodramatic equal, with a lovelorn Fry tormented and cheerfully abused by luscious femme fatale (and future Real Housewife of Beverly Hills) Lisa Vanderpump. I have gone on to be completely wrong about many other groups—and, indeed, many other aspects of life, in general—but initially dismissing ABC was the most rewarding mistake I ever made.

LM: Not sure if you realize it, JB, but *The Lexicon of Love* is the reason we became friends. When you told me it was your favorite album of all time—back in the early nineties, when we were the only people who'd admit to liking new wave while working at a grunge-obsessed *Spin* magazine—I thought: *Now, here's a guy I can hang with*. While I love Spandau and Culture Club, neither ever released a flawless long-player like *Lexicon*. The talky bits were my favorite parts, like in "The Look of Love," when Fry says to himself, "Martin, maybe one day you'll find true love." He always came across as such a hopeless romantic—it was the beautifully tailored suits, the way he referenced Cupid and Smokey Robinson in his songs, how he pined for a more chivalrous era. For an eighties teenager experiencing the thrill (and then heartache) of her first crush, ABC offered a vision of love that I could only hope the real thing would live up to.

MARTIN FRY: Decades don't always begin at zero. They begin a couple of years in, the mood and style. A couple of years into the eighties, when I was forming ABC, I realized no one could be more Sex Pistol–y than the Sex Pistols or more Clash than the Clash. I loved punk, but it never seemed to go as far as it could have. Maybe Simon Le Bon and Nick Rhodes or Tony Hadley and Gary Kemp might say something different, but for me and for a lot of my generation, it was really frustrating the Clash were never on *Top of the Pops.* I wasn't going to try and be a proto-punk. I wanted to do the opposite.

That's why I got so excited by disco, which was a really dirty word at the time. I wanted to make music that was funky and radical. The early ABC was the "Radical Dance Faction"—that's what we called ourselves. I'd also grown up loving Motown, Stax, and Atlantic, along with Roxy Music— Roxy performing "Virginia Plain" on *Top of the Pops* in 1972 was my road to Damascus. So it made natural sense to try and fuse those worlds. When I think back, looking at stuff like the Pop Group, James Chance and the Contortions, Pigbag, and all the bands that came through just before and just after ABC—Duran Duran, Spandau Ballet, Depeche Mode—there was a whole generation itching to make dance music, populist music. I don't think it was any accident that all those bands became internationally known.

I interviewed Vice Versa for my fanzine, *Modern Drugs,* in 1979. They were kind of a fledgling Human League, only younger and less revered. When I went to interview Steve Singleton and Mark White, they said, "We're going on a train from Sheffield to Middlesbrough to open up for Cowboys International. We've not got a drummer, but we've got lots of synths in our holdalls. You can stand onstage with us." We got bottled off by these skinheads who didn't get us. We were mohair sweaters and post-punk and ironic, but I loved it. After that, they let me join the band.

MIXTAPE: 5 More Melodramatic Songs About Heartbreak
1. "Say Hello, Wave Goodbye," Soft Cell   2. "Waves," Blancmange
3. "No More 'I Love You's,'" The Lover Speaks   4. "The Promise," When in Rome   5. "The Promise You Made," Cock Robin

Sheffield was full of experimental bands: Cabaret Voltaire, Human League splitting off into Heaven 17, Pulp were on that circuit, Comsat Angels. You felt really isolated in Sheffield. You didn't feel linked to the rest of the country. People didn't really go there for any reason. So the majority of the audiences you played to were musicians, guys in other bands. Those are the toughest people to play to. We once did a gig in the Heaven and Hell club in Birmingham. If you took out the 5 members of Duran Duran✻ who came to see the show, there'd be about 24 other people there. But Sheffield was entirely subsidized, so you could get on a bus for 10p and go anywhere in the city. It was a great place to be poverty stricken and function. That's why the band was able to change and develop.

Mike Pickering, who went on to be the DJ at the Haçienda, was working as a chef in Rotterdam and said he could get us some gigs there. So we went and slept on his floor. He had a shop and threw a party and let us jam. I started singing, and Mark White said I should be Vice Versa's singer. But then Mark White was dogmatic that we should drop everything, change the name, and become something else. It was destroy, disorder, dis-orientate—smash it all up. Vice Versa were being played on John Peel, they'd done an EP, they were going places, but we decided to destroy it. Virtually overnight, we hooked up with a drummer, bass player, sax, and keys. Looking back, it was really ambitious. We had a vision of how we wanted to be. We showed up onstage in Sheffield wearing cyclists' uniforms. People would show up expecting Vice Versa, and we were this new band, ABC: the Radical Dance Faction. Overnight, we wanted to be a funk band but with a sort of angular lyric. We wanted to be as polished as Chic and Earth, Wind & Fire, a band that was nurtured on *Diamond Dogs* and Kool and the Gang. We didn't really have the musicality, but that's not something you think about when you're coming through. That's why they call it blind ambition.

It was a frantic time, 1980, '81. We always felt like we wanted to get there first. The Human League were an incredible band, but we'd seen how Gary Numan and Orchestral Manoeuvres had almost eclipsed them by having chart hits. Spandau Ballet and A Certain Ratio terrified us. Stimulin, Funkapolitan, Haircut 100—you'd hear about these bands on the grapevine and through fanzines and the *NME* and *Record*

✻ **JOHN TAYLOR, Duran Duran:** I remember that. They were amazing. That was before they made a record. I felt ABC were better than us. I mean, *The Lexicon of Love* is a perfect record, as is "Poison Arrow." But they couldn't keep it together—that was their problem. But when I saw ABC at Holy City, I thought, *Holy fuck!* They played so well. They were a great band.

Mirror. They were all unsigned. We were frantically writing songs and playing shows. We wanted to be a step ahead. It felt like we were running to a place we wanted to be. I look back, and it was like a mania. Everybody had their manifesto, and everybody had a big mouth back then. I used to do interviews and tell people we were going to conquer the world. It all boils down to wish fulfillment, making it a self-fulfilling prophecy. That's why Muhammad Ali did it: to try and psych himself up for the battle ahead. It was mildly irritating when Gary Kemp said Spandau Ballet were the best band in the world or when Simon Le Bon said the same thing about Duran Duran. But we all said it.

"Tears Are Not Enough," the first single we brought out as ABC, was great, but it was really angular. It was successful—it got into the Top 20—but we had greater ambitions. We were our own worst critics.

We spent the whole of the eighties being unsatisfied with everything we did. We wanted to make a record that was like "Good Times," and "Tears" wasn't as fluid, and it wasn't as funky. That's why we contacted Trevor Horn. He'd just done "Hand Held in Black and White" by Dollar, and it had this panoramic, wide-screen sound. That's what we wanted to sound like. We didn't want to be Dollar—they were cheesy. People said,

STYLE COUNCIL

"I really like Jerry Lewis in *The Nutty Professor*," Fry says. "He undergoes this transformation and becomes Buddy Love in the Purple Pit. I always thought that was very *Lexicon of Love*. I was this gawky, adolescent, invisible kind of guy, but in the gold lamé suit everybody was paying me attention."

> **"Everybody had their manifesto, and everybody had a big mouth back then. I used to tell people we were going to conquer the world."**

"You had a Top 20 hit. That's an achievement. Why are you changing it around?" But we hadn't got to number one—that's how foolishly ambitious we were. That was definitely the spirit of the times. It wasn't really about any wealth that would follow from it. It was a competition. It was a game.

Trevor got it straight away. He was amused by a lot of the stuff we were talking about, how we were going to take on the whole music industry and change it. He was really inspiring because he'd been a musician—he was a Buggle. He said, "If you make a record, it lasts forever, so you might as well make it as good as you possibly can."

Not to sound like Eminem, but you've got one shot. You've got to hit the bull's-eye. There is a big difference between "Tears Are Not Enough" and "Poison Arrow." The idea was to make "Poison Arrow" as un-rock 'n' roll as possible. It was a million miles away from the Pistols and the Clash. We didn't want to sound like anyone else. It

was almost like a song from the 1940s but with bass parts from Chic and the drums… the idea was to have them as big as possible. They don't sound that big now, but at the time, it was operatic in the sense that it doesn't fade out; it builds to a climax. Lyrically, "Who broke my heart" is almost like a matinee idol singing. I'm looking at the sleeve—it's all tuxedos. In the middle of the song there's this bit where I go, "I thought I loved you, but it seems you don't care." And then Karen Clayton, the receptionist in [Trevor Horn's studio] Sarm East, she did the "I care enough to know I can never love you" part. It was an attempt to be like Clark Gable rather than Johnny Rotten.

As a singer, looking back, I was completely inexperienced. I'd done a few gigs but I wasn't developing. In "Poison Arrow," the idea of the vocal was to be histrionic. It wasn't just describing the emotions; it was reliving them. And it rhymed. This whole idea of making a song that rhymed was against the grain to a lot of the young bands that were writing songs back then.

"Poison Arrow" is a very emotional song, really. It's that feeling you get when somebody doesn't want to know you and you want to know them. It's that gut-wrenching kick in the teeth when someone walks away from you. That's the core of it, and I think that's why it's been successful over the years, because a lot of people have had that emotion. And another thing: "Poison Arrow" unlocked the door for the rest of the songs on *The Lexicon of Love*. The idea of writing something very emotional and not about toothpaste or electric pylons or the brutality of living in a high-rise block. Our songs were about heart and love and trying to make sense of that but, because we were very self-conscious, in an un-cheesy way.

I liked to write very bright, audacious, hyper-real love songs. But when I look back, I think I was hiding more than I was showing. Today's writers are very vulnerable and very specific about how they feel, but "Poison Arrow," "The Look of Love," "All of My Heart," they're kind of brash and larger than life. I wanted it to be art. I didn't mind the idea of being pretentious. What did Adam Ant say? "Ridicule is nothing to be scared of."

THAT WAS THEN BUT THIS IS NOW

 ABC made a classic eighties attempt to blow up the formula that made them successful by following *The Lexicon of Love* with 1983's austere, unglossy *Beauty Stab*, which was shunned by the mass record-buying audience who had previously embraced the group. (FYI: The title of this little recurring feature takes its name from *Beauty Stab*'s famously alienating first single, "That Was Then But This Is Now.") Subsequently, they turned themselves into cartoon characters for the great *How to Be a Zillionaire!* (1985); countered the confusion caused by the previous two albums with *Alphabet City* (1987), a semi-successful attempt to rekindle the ABC that had won widespread acceptance; and tried their hands at a British house record that worked hard to sound jubilant and celebratory with *Up* (1989). It was their last album of original material to make any chart appearance.

FRY: In 1997 I started playing live again. I still play gigs with people like Belinda Carlisle and Heaven 17, and there's an element of competitiveness even now amongst the veterans doing their victory laps.

The audiences we're playing to, those songs meant a lot to them. That really illuminated things for me. Up to then, playing old hits was a millstone around my neck. I was like, "I want to leave the past behind, what's next?" But it was fantastic to stand in front of an audience and feel the reaction, to read an audience and learn some stagecraft again. You sense all of that when you're standing in the spotlight. I still take pleasure in singing "Who broke my heart—you did!" and pointing the finger, and all those fingers point back at me and sing along. Thirty years on.

"WHIP IT"

For Akron, Ohio, natives and fellow art students Mark Mothersbaugh and Gerald Casale, and their various siblings and co-conspirators, the combination of multinational corporations, religion, government, and TV pointed them toward an inescapable conclusion: The world wasn't just getting dumber; it was actively devolving into a state of passive, drooling idiocy where any kind of atrocity was acceptable as long as it was wrapped in a bright package. Devo began life as an expression of outrage and disgust at the inevitability of a future where the world has mutated into unblinking blobs capable only of obedient consumerism. But that was a lot less fun than actually getting down in the dirt and wallowing inside the same corrupt, desensitizing system that was enslaving the nation. Devo should have been KISS's evil twin, a merchandisable monster that plastered its logo over every moment of our mindless existence. They were too weird to succeed. But with "Whip It," Devo collided with mainstream pop and allowed a momentary glimpse of what the world would have looked like if it danced in time to their tunes. It would have looked a lot like it does now.

JB: Getting older has its drawbacks. You pay doctors to fumble their way around your prostate. Also, you will probably never again listen to a piece of music and think, "I have never heard anything like that before!" Such was my reaction the first time John Peel played "Jocko Homo" sometime in 1978. It blew my teenage mind. If the taste-making late-night BBC DJ had announced he'd just played a record made by aliens, I would have believed him. "Jocko Homo" sounded like a national anthem of a country I never wanted to visit. Devo's problem was their timing. If a group like that, with their visual aesthetic, their brand awareness, and their dud-free early repertoire, emerged now, when nerds rule the world, they would be ubiquitous and instantly accepted. Instead, they had to settle for being the house band of the outcast, the socially awkward, the overexcitable, and the conspiracist. My kind of people.

LM: Devo scared the hell out of me. The "Jocko Homo" video seemed like a trailer for some freaky, sci-fi horror flick, and to my innocent, preteen eyes, the "Whip It" video might as well have been pornography. Mothersbaugh whipping the clothes off the black woman. The cross-eyed Asian girl with the gun. The guy who forces himself on the Asian girl while his white girlfriend cheers him on: "Ride 'em cowboy!" I'd yet to learn about S&M or rape or masturbation, but I knew enough to run to the TV set to turn the dial if "Whip It" was on and my mother was coming down the hall. Years later, I'm impressed by Devo's brilliance and the obscure literary references and subversiveness they sank into their songs. Hard to believe that MTV, now a playground for reality-TV smut, was once the home of such edgy cultural commentary. But in the early eighties, those plastic-helmeted Devo dudes were as nightmarish—and as compellingly watchable—as Freddy or Jason.

MARK MOTHERSBAUGH: Our goal wasn't to piss people off, but we were in a part of the world where there were a lot of things that were frustrating and crazy. Like people my age would sign up to go to Vietnam and defend democracy, and they'd come back and capitalism and democracy had decided that the reason why we were blasting away at people over in Asia was so it would be easier to set up factories over there so that our jobs in Akron could go over to Malaysia. It was a crazy time, and we decided that what we were observing was not evolution; it was more like de-evolution.

We were around for all the upheaval at Kent State. We were there for the shootings, and we saw all these people who had high ideals and wanted to change the world. Once people started shooting at them, they were like, "This is too heavy. I need to go back to being a student and not stick my head up and get shot at." We ended up looking around and saying, "How do you change things in this country?" It's not by rebellion. Rebellion gets hit over the head with a club and stopped very successfully. We were looking at who did change things and how they did it, and I remember feeing that the people who changed the culture the most were all on Madison Avenue. They were talking people into buying that new car they didn't need. They were convincing people there were germs in their sink even

though they couldn't see them, but they could possibly be dangerous so you have to buy this special miracle blue cleaner. And yes, there is a cure for balding: It's called brown spray paint. You just spray it on the top of your head. They were selling all these insane products and doing it in an artistic way, and we thought that was subversive. We thought, *If we're going to effect any change, the way to do it is you go into the belly of the beast.*

GERALD CASALE: We became a performance art group, and a lot of it was based on aesthetic confrontation that wound up in verbal and physical confrontation. The more that happened, the more excited we became. The kind of crowds we were able to get in front of irritated us. The feeling was, *If these people hate us, we're on the right track because we don't respect them either.* We wore black plastic trash bags, poked holes in them for our legs to come out, taped them up around our necks so they wouldn't fall down, and we'd be naked [underneath]. And we wore clear plastic masks; they were creepy, they had lips and eyebrows. We would play local bars, and it would get really nasty. A guy would scream, "You guys are assholes!" And I'd scream back, "No, you're the asshole." Then he'd go, "I'm gonna smack your fucking head in!"

And the club owner would come over with a couple of roadies, and we'd be forced to leave the stage. A guy gave us $75 once to stop playing. We really enjoyed that.

At the end of 1976, we were in a basement in a house in Akron practicing many nights a week for many weeks over and over and over. We were getting excited by the fact that we could really play together, and the excitement of live performance sped up our music. We saw the Ramones when we were in New York, and we were suddenly becoming part of something.

[A&R man] Kip Cohen called from A&M out on the West Coast. We were invited out to L.A. to showcase. He famously rejected us and hated us when he saw us. But we weren't going to take no for an answer. At our first performance, I had met Toni Basil, and she was friends with Iggy Pop, and she had dated Dean Stockwell. They had been hanging out with Neil Young. Pretty soon, we had four or five gigs lined up. It snowballed when unscrupulous managers and entertainment lawyers and record company A&R men started attending those shows, and pretty soon we had a bidding war.

We thought about Devo from the beginning as a multimedia band. Mark and I were visualists. We were art students. We thought we were going to put out video discs. We were reading all this stuff about video disc technology, and we thought, *This is the future. We'll be like the musical version of the Three Stooges. We'll do short films that will feature a song we wrote. The productions will be music-driven, and we'll do enough of them to make an hour program, and we'll put one out every year.* Oddly enough, that's not the way it worked out.

MOTHERSBAUGH: The first thing Warner Bros. said to us was "Why are you wasting your time making these movies?" We said, "That's part of our art—we're visually oriented artists. We're not just writing songs; we're making pictures to go with them." It took a number of years before MTV showed up and record companies noticed and went, "Oh, that's what you tricky bastards were doing." For the most part, they would use terms like "wacky" and "quirky." "Quirky" was a term to take anything we talked about that was serious and marginalize it.

CASALE: With MTV, we were the pioneers that got scalped. We'd had five videos done before MTV existed. Then MTV was just starting out in 1981, and they came to us and blew smoke up our butts. They told us how we were the future and so were they, and how we had anticipated how things were going and they were going to show the whole world our videos and make us huge. MTV came on in three cities, and, yes, they were playing Devo videos all day long. Then, as soon as they went national, they tied themselves to Top 40 mainstream-radio hits, and they started pulling Devo videos because the songs weren't on the radio. That was their excuse: "You guys don't have hits."

MOTHERSBAUGH: For survival, we needed to have some kind of an income. We were so far ahead of the curve that it really made sense at the time to crawl into the colon of Hollywood and attempt to impart our message through that methodology, to allow ourselves to be on *The Dick Clark Show*, to be on *The David Letterman Show*. We said, "How far can we get into this?" We thought the Devo aesthetic was strong enough, we believed in it enough and thought we were different enough that it could survive the acid test of Hollywood, and we had a modicum of success. We finally had a hit.

CASALE: We were still a band that cared about ideas and aesthetics, not sitting around trying to cynically write hits, and we didn't put something on a record unless we liked it. We didn't have any sense of "Oh, here's the hit!" The record company types came into the studio when we were making *Freedom of Choice*, and they all decided either "Girl U Want" or "Freedom of Choice" were the only viable radio songs. They went with "Girl U Want," and it promptly stiffed.

They didn't even want to put out "Freedom of Choice." They were still arguing about spending any more money on us when [legendary radio influencer] Kal Rudman, independent of all that, made "Whip It" a hit. It isn't like Warner Bros. paid some independent promo man $200,000. They didn't spend money on Devo.

Lyrically, it was a parody. We were all big fans of Communist and Red Chinese propaganda, because intellectually you can't help but be drawn to it, and because it's so funny and the graphics that go with it are so powerful. It was really Thomas Pynchon's book *Gravity's Rainbow* that made me write the lyrics. In *Gravity's Rainbow*, he's writing these poems and lyrics, and they are parodies of Horatio Alger: You're number one! There's nobody else like you! You can do it! Americans, pick yourselves up by your bootstraps and you can make it! We thought, *This is perfect. This is like the American version of Red Chinese propaganda.* Our graphics taste ran toward Russian constructivism and Chinese government propaganda but, obviously, lyrically, we were more American. So I thought, *I'm gonna write a Pynchonesque parody*, and "Whip It" was my attempt at that.

Some people assumed it was an S&M song, so we wanted to fulfill their expectations with the video. Others thought it was about jacking off. Every time we'd do a radio interview, typically the DJs would be these leftover seventies hippies. They'd have the satin baseball jackets from the record company and the big pile of coke, and they'd go, "Whip it, dude. Heh heh heh!" and they'd make jerk-off moves. We'd start by telling them what it's actually about and that would bum them out, so then we realized we should just go along with it—"Right! Whip it! Heh heh heh! Ya know it!"—and then they liked it. We made sure the video reinforced the whipping idea by having Mark literally whip the clothes off the black woman in the ranch corral while the cowboys cheered him on. It was satire of all the horrible right-wing racist values.

Suddenly we were playing 10,000-seat arenas and getting taken a lot more seriously, and that gives you a lot more tools.

> **"We thought, If we're going to effect any change, the way to do it is you go into the belly of the beast."**

But then, foolishly, we didn't change our aesthetic or our message or our disdain for stupid people or fundamentalist religion or power abuses.

MOTHERSBAUGH: We were a divisive entity throughout our whole early record career. You would get people who were inspired by it—the future geeks, the people who turned into the Steve Jobs and Bill Gates, and the people who embraced technology and understood ironic humor. But Devo were never Bon Jovi–big. We were always on the outskirts of the culture. When we had a hit, it was a double-edged sword. When the next album came up, the record company, who had ignored us for the last three albums—it was great: They would give us enough money to put out another record, and we got to do what we wanted. By the fourth album, they were like, "Wait a minute.

These guys brought in millions of dollars for us. We better keep an eye on them, make sure they don't fuck up." So the president of the company was like, "Hey, guys, do anything you want. Just do another 'Whip It.'" But we'd just done the same thing we'd always done, and "Whip It" just happened to connect with DJs.

We wanted our songs in commercials. People like Neil Young were like, "I would never let that happen to one of my songs." We thought, *We want kids to hear those songs*. "Freedom of Choice" is in a Target commercial. They go, "What is that song?" Then they go listen to the record, and they go, "Wait a minute. It says, 'Freedom of choice is what you got / Freedom from choice is what you want.' What does that mean?" We wanted kids to get sucked into our music, so we took advantage every time we got offered to license our stuff to commercials. That's how we'll affect people and change them. It would be kind of like letting evil Big Brother serve you up and Big Brother didn't even know he was doing it. These are the exact people who needed to hear our music and would never have heard it in a million years if it wasn't for one stupid song that fit into a dance club format. Some people came to our shows, and they're doing their stupid white-people dances to our song, and they're singing "Whip it good!" And then they buy the album, and

they take it home, and they get served up a whole load of Devo.

CASALE: We were constantly trying to explain ourselves and present ideas, and they would get ignored or shot down. It was like the old TV series *The Prisoner*—you can't get out of the village. That was the irony, and that was exactly what Devo had been telling everyone: All this fake rebellion rock 'n' roll was just posing, and corporations were selling it. It had all been totally co-opted. We were elevating the whole idea of co-option as satire. When we said, "We're all Devo," we meant it.

THAT WAS THEN BUT THIS IS NOW

Devo split in 1991. Mothersbaugh went on to a successful career scoring movies and TV shows. Casale has directed commercials and music videos. "Whip It" lives on in many commercials for household products, including Swiffer. In 2006, Disney attempted to launch Devo 2.0, a group of child actors performing songs from the Devo catalog aimed at the preteen market. The project was not a success. Devo 1.0, meanwhile, having re-formed in 1995, continues to release new music and tour.

"We made sure the video reinforced the whipping idea by having Mark literally whip the clothes off the black woman in the ranch corral while the cowboys cheered him on. It was satire of all the horrible right-wing racist values."

CASALE: Disney said, "We'd really like to do something with kids and Devo songs." They wanted the songs skewed for four- to seven-year-olds. I said, "What if we cast around for a kids band that can actually play, and we'll record them, and I'll shoot videos for the songs, and we'll make the kids into personalities and take them on tour for a year?" Disney loved it.

I spent a good part of a year getting the band together and ready to go out on a tour of middle schools. We were practically done, and the top brass at the Disney label wanted to see some of the video cuts. Suddenly, we were being asked to send over the lyrics to

every Devo song that we'd shot. We get the big call: "You're gonna have to redo the lyrics." They were like, "'That's Good,' the whole third verse: 'Life's a bee without a buzz / It's only great till you get stung.' We know what you're saying. It means life's a bitch unless you're getting high, and life's only great until the cops pop you!" I was like, Wow, here's some suits that were raised on a breakfast, lunch, and dinner of hip-hop mentality, because those words were written in 1982, and it didn't mean any of that. We might as well be in Red China. The best was "Uncontrollable Urge." They said, "We know what an uncontrollable urge is!" We never said what the uncontrollable urge was. They said, "Exactly! It's the lack of definition. Those kids are going to think it means sex. Make it about junk food." This was going to play on the Disney channel in the afternoon. And what do they advertise: junk food and sugary cereals. I changed the lyrics. I wrote, "Before dinner and after lunch / I get so out of control I know I gotta munch," and our lead singer in Devo 2.0 is a 13-year-old girl, Nicole, and so they show it to their top brass, and they go, "We love it!" It sounded so filthy!

MOTHERSBAUGH: The Swiffer commercial was maybe the most pervertedly like a Devo video. Like, we would have found that footage and gone, "Let's use that!" 'Cause it was such hideous, moronic footage of a housewife dancing around her kitchen with a wooden floor mopping up with this stupid miracle mop. But by that point, "Whip It" had already been "Flip It," "Chip It," "Dip It." It's like they're injecting people with their stupid messages; they're the host mechanism for our virus. What did I just get? It wasn't "Snip It." Maybe it was "Clip It"? They did this commercial where they have factory workers singing "Rip It" for packaging things on pallets that are going to be shipped overseas. They have all these workers singing in this video that's one step above homemade. I really like it.

CASALE: Devo have been offered a ton of opportunities all the time that Mark scuttles, and I keep trying to see how many of them can survive. I'd be doing a Devo musical and a Devo movie, a Devo store, Devo products. Mark's the one that puts it into retirement. All he wants to do is composing for TV and films. At this point, I wouldn't even have the expectation of cooperation, just agreement not to stop it.

MOTHERSBAUGH: He's not being 100 percent honest. He is, in the sense that I put my attention in other places, but neither one of us can show the other a script they've come up with for a Broadway show that anybody wants to sign on to. Whatever the appearance is, my intentions are for the health of the band. If someone has a script that centers around the Devo songs or the band—although that, to me, seems less appealing than something that centers around de-evolution; you could do something very entertaining that talked about de-evolution—I haven't seen that script. If he knows about a script that I turned down, he should send it to me immediately.

CASALE: I just came to realize that what I think should be any opportunities and potentials that should define Devo are not reality.

MOTHERSBAUGH: I feel like Devo should have done what Kraftwerk did, connecting with the Museum of Modern Art. Maybe I am the source of all the problems, but I don't really think so. Who knows? Maybe there's still time for Devo, part 3.

MIXTAPE: 5 More Songs by Bands of Weirdos 1. "Making Plans for Nigel," XTC 2. "Rock Lobster," The B-52s 3. "The Number One Song in Heaven," Sparks 4. "Human Fly," The Cramps 5. "Once in a Lifetime," Talking Heads

ECHO

AND THE

BUNNYMEN

"THE KILLING MOON"

In London, they preened. In Manchester, they brooded. In Birmingham, they danced. But in Liverpool, the bands of the eighties hallucinated. You didn't even have to listen to the music; you just had to look at the names—the Teardrop Explodes, Orchestral Manoeuvres in the Dark, Dalek I Love You, Pink Military Stand Alone, the Icicle Works, Nightmares in Wax—to know that someone had slipped something particularly potent into the Mersey. The city's most prominent act at that time, Echo and the Bunnymen, were on a different type of trip, and it wasn't a joy ride. The opening bars of their debut single, 1979's "Pictures on My Wall," are a portent of doom. For the next four years and the subsequent quartet of albums, the Bunnymen made music choking with paranoia, confusion, and despair. Few singers embodied heavy-lidded, drugged-up dread as convincingly as Ian McCulloch. The Bunnymen's brand of woe-is-me intensity is hard to maintain without collapsing into self-parody, and as the decade progressed, they evolved into a more traditional band. But to this day, those first four albums are like a long, scared shiver in the middle of a dark, lonely night.

JB: I wonder what it must have been like to be Ian McCulloch back at the height of his U.K. fame, to show up for concerts and find himself confronted with crowds of clones, adolescent doppelgängers swamped by their oversize army coats and baggy camouflage pants, attempting to duplicate his graveyard pallor and painstakingly unkempt hairstyle. I imagine he was enough of a narcissist to enjoy the effort and exult in the failure. (It's possible he gave me a comprehensive account of what it was like while we were chatting, but that Scouse accent: impenetrable.) We live in a time when the words "rock star" are peppered liberally and inappropriately across all facets of everyday conversation. Actual living, breathing examples of rock stardom, though? They're way up there on the endangered species list. In his heyday, Ian McCulloch embodied most of the attributes we want from our rock stars: He was aloof, self-obsessed, arrogant, insecure, and convinced that he was the center of the universe. And with "The Killing Moon," he presented a cast-iron case that he was correct in that belief.

LM: When I saw Echo and the Bunnymen in concert a few years back, McCulloch introduced "The Killing Moon" by saying, "Some say this is the best song ever written. I happen to agree." You won't get an argument from me. Whenever I hear that eerie intro and he starts to sing about taking me up in his arms, it stops me dead in my tracks, whether I'm mid-workout at the gym or mid-shop at Trader Joe's. "The Killing Moon" is mood music that never fails to remind me of what it's like to be young and wistful—not sad, exactly, but brimming with the kind of longing and melancholy that only a restless romantic can truly understand.

IAN McCULLOCH: "The Killing Moon" came in stages. I had the chords and the verse and melody, then one day I woke up, and it was sunny, and I sat bolt upright—if you can sit bolt upright—with the words to the chorus, which I hadn't known any of before. I think it was the Lord himself saying, "It would be fantastic if you said these words." I woke up and there they were. It was the whole thing: "Fate / Up against your will / Through the thick and thin / He will wait until / You give yourself to him." That is up there with "To be or not to be." Whoever Him is, is up to you. For a long time the Him in the chorus was me, and then I realized, it isn't me at all—it's Him, the fucking higher power. It's basically a hymn or a prayer. It's probably my "How

Great Thou Art." It sounds like a love song, it sounds adult, it sounds European—like it's got subtitles, and everyone's got fantastic hair. I've said a lot of times that it's the greatest song ever written, and the reason it is, is that it's more than a song. It's way beyond being a song. It's about everything. It's not about football or fucking celery, but it's about most other things.

I loved the Pistols and the Clash, but a lot of the punks were just dodgy Cockneys. It was backwoods music. At [legendary Liverpool club] Eric's, it was always a mixture. It inspired the likes of me, Holly Johnson, and Ian Broudie. It wasn't a fashion, leather-studded thing; it was more about listening to pretty obscure records that I'd never heard—everything from reggae to punk to shit like Roogalator. It was a melting pot. It started because of punk, but it wasn't drenched in that one-dimensional thing that the clubs in Manchester had. They all wore cloth caps with their hair sticking out at the back. And tank tops. [Editor's note: He doesn't mean tank top in the American sense of the filmy garment that clings to Kate Upton's curves. He means it in the grim, British sense of the shapeless, sleeveless, sludge-colored V-neck sweater that strained against many a British belly in the latter part of the previous century.] Liverpool was different. We had the Jobriath look amongst us with Pete Burns and Holly. It was a mad smorgasbord that I never got bored of. It was easy being in the same place as these . . . not weirdos, but lost souls. We couldn't play any instruments, but it was only a question of getting a guitar off someone. The Crucial Three [McCulloch's much-written-about-and-discussed first band with Julian Cope and Pete Wylie] didn't exist. The other two wanted it more than I did. It lasted for about an hour. We played one horrible song in my mum's front room. Julian had a silver bass. He'd painted graffiti on it, like "I Am a Punk" or "Get Punkitude." He was a dickhead extraordinaire. Wylie played some kind of Les Paul the color of fudge. I stood there with a bog roll [toilet paper] and a sponge on my head mumbling some kind of crap. It was an hour of abject bollocks. The other two still believe that we toured.

Then there was another group, A Shallow Madness. We rehearsed in my flat, in my bedroom, but I used to go to my mum's down the road to have my washing done to avoid being there. I'd go and have egg and chips, processed peas, HP sauce, bread and butter. I'd have eaten fucking rat rather than rehearse with them. They were rubbish. I thought, *I'll never do that show at the Rainbow, that David Bowie show I dreamed about. I'll never be Ziggy Stardust.* I thought at best I was going to be the tambourinist in XTC.

"[*The Killing Moon*] is up there with 'To be or not to be.'... It's probably my 'How Great Thou Art.'"

But then I bumped into Will [Sergeant, Echo and the Bunnymen guitarist], and it was like, *Fucking hell, this fellow has befriended me in one of the least-friendly ways possible*. He was taciturn, and he was shy, but also he had an aura that could melt volcanic lava even more than it had already melted. He had a sneer—not even a sneer, just a kind of flick of his lip. I thought, *Okay, you're the cat for me*. This fellow, he said, "I hear you're a pretty good singer." I said, "Who told you that?" I hadn't ever sung in my life except when I was 14 in my bedroom to Bowie records. But I look like I'm a great singer. So he said, "Fancy doing some music? Come to my house in Melling." I was like, "Where the fuck is that? Somewhere near Hadrian's Wall?" It was not far off. It was a remote subcontinent outside of Liverpool. I took five buses to get there, carrying my Hondo guitar. I wanted all the people on the bus to look at me like I was a musician, but this was just a plank of wood with some strings on it. It wasn't going to further my stardom.

When I got to Will's, he had a drum machine and a guitar his dad made. I don't know how he made it—he had no background in music or making instruments—but it bloody worked. I had my acoustic. We plugged in, put the drum machine on. He said, "What do you think: Bossa Nova or Rock 1?" I said, "Let's try Rock 1." The drum machine went boom-cha-cha-boom-cha-cha. I went ching-ching-ching on my acoustic, and he went ding-ding-ding on his guitar. I said to him, "Hang on, we are the best band in the fucking world." I thought, *Fucking hell,*

MIXTAPE: 5 More Songs from Liverpool

1. "Reward," The Teardrop Explodes   2. "Touch," Lori and the Chameleons   3. "The World," Dalek I Love You   4. "The Story of the Blues," The Mighty Wah!   5. "Flaming Sword," Care

"Liverpool was different.... It was a mad smorgasbord that I never got bored of. It was easy being in the same place as these... not weirdos, but lost souls."

it took five bus rides to get here, but there's something going on. That brittle twanging and some kind of spindly outer-space guitar and me singing something—it sounded interesting already. I thought, *This sounds great. All I've got to do is recite or half-sing some pretentious crap over the top.* And lo and behold, "Pictures on My Wall," which sounded pretty decent: "People burning, hearts beating…" It was a bit like the apocalypse, Liverpool 11 stylee.

The first time we played Eric's, we only had the one song. We got up and the drum machine wouldn't work, and we were wearing headphones, so none of us could really hear anything. I was ready to go with our one song that I didn't really know, but I had the line, "Talking to you about evolution /

All you want to do is swing like a monkey." I thought the cognoscenti of Liverpool would be digging that, and then after that line I should try and come up with a few more so it would keep going. Will was on his knees, going, "It's not working! I plugged it into the PA, and it's not working!" I was like, "It's my first time, and your drum machine's fucking crap." He said, "Do you want to go into the dressing room and wait for me to fix it?" I said, "That'll look good, won't it? Leaving you onstage like you're the sodding electrician. No, I'm going to stand here." And it was pretty hot. I had this fantastic red polo neck on, the kind David Attenborough would have worn on the telly in the fifties. I was like, "Come on, get them ohms and watts going!" It could have been embarrassing. There were about 70 people. I just stood there and looked at them, and I think they all thought, *Fucking hell.* I didn't say much. I coughed, and I did a full-on whistle into the mic, and then finally, after about 10 minutes, the drum machine started and we were off and running. People were spellbound. We were in our flow. No, honestly, we were. Pete Wylie was like, "Bloody hell, Mac, that was out there. That was avant-garde." It was better than being in a proper band with a drummer churning out all that new wave bollocks. All those bands wearing school blazers and gray jeans? I mean, what the fuck have you got gray jeans on for?

THAT WAS THEN
BUT THIS IS NOW

Echo had a modicum of modern-rock success with the singles "Lips Like Sugar" and the Doors' "People Are Strange" from *The Lost Boys* soundtrack. In 1988 McCulloch split from the Bunnymen and embarked on a solo career. Nine years later the singer reunited with Sergeant and bassist Les Pattinson. The group continues to tour and record. Meanwhile, McCulloch continues to be irritated by Bono (who's gone on the record as saying he's an Echo admirer) and the U2 singer's messiah complex.

McCULLOCH: I heard they played "The Killing Moon" on *Dancing with the Stars*. That's the most difficult song to dance to. You can't even do a funeral march to it.

With my songs, I always like to push things and make them cryptic but also make them easy for moderately intelligent people to get. I always want to push on and make those lyrical delights that can stand alone outside the song. That, to me, is the longevity of it. I know there are people out there who appreciate it and love it. It might not be right for 100,000 people with cowboy hats on singing "Where the Streets Have No Name." I suggest they get their fucking local sheriff on the case if their streets have no name. Bono—Nobo, that's his fucking name. What a gibbering, leprechaunish twat. He's up to no good. He's more out of his mind than I've ever seen anybody, and that includes Mel Gibson on the David Letterman show when his head spun around 360 times. He's the most banal, buffooneried-up, fucking leprechaun. He's kissed more Blarney Stones than I've had hot dinners. I wish they'd been toxic so he'd fuck off.

"**F**rom half-spoken shadows emerges a canvas. A kiss of light breaks to reveal a moment when all mirrors are redundant. Listen to the portrait of the dance of perfection: the Spandau Ballet." Thusly did scenester journalist Robert Elms announce the group's arrival, circa 1980. London's painfully exclusive, agonizingly fashionable Scala club served as the backdrop for their debut gig, quickly sealing their reputation as the most despised—and discussed—band in Britain. Inviting envy, derision, and open antagonism, Spandau Ballet (their name a term used by Nazi guards to describe the twitches made by Jewish hanging victims at Berlin's Spandau Prison) stretched an invisible velvet rope between themselves and a music media still infatuated with Joe Strummer and Johnny Rotten. As members of the notorious Blitz Club clique, the Spands positioned themselves as an androgynous fraternity, sneering down at the ripped T-shirts, dirty sneakers, and beer-soaked jeans worn by the nation's sheeplike, style-free rock audience. And their clannish demeanor proved a cunningly effective marketing tool. After initial success with a few chilly, Teutonic hits, Spandau started smiling and wearing sensible suits, and by the time they'd released the international number-one "True" in 1983, they were embracing a mass audience who would've never passed the rigid dress codes at the nightclubs the band once frequented.

BALLET

"TRUE"

JB: One of the youthful pleasures of punk was the opportunity to tell your elders and betters, "You're a dirty hippie—you don't get it!" Ever the sharp operator, Spandau songwriter Gary Kemp flipped the script, addressing his detractors with a sneering, "You're a middle-class wannabe; we're working-class royalty—you don't get it." In the post-punk environment of the early eighties, hurling that "middle class" label was an insult tantamount to sinking a shiv between an opponent's shoulder blades. It meant you were inauthentic, that you were culturally blinkered, that you couldn't dance. It hurt.

 But Spandau Ballet weren't in the class-war business. Once they'd wedged an elegant boot in the door, they were all about transitioning from exclusive to inclusive. And there's no better way to win over the masses on whom you'd once looked down than with a sincere, hand-on-heart, "I'm just a poor boy" ballad. "True" is a classic end-of-the-dance song. It's one of the few legitimate examples of British baby-making music.

LM: Like the rest of America, my love affair with Spandau Ballet began with "True." Unlike the rest of America, my relationship didn't end there. Thanks to the glorious Newark, New Jersey–based video channel U68—a mid-decade, UHF alternative to MTV—I retroactively learned that Spandau had been New Romantics. There was their synthy 1980 debut, "To Cut a Long Story Short," and 1981's funky disco jam "Chant No. 1." But my favorite had to be 1982's artsy "She Loved like Diamond," a melodramatic mini-movie in which a black-veiled ghost of a woman drifts through dry ice and falls to the floor with blood pooling out of her mouth. "She loved like diamond," Tony Hadley crooned, "and cut so hard she died." (Even then I struggled to find meaning in Gary Kemp's lyrics.) Watching that today is like unearthing an ancient artifact, yet nothing about "True" feels like it belongs inside a time capsule—not the sharp, double-breasted suits they wear in the video, and certainly not the music. With that song, Spandau Ballet went from New Romantic to just plain romantic and, as a result, ended up with arguably the most timeless song in this book.

GARY KEMP: In 1978 we found this wonderful little club called Billy's, which had a Bowie Night. It was put on by a guy called Steve Strange and another one called Rusty Egan, and they were playing records that they had found in Berlin—Kraftwerk, Gina X, Nina Hagen—mixed up with Bowie, Iggy, Lou Reed, and Roxy Music. It was the first time that a youth cult had begun without a band. It's really almost going back to the mod time, when they were dancing to Motown. They weren't interested in watching bands; they just wanted to dress up cool and watch each other. And suddenly a manager thought, I'll make sure there is a band for them, and the Who were formed.

In a way, we did that too. These kids were down in Billy's in Soho, dancing this extraordinary slow jive to this electronica music. We arrived and we thought, *This is our time. This is our generation. We have a responsibility.*

We already had a band, but we were on a sort of post–power pop hiatus. The band that we liked up to that point, who we all wanted to be, was Generation X. We thought Billy Idol was the best thing we'd ever seen. Ironically, after Billy saw our first gig at the Blitz, he went up to Steve Dagger, our manager, and said, "This is the future of rock 'n' roll, man."

We decided we'd do a private gig for these kids in Billy's. By then we'd rewritten our entire set list. We'd bought a synthesizer, and we had a bunch of electronic songs—all four-on-the-floor drums, dance-y, groove-y, but with this very white, European sound to them. It was a mixture of Kraftwerk and what David Bowie had done in Berlin—that sort of extraordinary amalgamation of Iggy Pop and Edith Piaf.

Then we started playing these gigs in extraordinary places for our friends. We knew that they would not go to some rock 'n' roll pub. We did one on the HMS *Belfast*; we did one in a cinema. They were events. No record company had seen us at this point, and they all wanted to sign us. Record companies weren't allowed into our gigs. The only way they could see us was through this documentary that Janet Street-Porter filmed in black and white. Nowadays you can't have a mystique. Somebody videos you on a phone, they put it up on YouTube, and someone else writes "bollocks" underneath.

When the club moved from Billy's to the Blitz in Covent Garden, our mantra to the press was that we are a movement; we're not just interested in being in a band. There are people in this club who will be photographers, filmmakers, clothes designers, and dancers—which is to say, you had Stephen Jones, the milliner; Michael Clark, the dancer; John Maybury, the filmmaker;

Dylan Jones, the magazine editor; Robert Elms, the journalist; and it goes on. Boy George was there, Steve and Rusty. There was a sense that there was going to be a multimedia success, and I don't think that had happened since the sixties. A lot of the kids who became successes in the sixties had stayed in charge all the way up to the eighties. I remember that suddenly, in about 1980, everybody wanted to have someone with colored hair come and work for them. It was like media companies were just recruiting people as they walked out of the Blitz.

I clearly remember going up to Birmingham on our first gig ever outside London. It was December 1980, and our first single, "To Cut a Long Story Short," was out. We decided to play in this place called the Botanical Gardens. It wasn't even a venue—it was, literally, a botanical garden. We knew that there was a club up there called the Rum Runner and that everyone was doing a similar thing to us. So about a hundred of our lot all went up there, and it was like the Wild West: the two sides slowly approaching each other. I remember someone asking our manager if they could support us that night and, of course, he answered, "No one supports us. We're the only band onstage." Then, after the gig, we went back to the [Rum Runner owners] Berrow brothers' flat in Birmingham, and I was sitting on the floor, and we were all drinking, and I realized

"We arrived and we thought, *This is our time. This is our generation. We have a responsibility.*"

▬▬▬▬▬▬

that some of these guys in the flat were in the band that had wanted to support us. I distinctly remember this blond boy I was talking to saying to me, "We've got this band—it's called Duran Duran." And we soon found out about them.

The electronic thing became popular very quickly, and we sidestepped it into doing a brazenly funky song called "Chant No. 1." I don't know why that worked. You just get things right sometimes. It was a song about Soho, a film noir of the Soho streets filled with drug-induced paranoia. It was sort of achingly, archly hip, and you can't sustain that. That's why we jumped ship. We could have been like Depeche Mode and just played the same music for 35 years and had great success with it, but we were bored. We wanted to move on.

For me, the only way to go after that

was to write damn good songs, songs that would last forever. I'd been listening to a lot of Al Green, Marvin Gaye, Daryl Hall and John Oates. Steve Norman, who at that point was really Spandau's second guitarist as well as the percussionist, had picked up the saxophone and utterly fell in love with it. I found myself writing songs that weren't just for Tony but also for Steve's sax. Spandau has two things that make us sound like no other band: Tony's unique and powerful voice and Steve Norman's amazing saxophone that we always like to include. It's the sound of our soul, if you like.

"True" was about the fourth or fifth song I wrote for that album. Originally, Trevor Horn was going to produce, but I don't think he ever really got the idea of recording a band that was very into controlling their own sonic destiny, so we mutually dropped each other, and we found [Tony] Swain and [Steve] Jolley. They were white guys who were doing black music with a band called Imagination, and I loved the sound they were making. We thought we should get away from London, because we needed to find a sound for the album that wasn't reliant on Soho. We went to Compass Point in Nassau. Robert Palmer had recorded there, so had Bryan Ferry. Talking Heads were there when we were there.

Nobody thought "True" was going to be the single. Musically, it was me trying to write an Al Green song. What made the difference was the backing vocals. I went and started tracking up the backing vocals, and they became the unique selling point of that record. I put on this Motown-influenced guitar, we laid down the keyboard, and the drums were all done, and then we made this strange decision not to include my brother, Martin, on the song. We wanted a bass synth because we really loved the bass synth on the Imagination records. Martin stepped aside and let Tony Swain play it. If he had known it was going to be one of our biggest songs ever, he might have argued the point.

You never know what's going to make a record work, but there was something about the aural quality of that song that suggested

MIXTAPE: 5 More Blue-Eyed British-Soul Songs
1. "Careless Whisper," Wham! featuring George Michael 2. "Digging Your Scene," The Blow Monkeys 3. "Bad Day," Carmel 4. "Closest Thing to Heaven," Kane Gang 5. "Oh Patti (Don't Feel Sorry for Loverboy)," Scritti Politti

it was just going to be important. But we still didn't think it was a single—it was a six-and-a-half-minute track. It was going to be the last song on the album. Can you imagine that now, sticking one of your best tracks last? No one would do that. In those days, though, you approached an album as an actual piece of work, and where you placed your tracks was all about how people heard the piece as a whole. Movies have denouements, plays have denouements, and albums had denouements too. Nowadays they just peter out.

At the time, I was having a very unrequited romance with [Altered Images singer] Clare Grogan. It was unrequited on both ends. It was courtly—I think that's the expression I can correctly use—but it was romantic. She gave me a Nabokov book, *Lolita*, and that sort of represented

> ## "We were getting back reports from America that it was getting played on black radio. They had no idea we were a white band."

her. I took two lyrics that I based on lines in Lolita. One was "seaside arms," which was an expression that Humbert Humbert used about Lolita. I thought that was rather beautiful, and I was ridiculed for that for years. "What's that line about? It's stupid!" Well, go and argue with Nabokov. And the other one was "With a thrill in my head and a pill on my tongue," which I kind of paraphrased.

"True" became a song about writing a love song. Why "Why do I find it hard to write the next line? I want the truth to be said"? Because I didn't want to write it down—because there's nothing more embarrassing. That's partly what the song is about. But it's hard to be truthful in a song. As a songwriter, you're not writing love letters all the time; you're using real life to help you fantasize about a greater, more powerful life. What you really love more than anything else are the songs you're writing.

Eventually "True" made number one in the U.K.—in those days no records went straight in at number one—and we were getting back reports from America that it was getting played on black radio. They had no idea we were a white band. The proudest legacy of that song for me is that it turned on black kids, and there are so many black artists—Nelly, R. Kelly, will.i.am, Lloyd, P.M. Dawn—who dug it and made it part of their aural landscape.

"Gold" was a little bit of a hit in America,

but we had issues with our record company there. They weren't very powerful, and they made a lot of mistakes. I remember meeting John Taylor when Duran had their reunion in the early 2000s. I went along to the gig, and immediately afterwards, he said, "You guys had Europe, we had America." Which is kind of how it was. It's rather ridiculous that these two fey groups that sized each other up in the car park of the Botanical Gardens in Birmingham should then decide that one had one continent and one had the other, but musically that's what happened.

I'm not bothered by the fact that Spandau's American career didn't last as long as it did in the rest of the world, because what we ended up with was a song that has completely altered the American landscape of music. I'd rather have one of those than a much longer career that left less of a song legacy behind. That's really where my heart is, with my songs. They're my children.

TONY HADLEY: The name Spandau Ballet was chosen out of naïveté. Robert Elms had been to Berlin for the weekend, and he was having a leak in the bathroom in some grotty club, when there, graffitied on the toilet wall where he was standing, was "Spandau Ballet." Spandau is an area of Berlin—a region, like Brooklyn. He came back and said, "I think I've got the name for the band." We went, "Spand–what?"

"Spandau" is not a word that trips off the tongue. He said, "It's great: It's got some sort of German vibe to it; it's ballet—it's about dance. It's creative." We were looking for a name that was going to really stick in people's minds. And Berlin was a very cool city. Everything was very angular, very stark. There was East Berlin and West Berlin—it was like the forces of good and evil pitted against each other.

By that time we'd all convinced ourselves it was brilliant. And it was brilliant, until we hit a bit of a roadblock in America. There's a massive Jewish community there, and certain people started to say that we were an anti-Semitic band. People have told me over the years that there is sort of a Nazi reference, which was nonsense from our point of view. But I could understand people who were a bit more knowledgeable than a bunch of 19-, 20-year-old kids going, "Hey, man, that's got an implication."

No one in America had had the prior history of Spandau Ballet. They just thought we were a nice bunch of guys who sang this really lovely ballad. They didn't realize that there had been previous albums—*True* was our third album. Although, I don't think "True" or even the album is totally representative of the group. We were much tougher live than we were on record.

If we'd been signed today, we probably would have been dropped on the second album and never have gotten to *True*, but in those days record companies kept the faith. So we were allowed to make the *True* album, which obviously was a much more commercial-sounding album. That song and album took us from a cult band to an international success. It was number one in 21 countries around the world. All of a sudden we were traveling in a private jet and going, "Wow, this is amazing!"

I don't think "True" is Spandau's best song—for me, "Through the Barricades"

is. But "True" had some connection, and I don't really know why. It's not a specific lyric, is it? "Head over heels when toe to toe"—sometimes you'd be like, "Right, Gary, what's this about, mate?" Is it "I'm head over heels in love?" "Am I in bed because our feet are touching and …?" I don't know. But then, I suppose, we grew up on David Bowie and Roxy Music. "Virginia Plain"—what's that about? Half of the Bowie songs, I couldn't tell you what they're about. With "True," you have to create the imagery for yourself.

THAT WAS THEN *BUT THIS IS NOW*

Gary Kemp left Spandau Ballet in 1990 to pursue acting and a solo career. He and Martin starred as the notorious gangster twins in *The Krays* before the latter joined *EastEnders* as one of the soap's most popular villains. In 1999, Hadley, Norman, and drummer John Keeble failed in their attempt to sue Kemp, the group's sole credited songwriter, for unpaid royalties. After a decade of sullen silences and hurt feelings, all five embarked on a 2009 reunion tour. However, the curtain has since fallen on the Ballet yet again, with the singer returning to the Tony Hadley Band—featuring Keeble on drums—and his duties as a part owner of Red Rat Brewery.

KEMP: As the decade wound down, there was a sudden interest in club culture, which was sort of inspired by us. Back in 1980, we used to say we wouldn't tour, we'd only release white labels, and DJs could play our records, and anyone dancing to them were the stars. In the end, that monster we'd built came

back to destroy us all. The second summer of love and the rise of the DJ at the end of the eighties was really the death knell for the bands. Remaining at the top of the tree was going to be difficult. Even bands like U2 took a bit of time to regain their speed.

I had an opportunity with my brother

to go into acting. I got bored with working with the band. I was frustrated at being the only songwriter. Ten years later, we ended up in a big court case punch-up. I'd had a child, my marriage [to actress Sadie Frost] was breaking up, and I was in the middle of a solo album. [Hadley, Keeble, and Norman] realized that the publishing makes lots of money, and the songwriter makes more money than the performers, and there's a bitterness that comes from that. We ended up in a dispute, and it took a judge to sort it out. Once that happened, there was going to be at least 10 years before we could face each other again.

I'm so glad we did, because we ended up coming back and selling more tickets on that tour than we ever sold in the eighties. I think there's a future for Spandau still, because if you fall in love with songs or an artist in your formative years, you pretty much love them for the rest of your life.

HADLEY: The reunion wasn't an easy decision. It took about six months of soul-searching before I thought I could meet with Gary. We met at the Flask in Highgate in North London, with John Keeble as the Henry Kissinger. We got a pint, and I said, "Right, before we go any further. . . . " I launched a few grenades. Keeble was sitting there going, "Oh, Christ! It's all falling apart already!"

Then Gary said a few things, and we sort of looked at each other. "Is this going to work?" he said. I said, "I'll tell you what: I've said my piece. If this is going to work, then we have to draw a line under it and not talk about this again. What happened has happened. Do you think we could work together again?" And he said, "I'd really like that to be the case, and I think we can."

So, I agreed. I said, "Look, happy to get together again, but I'm a solo artist. I'm not going to go back in Spandau Ballet [full-time]." I mean, I've been a solo artist for longer than I was ever in Spandau Ballet, and I have a good career. My allegiance, really, is to my own band, the Tony Hadley Band, who have been with me for years.

I suppose the question on a lot of people's lips is, "Will we get back together again?" I would like to. There's still a little bit of politics.

The Christmas before last, John Keeble said, "Have you heard from the rest of the guys?" I'm, "No, no, and I'm not expecting to either." We're all older. What you were when you were focused on music when you were a young fella, and what you become when you get married and you have children—you pick up other friends, and they become more of your best friends.

But we're still old friends, which is great. We can all go out and have a pint and a meal, and we'd all laugh and joke and tell stories. But it's not the same, and it never will be.

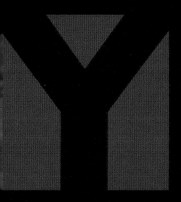

You know the famous Human League story? The one where the founder is pushed out, leading to the departure of its creative axis and leaving only the singer and the guy who operates the slide projector? And you know how the singer, Phil Oakey, recruited two teenage backing singers who'd never sung a note just because he liked the way they danced at the Sheffield disco the Crazy Daisy? And you know how, a year later, that version of the group beat ABBA out of the coveted U.K. Christmas number-one spot with "Don't You Want Me," a record that would go on to kick open the doors of America to all manner of British synthesizer bands with fascinating haircuts? This is not that story. We approached the Human League on numerous occasions—occasions numerous enough to be innumerable. And each time, Oakey politely but firmly turned down our request for an interview. So while we don't have that Human League story, we don't *not* have a Human League story. We talked to Martyn Ware for our Heaven 17 chapter (see page 98), and he spoke in some depth about the early days of the Human League, the singular talent of Oakey, and the writing and recording of "Being Boiled," which left us with a dilemma: Do we memorize this stuff to use as anecdotes during one of our enjoyable new wave dinner parties? Or do we cheekily run it under the Human League banner because "Being Boiled," released in 1978, is one of the foundations upon which the era we're celebrating was built? We're probably going to do both. So, this story does not appear with the cooperation of the current incarnation of the Human League. But it is a story about the first Human League single, told by a member of the group who helped write and produce it. Caveat emptor!

B: While I was interviewing Martyn Ware, I stated that the first two lines of "Being Boiled" are the electronic-music equivalent of Mick Jagger's opening couplet in "Sympathy for the Devil." Sometimes words just pop out of my mouth, but in this case, I made sense—at least to myself. When Oakey intones, "Listen to the voice of Buddha / Saying stop your sericulture," you instantly know you're in the hands of someone who sees the world in a very different way, and you've just made the decision to hang on for the ride. This early, indie version of the Human League was awash in nerd influences—Michael Moorcock, Dark Star, Gerry Anderson, the dot matrix printer—and together they coalesced into the woozy, nightmarish narratives of *Reproduction* and the heartbroken, dystopian ballads of *Travelogue*. I've loved a lot of the music the Human League and Heaven 17 went on to make, but separately they never created a world quite as compelling as the one they built together back in their formative days.

LM: Nowadays, you know exactly wh every pop song is about. It's right the in the title: You're a firework. You c stand under my umbrella. But there w a time that bands made us work for I had no idea what "Being Boiled" w about. *Sericulture*? But the music was ominous and Oakey's voice so hypnotizi so meditative, I really wasn't bothered the coming years, Oakey would be writ songs based on human emotions, but this low-fi warning to the silk industry th really makes my blood flow.

MARTYN WARE: Phil [Oakey] was my best mate from the fourth form, King Edwa School in Sheffield. When I say "best mate," I don't mean there were a few of us who we best mates; I mean it was, literally, me and him. It was a real bromance thing. We used to ri around the Derbyshire countryside on motorbikes, [had] formative sexual experiences ar drug experiences, parties at his house—all the things you go through when you're a teenag We shared everything.

[I didn't know if he could sing, but] I knew he looked great. He had the floppy haircut, a he always dressed interestingly. He was a very quiet guy. He didn't seek approbation from h peers. He was kind of otherworldly, but then the other half of his character was very dow to-earth. He has always been like this, and he always will be a complete contradiction. He's like the best chum you could ever have, and at the same time, he's kind of distant and aloof. I've never met anyone like him.

We'd grown up in our musical tastes together, and I knew how weird his tastes were. He turned me on to Frank Zappa and Carla Bley's *Escalator over the Hill.* We both loved anything we could find that was electronic and experimental. I knew he was conceptually right [for the Human League]. What I didn't know was, could he write top lines to the backing tracks? That wasn't really a block anyway, because we could easily have written some lyrics together with him. But as a test, we gave him the backing track to "Being Boiled" and told him to go away for a couple of days. He came back with a bonkers lyric and his voice, not out of tune but a bit deadpan, without expression. It was clear he could hold a tune of some kind, and his voice was unusual. I likened it to the deeper-range side of Bowie. But really, his influences at the time were more like mine. He really liked Neil Diamond and Leonard Cohen and, to a certain extent, Peter Hamill. He was just a genuinely odd person who was very musical. He heard the musicality in everything without prejudice. We would apportion equal weight to the most banal disco tunes like "Let's All Chant" by the Michael Zager Band and also, from a

lyrical point of view, we liked it. [Early Human League song] "Dance Like a Star" is based on that same idea of what is the blandest lyric we can think of? Can we get to that crystalline thing? Can we think down to that level of the great disco masters? And at the other end, we were experimenting with extreme philosophical sci-fi narrative and a lot of philosophical musings.

I didn't know what to think [about "Being Boiled"], to be honest. I just liked it. I didn't think, *Fucking hell, we've hit the jackpot!* It was more like, *Who the hell is ever going to hear this?* I played it for Paul Bower, who was in a punk band called 2.3 in Sheffield, who were signed to [indepen- dent Edinburgh label] Fast Product. He sent a cassette to [label boss] Bob Last. Next thing we know, he's on the phone saying, "We want to put it out." We were actually going to have a record out—a real record. Even though I'd had no experience in graphic design, I immediately determined that we wanted to control artistically how we appeared. I went down to Andrews, the stationers in town, near the city hall, and bought a bunch of Letraset [sheets of trans-ferrable lettering beloved by fanzine writers in the seventies], and knocked together the cover for "Being Boiled."

Culturally speaking, it was quite a different environment. It was in the immediate post-punk phase, and record companies were looking for acts that were unusual, as opposed to similar to something that was successful. It was a unique point in pop history in Britain. We just happened to be around at that moment. We thought what we were doing and the way we were using the limited tools we had was unique. The Korg, which I've still got in my studio now, cost 350 quid [about $500]. The main workhorse synth we used was a Roland System 100, which I still have as well. That cost nearer the 1,200-pound mark. They were both bought on hire purchase [layaway]. That's why, when we were touring in the late seventies, Ian [Craig Marsh, League cofounder] built a structure out of steel frame and Perspex to protect them. The journalists at the time were going, "What a powerful indication of the alienation of contemporary youth," but it was just to stop the skinheads from gobbing on them.

We were pleasantly surprised by the open-mindedness of the punk audiences.

But our punk epiphany was in the early to mid-seventies with bands like the New York Dolls, Suicide, even Parliament and Funkadelic, as well as the punkier bits of the German new wave of the seventies: Amon Düül, Can, Neu!, and Faust.

I was confused by the reaction to ["Being Boiled"]. I was amazed that anyone would be interested. I'm not being self-effacing; I just thought it was such an out-there piece of work. I felt like it was a novelty record, to be honest, but then when you get a couple of compliments from people you respect, like noted reviewers in music magazines, you start thinking quite differently quite quickly and thinking, *Maybe it is really good*. One of those music papers, *Melody Maker*, had guest columnists who came in and did reviews. John Lydon reviewed "Being Boiled," and his review was "Trendy hippies." Two words. At first, I was really upset, but then I thought, *John Lydon's taken notice of us. It must be having some kind of impact.*

MIXTAPE: 5 More End-of-the-Seventies Songs That Pointed the Way to the Eighties 1. "Boys Don't Cry," The Cure 2. "Bela Lugosi's Dead," Bauhaus 3. "Hong Kong Garden," Siouxsie and the Banshees 4. "At Home He's a Tourist," Gang of Four 5. "Public Image," Public Image Ltd.

It sold something like 5,000 copies in three months, and that was a lot for an independent single. And of course, that's when the record companies start sniffing around, because they see something underground that might break big. EMI were interested, and though we could have got more money out of them, they were just too corporate, and we wanted to keep complete control. It wasn't because we were control freaks. We had such a clear artistic vision that we couldn't afford to sign to someone who was going to change it. So, besides the fact that Virgin wasn't the biggest advance we could have got, that was the home we wanted.

The Human League had a manifesto, a set of guiding principles. It exists as a written document. I can give you the gist of it: Only electronic instruments—there was no such thing as samplers or even MIDI at that point. No found sounds, although that's not quite true; we did use some sound effects on "Circus of Death." We were never going to sing songs about love or use the word "love." There was a list of words that were banned, and "love" was one. We created quite a challenge, because we had to find different subjects to sing about. If you take love, sex, and human relationships out of the game, you're not left with a whole heap. That's how you get science fiction and philosophical tales. We really wanted to create this holistic—although we didn't know the word at the time—almost hermetically sealed world of meaning and narrative. Right from the start, we wanted people who listened to us to regard it as entering into our world, where we could, over a period of time, flesh it out with our artistic content. So it's not just about music. It's about lyrical content, it's about the kind of films you watch, it's about the kind of novels you read, it's about the kind of visual art you like. It all fed back into a worldview.

THAT WAS THEN BUT THIS IS NOW

 The Human League achieved cult success in the U.K. over the next couple of years before corporate machinations resulted in their implosion and the end of the Ware-Oakey bromance. As for "Being Boiled," British producer Richard X, renowned and dismissed as the godfather of the mashup, revived the seminal synth song twice: First in 2001, on his *Girls on Top* EP, where it was used with the vocals from TLC's "No Scrubs" and titled "Being Scrubbed"; second, as a Top 10 single for U.K. reality show–reject supergroup Liberty X, where it was mashed up with Chaka Khan's "Ain't Nobody" and titled "Being Nobody."

After producers-musicians Martyn Ware and Ian Craig Marsh were ousted from the Human League, they seemed poised to steamroll their former workmates. They formed the production company British Electric Foundation, which they used to launch their new incarnation, the trio Heaven 17 (the name was taken from the fictional pop group invented by Anthony Burgess in *A Clockwork Orange*). They presented themselves as hardworking executives armed with spreadsheets and shoebox-size cellphones. Despite being showered with plaudits on its release, Heaven 17's 1981 debut, *Penthouse and Pavement*, was not a source of successful singles. The music produced under the B.E.F. banner—the yellow cassette *Music for Stowaways*, the B.E.F. covers album *Music of Quality and Distinction, Vol. 1* (which nevertheless helped relaunch Tina Turner's career)—were appreciated by similarly slim audiences. Meanwhile, the Human League's *Dare* just kept getting bigger. However, the success of Heaven 17's second album, 1983's *The Luxury Gap*, evened the playing field.

HEAVEN 17

JB: I'm not one of those people who weeps tears over the wonder of vinyl. I don't have a side in the analog vs. digital debate. I like not having to get up to turn the record over just as much as I appreciate not having to lumber over to the TV for the pleasure of manually changing the channels. But after listening to both sides of a record, it is a particular pleasure to realize that one of them is your favorite. Side one of Heaven 17's *Penthouse and Pavement* is a smug, accomplished powerhouse. If you wanted to introduce your new incarnation and extinguish any lingering comparisons with your former workplace, you couldn't do better than the one-two punch of "(We Don't Need This) Fascist Groove Thang" and "Penthouse and Pavement," followed by "I'm Your Money" and "Soul Warfare." Side two has its highlights—"At the Height of the Fighting," "Let's All Make a Bomb," for instance—though it's hard to prevent the needle from returning to the breakneck beginning of "Fascist Groove Thang" a few more times. But as much as I love that side of that album, I have never been quite sure if Heaven 17 were a pop group or an ironic comment on being a pop group. When we spoke, Ware confirmed that I was correct to be confused, saying of "Fascist Groove Thang": "We thought it was a comedy record."

I was less confused about *The Luxury Gap*. Thematically, it dealt less with corporate culture and socioeconomic downfall than with broken hearts and doomed relationships. *The Luxury Gap* had the electronic age's own wee-hours Frank Sinatra song in "Come Live with Me," it had the tense "Let Me Go," and it had Heaven 17's first genuine hit, "Temptation." Glenn Gregory's deep, burnished voice has always sounded better alongside a female vocalist, and he's never had a better partner than session singer Carol Kenyon. Even without Kenyon's contribution, the track is punchy and melodramatic, but she inflames it, and she brought it even further to life via a series of star-making TV performances with the band. Heaven 17 may have adopted the image of captains of industry, but "Temptation" put them firmly in the executive suite.   LM: What he said!

MARTYN WARE: The Human League were two albums into our deal with Virgin and tens of thousands of pounds in the hole, unrecouped because of tour support. The albums weren't particularly expensive to produce, but they were just about covering their costs. Despite the best efforts of Virgin to break us, in inverted commas, we were only appearing to be popular with the cognoscenti, as opposed to the general public, and we didn't know why. Our live following was still building, we were planning a European tour, we'd got all the slides sorted out, but there was pressure being exerted on us. [Manager] Bob Last was talking to the record company, and he was filtering it back to us through his perception: "You need to have a hit album, boys." We never felt that we were going to get dropped, but it did cause tension, and I'd known Phil [Oakey] as my best friend for God knows how long—six years, I think. That made the split even more upsetting.

Bob, unbeknownst to me but not unbeknownst to Phil and Ian [Craig Marsh], had secretly been having talks with the record company to destabilize the situation and dropping words in Phil's ear that maybe he could be a solo singer. Bob was confident he could manipulate the situation so that he could keep the band name and bring in new songwriters like his mate Jo Callis, who's a good friend of mine—no blame apportioned there. This was all presented as a fait accompli one day when I turned up at the studio. With no inkling there was anything going on, I said, "Hi, boys, what's going on?" and they said, "We're throwing you out of the group, Martyn." I couldn't believe what I was hearing. Then my automatic Sheffield-ness kicked in, and I said, "No, you're not. It's my group." Like Jack Black in *School of Rock*. Because it was my group—it was mine and Ian's. The presumption was that Ian was going to stay in the group, and the justification for him staying was that they needed the name, otherwise they'd be breaking the contract for the upcoming European tour. They were willing to compensate me somewhat; however, there was no money to do it. What threw a spanner in the works was, the day after that, Ian called me up and said, "I can't do it. I want to go with you and do something. I feel more of an empathy with what you're doing than all the machinations that have been going on behind the scenes, which I don't agree with." That was not what they reckoned on at all.

I tried to absorb it for a couple of days, then I thought, *Fuck 'em. Our success didn't depend on Phil. We'll just find another singer*. Within 48 hours I'd approached Glenn Gregory. Had Glenn been in Sheffield at the time we were looking for vocalists when we sacked Adi Newton from the Future [Ware and Marsh's pre–Human League incarnation], he would have been in. But he had just moved down to London with his little handkerchief on a stick, so it was impractical to ask him to move back to Sheffield. Glenn said yes and moved back up to Sheffield, and within a week, Heaven 17 was born.

I'd already got the name lined up. Bob's strategy had been to say to me, "Your strongest suit is in the studio. You and Ian should form a production company." Which was quite a forward-thinking thing. I immediately liked the idea and said, "If I'm going to form a company, I want it to sound like it's always existed, like a grandiose entity that has just slipped under public notice but is, in fact, gigantic." We tried a few names, and I quite liked the idea that it would have "British" in it, but it would be like some kind of brass plaque on the wall in the city of London. And I liked the word "electric," so we thought British Electric Company.

Couldn't call it that, but we thought, *How about something that sounded like a philanthropic corporation?* So we settled on British Electric Foundation. Bob Last was a graphic designer, so I said, "Bob, as part of your role in this, you've got to come up with a logo that is like a 1930s recording company." Hence the tape reel, even though tapes didn't exist back then, and the font looked like it was carved out of metal. Within a week of that, we'd formed Heaven 17 and started work on the first music we recorded.

The manifesto we had with Heaven 17 was suddenly this freeing from the shackles of electronic music—the ability suddenly to use anything you wanted. When we were off duty from the Human League, the music we'd all been listening to at parties and loving and buying was American dance music. Heaven 17 emerged from that set of influences. Kevin Saunderson and Chicago and Detroit house credited Tubeway Army, Kraftwerk, and Heaven

MIXTAPE: 5 More Songs from New Groups That Grew out of Old Groups
1. "Rush," Big Audio Dynamite   2. "Rise," Public Image Ltd.
3. "Oh L'Amour," Erasure   4. "My Ever Changing Moods," The Style Council
5. "Johnny Come Home," Fine Young Cannibals

17 as influences more than they credited the Human League. I thought that was an enormous compliment.

Penthouse and Pavement allowed us to incorporate our take on politics and socialist beliefs but keep it pop and shiny. The "Pavement" side, which was the electronic side, was largely tracks that we had already been writing for the Human League. Not the lead lines—we'd not written the lyrics or anything like that—but the actual backing tracks. Although we already knew Glenn could sing, the audition piece for Glenn to join Heaven 17 was "Wichita Lineman," which was to be on the B.E.F. album [*Music of Quality and Distinction, Vol. 1*], which was something else we'd planned on doing with the Human League on the next album. The concept of "Penthouse" and "Pavement" sides happened because we thought, *If we try and evenly distribute tracks amongst the album, it might sound a bit disjointed. Why don't we use the electronics side almost as a good-bye to the purely electronic, easing our audience into a new era?* The logical thing to do would have been to put the "Pavement" stuff on the A-side, which would have been the transitional thing, but then, in typical contrary manner, we loved the new direction so much that we decided to put the new stuff on the A-side.

[While recording *Penthouse and Pavement*,] we'd actually take a sneaky

> **"I tried to absorb it for a couple of days, then I thought, *Fuck 'em. Our success didn't depend on Phil. We'll just find another singer.*"**

listen [to the Human League, who were recording *Dare* at the same time and in the same studio]. The first thing we heard was "Sound of the Crowd," and we thought, *Mmm, this is a bit rubbish, isn't it?* I was demented, of course. I was so motivated by the disrespect I'd received from the opposite team that I was bitter and twisted for a while. And I still think "Sound of the Crowd" is a bit rubbish, but charmingly rubbish. And they had to get a single out quickly. "(We Don't Need This) Fascist Groove Thang" was about to come out. They were released at fairly similar times. We thought we'd got daring and sophistication while they were just sort of going through the motions. But then *Dare* came out and went stone-cold big time, and the rest is history. But to give the Human League the right to use the name and to disavow ourselves of the rights, myself and Ian each took 1 percent of the next album, which happened to be *Dare*. That enabled me to pay for my first flat in London. So, hurrah.

We didn't really have any idea what huge commercial success was, so, to us, *Penthouse and Pavement* was a huge commercial success. Compared to the first two Human League albums, it was massive. It was an album that people coveted, and it was in the [U.K.] Top 75 for a year and a half. That meant that they gave us carte blanche in order to do *The Luxury Gap* album. If we were Rihanna, we wouldn't get an unlimited budget. There was a contractual limit, but in reality, if we'd said we'd run out of money halfway through, they'd have fronted the rest. *Penthouse and Pavement* cost 40,000 pounds. *The Luxury Gap* cost 180,000 pounds, and *How Men Are* cost 300,000 pounds, because, by that time, we'd had massive hits. They thought we could do no

"*Penthouse and Pavement* allowed us to incorporate our take on politics and socialist beliefs but keep it pop and shiny."

wrong, which, of course, is always a fallacy.

Dare had been out and been a big hit, so the motivation for us was very much direct competition. As far as we were concerned, all bets were off the table. "Temptation" was very much an idea I had about an Escher staircase that continually seemed to be going upwards and upwards and creating a kind of structural tension. The motivation was to make something that was timeless and classic, and that's what happens when you employ big orchestras. It's not only a stamp of quality but a stamp of timelessness. I remember going into Virgin and saying, "Wouldn't it be great if it sounded like one of these big sweeping Western soundtracks? An orchestra would be truly epic"—before "epic" was an overused word. It worked amazingly well. Virgin were open-minded. They didn't go, "How much is it going to cost?" They said, "When do you want it?" Within the week, we were in the studio with a 50-piece orchestra. Once we'd written the lyrics, it was always the idea that it would be a duet, even though we didn't have a girl member of the group. We'd always loved the delicacy of the female voice against Glenn's. Virgin didn't want to release it as a single because they didn't have Carol Kenyon signed up. We said, "We beg of you, please just release it, and it will be a hit." It was the only time in our entire career we

didn't see eye to eye with [Virgin managing director] Simon Draper, and we were right and he was wrong. It was a most expensive enterprise, but we got a lot of value out of it. It made a lot of money, that album. It used to be a high-risk, high-reward business, and now it's a low-risk, low-reward business.

Carol Kenyon was a bit arrogant. Even though she knew what the deal was when we brought her into the studio—we paid her, and she signed a release form—she approached us after the fact and said, "I think I deserve some royalties on this." No: We wrote the song, we paid you to do a performance, you were happy with those terms—see ya. Fast-forward a few years. The Ibiza version of "Temptation," the Brothers in Rhythm remix, is a big hit. The day before we're due to go on *Top of the Pops*, she attempts to blackmail us: "I'm not going on *Top of the Pops* unless you pay me a percentage of the record." And again we went, "See ya," and got the woman who'd been in the video, who couldn't sing a note to save her life, but she looked hot.

We were not typical pop stars. We never courted that. We carried on with our lives and our friends. All that happened was we had more money. We weren't trying to be celebs—in fact, we completely eschewed it because we viewed ourselves as valid artists and musicians. The flip side of that particular coin is we didn't perform live except for TV shows and MTV. We thought we could better spend our money making great videos. It enabled us to service different markets without having to tour the world for months on end. But it got to a point in the mid-eighties where we were using more session musicians, and we could easily have toured. That would have been the sensible time to move on to that, and we never did. It became a sort of dogma, which I regret because we had a shit-hot band. Around 1985, we were offered a million pounds to tour the West Coast of America with Coors sponsorship, and we turned them down because we said we don't do that. It made it very difficult for us to break America, because all we had were videos. Plus, the relationship with us and Virgin started falling apart. We found out that, by stealthy means, they had licensed us to Arista in America for three-quarters of a million dollars, and we didn't see a penny of it. It was added to our unrecouped account. We were so pissed off. We put out one more album, which, admittedly, wasn't all that great, and it all fell apart from there.

THAT WAS THEN BUT THIS IS NOW

Heaven 17 went on hiatus at the end of the eighties. Ware produced Terence Trent D'Arby's multiplatinum debut album, *Introducing the Hardline According to Terence Trent D'Arby*. He turned down subsequent production work with Rod Stewart ("I didn't like his politics") and Bette Midler, but helmed records by Erasure and Marc Almond. He is also active in the hard-to-explain field of 3-D sound installation. A 1992 remix of "Temptation" returned the group to the U.K. Top 5. Ian Craig Marsh left the group in 2007. In 2008, Heaven 17 toured with the Human League. ("We're mates now," Ware says of him and Oakey, "but I wouldn't say there's been closure.") The group collaborated in 2010 with squeaky-voiced beanpole new wave revivalist Ely Jackson of La Roux on a new version of "Temptation" recorded for the BBC. In 2013, the third British Electric Foundation album, *Music of Quality and Distinction, Vol. 3: Dark*, was released, featuring contributions by Boy George, Andy Bell, and Kim Wilde, among others.

WARE: After I produced Erasure's *I Say I Say I Say* [in 1994], Vince Clarke said, "Would Heaven 17 consider supporting us on our [1997] arena tour?" We'd never performed live, but the next thing you know, we're performing in front of 15,000 people at the NEC [National Exhibition Centre in Birmingham, England]—the first major gig we'd ever played. We've not looked back since.

I'm not surprised the material has lasted, to be honest. I'm flattered, but good songs are good songs. It makes no difference to me when they were made. We're not nostalgists, so we don't perform them in that sense. We're always looking to refresh the way they sound, and we keep getting younger and younger players in the band to make us look even more old. People go, "It's a nostalgia trip," and the majority of our audience is people of our age, but there is a significant proportion who caught on via their parents or who go to eighties clubs. There's an eighties club at least once a week in every town, village, everywhere in the U.K. The people who go to these clubs are 20-somethings; they're not people my age. The collaboration with La Roux, for instance, was instigated by her, not us. She was talking about how her major influence was Heaven 17. To her, we were almost as relevant as Bowie. The thought that you were being accorded that kind of status is almost inconceivable. Looking back, we always believed that we had longevity, but 30 years? I could have seen 10, but not 30.

DEXYS MIDN

"COME ON EILEEN"

WHO has a worse problem than a one-hit wonder? An unjustified one-hit wonder. A group with a history, a following, and a bulging back catalog in their home country who are known elsewhere only for a single song whose success they are frustratingly unable to repeat. Spandau Ballet suffered from this stigma. So did A-ha. But no one was less deserving of this fate than Dexys Midnight Runners. America knows them for one song: a fiddle-and-banjo-fueled, knees-up staple at weddings, wakes, and bar brawls. But there was so much more to Dexys than that. "Come On Eileen" caught them in the middle of a constant evolution. The Dexys of 1980 were an enraged, Stax-style soul revue with a bludgeoning horn section who dressed like New York dockworkers. By the time they'd reached their third album, the horns were gone and the band were clad in preppy attire. Every musical phase, every visual transformation, sprang from the feverish, churning imagination of Kevin Rowland. A lightning rod for controversy and, on occasion, a laughable figure, Rowland took himself and his band deadly seriously. When he was unhappy with the quality of the band's debut album, *Searching for the Young Soul Rebels*, he made off with the master tapes, refusing to return them until the label acceded to his demands. Unhappy at how he was portrayed in the British music press, he stopped doing interviews and had his hapless label pay for advertising space for him to pen essays about his various philosophies. Ironic that such a driven, obsessive, humorless figure would end up being best known for a silly sing-along song, but such is the fate of the unjustified one-hit wonder.

IGHT RUNNERS

JB: You know that Adam Ant lyric from "Goody Two Shoes," the one he addresses to a guy who's kneeling, crying words that he means, opening someone's eyeballs and pretending that he's Al Green? That's about Kevin Rowland. The image conjured up is one seared into the memories of British Dexys fans: Rowland, wild-eyed and unsmiling, clad in black, haranguing the audience over an endlessly repeating brass riff about soul and passion and some revelation he was forever trying to explain to us but could never find a way to express. We hung on his every word, or more accurately, every yelp, because the music was so consistently brilliant and so consistently different. The debut album, 1980's *Searching for the Young Soul Rebels*, was a blast of anger and contempt that crucified hipsters and anti-Irish jokes while lionizing sixties soul footnote Geno Washington, the subject of Dexys' first U.K. number one. *Too-Rye-Aye* emphasized strings over brass and uplift over outrage. The contentious *Don't Stand Me Down* is a six-song epic featuring more monologues than actual singing. The 27-years-late follow-up, 2013's *One Day I'll Soar*, is a stripped-down, affecting album that sounds like it was made by a man who's lived a long, hard life. There comes a time when you're happy not to hear any new music from your idols, no matter how much time, love, and money you've invested in them over the years. It's not like that for Dexys fans: We're in it for life.

LM: Rowland and my aunt Eileen are of Irish descent. So, I'd always believed, was Dexys and the knee-slapping, jig-inducing "Come On Eileen." I was shocked when I learned that Rowland and Co. actually hail from Birmingham, England—the same hometown as my beloved Durans, who would never be caught dead in Dexys' "Eileen"-era overalls. Decades and countless listens to "Come On Eileen" later, I still have no idea what the lyrics are beyond "Poor old Johnny Ray," but I have to hand it to Rowland: He penned the most well-known song in this book.

KEVIN ROWLAND: I had nothing to lose. Nothing. I was going nowhere. I could have ended up in prison. That is not being dramatic. I miraculously escaped prison. I don't think I would have survived. Music saved me. I was the kind of guy who would get into a lot of trouble, a lot of fights. I felt I was a fuckup, and there was no way I was going to take this music thing lightly.

We started with a blank canvas. I remember waking up in the summer of '78, two or three weeks after [Rowland's punk band] the Killjoys had broken up, and thinking, *Hang on a minute, let's start something completely fresh. Let's dream it first.* I literally did just that. I dreamed, "It's going to sound great, it's going to have a brass section, and we've got to look great." I felt hemmed in by punk at the end, and I just thought, *Everything had been leading me to this. This is going to be more than a band.*

It wasn't about aping soul. I know we said "soul" a lot. *Searching for the Young Soul Rebels.* We probably shouldn't have done. I think that limited us slightly. It was more than soul; it was soulful, it was pop. I think we just thought it was really cool to say "soul" at that time because nobody was talking about soul in 1978, so we saw the potential to be a bit radical.

It happened a bit too fast. Christ, it happened really quick. We did a tour in March–April [1980]. It was called the Straight from the Heart tour. It was fantastic. We really felt we were building something. You'd go on stage to about 400 people a night, and they didn't know anything about it except for the first single, "Dance Stance." We'd probably recorded "Geno" then, but it wasn't out. We'd win the audiences over every night—by the end of the show, they were all on our side. Then we had the number-one single,

which was great. But then we did shows, and the album hadn't come out yet, so most people, all they knew was "Geno," and they'd come along to the show wanting 10 "Geno"s. But we had some versatility, some variety, different moods. I found that tour a bit of hard work.

We didn't really have much experience, we didn't have experienced managers, and we were going out on these tours and no one was looking after the money. We signed two 50-page contracts: one publishing, one recording. I started to read the front page: Hereafter… thereby… whereby… wherefore. In the end, I just said, "Give us a pen." That's show business.

I was a bit uptight. I don't think I was angry—I probably was. I was always trying to stop smoking. I was always two days on, two days off. I was forever withdrawing from cigarettes. I was probably angry about that. I probably wrote a lot of these songs when I was two days off the fags.

Before "Come On Eileen," we were on our uppers [U.K. slang for "going through hard times"]. It had been two years since the previous number one. We'd changed labels, and the records had done all right but not great, and at least one hadn't done anything at all. We weren't exactly flavor of the month at the record company. There was talk of them dropping us, and a lot of other people like Adam Ant had come through. I always want what I haven't got—or I used to. I was hankering after pop success at that point. I'm not saying we wrote it with that in mind. Oh, that I would be that clever. But we did write it, like everything we did, the best we possibly could. We worked our arses off. Every detail counted.

We weren't trying to make a happy song. I liked songs that reminded you of the summer, like the Beach Boys, like "Do Anything You Wanna Do" by Eddie and the Hot Rods, like "Concrete and Clay" by Unit 4 + 2—good songs that sounded good in the summer. And ["Come On Eileen"] really worked. It's got so many different rhythms going on. It's got the [sings intro] bom-bom-bom, bom-bom-bom. It's got the banjos, and then you got the piano. We worked really hard on it.✱

We really enjoyed it when it was going up the charts, but I must admit the tread-mill of going around touring everywhere and doing promotion I found exhausting. You're going to America and you're doing an interview while you're having your break-fast. I'm not very good as a pro, and I wasn't prepared to schlep around America. We did two three-week tours, and after that I was like, I want to go home.

We did the demo for the next album [1985's *Don't Stand Me Down*], and when the manager came round to my flat and I played it for him, he made that noise, that intake of breath, like "Oooh, are you sure about this? You could lose everything you've got." And I was thinking, *What the fuck have I got?* I just felt like I was an arm of the record company. I felt I had to keep a smile up because everybody I knew was going, "You should be really happy. Things are going so well for you everywhere." And I was thinking, *Yeah, I should be happy, shouldn't I? What's wrong with me?* I didn't think I deserved it. I thought other people would be jealous of me, and I thought the band would be jealous. I just got really paranoid and withdrawn, but I had to keep on smiling, or thought I did. I didn't even have a car. I was in Birmingham. I would get on the bus and the driver would say, "Can you come back to the depot and meet everybody?" That happened in taxis too. I didn't want to disappoint people, but everywhere I went, it just seemed relentless. I liked it on the way up, the first couple of months, but the workload coupled with pressure, and suddenly, a whole organiza-tion developed around us, all depending on you and all smiling at you.

✱**"BIG" JIM PATERSON, Dexys trombonist,** "Come On Eileen" co-writer: "I can't understand how people can dance to it. It's an awkward tempo—the slow-down, stop, speed-up thing. How can you keep up?"

THAT WAS THEN BUT THIS IS NOW

***Don't Stand Me Down* divided critics and ended the band as a U.K. commercial force.** Subsequently, the album's cult following has blossomed, and it is revered as a neglected classic. The group called it a day in 1986. Rowland released two solo albums, *The Wanderer* (1988) and, 11 years later, the notorious *My Beauty* (a.k.a. the one where he wears a dress on the cover). After Rowland's protracted battle with cocaine and numerous attempts to reunite the band, Dexys started playing live again in 2003. Rowland announced a new album in 2005. Seven years later, that album, *One Day I'm Going to Soar*, was released to acclaim. The band has been successfully touring Britain since the record's release, including a stint in London's posh West End. They play the entire album every show.

ROWLAND: Not that I don't think ["Come On Eileen"] is a classic. It probably is. I'm not ready to look back. I'm just always thinking about now, and I'm grateful for the money. Not that we had the most amazing deal ever, but we get money from it, and it's enabled us to be where we are now. If I hear it, it's a double-edged sword. On the one hand, it's a really good song, and we're glad that it's been successful. But we're known as one-hit wonders in America, and that's not something I'm happy about. I know it's better than being a no-hit wonder, but over here [in the U.K., in case you forgot] we're known for a lot more. All right, the main thing we're known for is "Come On Eileen," and some would know us from "Geno," but there are quite a few people who know about our albums and what we're really about and who follow us now. We've had a great response to [*One Day I'm Going to Soar*], and, God willing, that's going to change things for us in America. But who knows? I haven't got the highest expectations.

MIXTAPE: 5 More Songs Named After Girls
1. "Louise," The Human League 2. "Christine," Siouxsie and the Banshees
3. "Charlotte Sometimes," The Cure 4. "Stand Down Margaret,"
English Beat 5. "Joan of Arc," Orchestral Manoeuvres in the Dark

You're Malcolm McLaren. The world sees you as the Situationist Svengali responsible for the Sex Pistols. But when your brainchild implodes as messily and unexpectedly as they exploded, what do you do for an encore? In 1980, McLaren kicked Adam Ant out of his own band and recruited a 13-year-old Anglo-Burmese schoolgirl to front his new creation. Like the refurbished Ants, Bow Wow Wow were a heady collision of Burundi drumming and twangy surf guitar. But in Annabella Lwin, the group found they'd recruited less a traditional lead singer and more a human popcorn popper. Her breathless shrieks, giggles, gurgles, and growls infused Bow Wow Wow's early material with a giddy innocence that, in the U.K. at least, would prove the group's salvation and undoing. McLaren's attempt to wring fresh outrage from the British public by putting his grubby fingerprints all over his underage leading lady's unspoiled youth was deflated by Lwin's natural effervescence. By the time America took notice, Bow Wow Wow had ditched the breakneck tempo and the flirtation with adolescent exploitation and evolved into a more muscular, more traditional pop band. A mere three years after they formed, the group unceremoniously kicked Lwin to the curb and brought the curtain down on Bow Wow Wow. It was a premature end to a career that might have had a little more mileage, but, then again, Bow Wow Wow was not a group that needed to grow up or get any older.

"I WANT CANDY"

JB: Was Malcolm McLaren a genius? Did he brilliantly choreograph every chapter in the Sex Pistols' short history? Did he simply hang on for the ride after the band swore up a storm on Bill Grundy's TV show in 1976? My inclination is to answer the preceding questions no, no, and yes. But the Malcolm McLaren of 1980? The one who got the then-mighty EMI Corporation to bankroll a band fronted by a girl singing about taping songs off the radio onto blank cassettes as if it were a seditious act that struck at the heart of the bloated music industry? That guy was a goddamn Nostradamus.

 I'm okay with "I Want Candy," and I appreciated producer Mike Chapman's steering the group in a mid-period Blondie direction. But the beautiful, frenetic music Bow Wow Wow produced between "C30 C60 C90 Go" and "See Jungle (Jungle Boy)" was the sound of a young woman's triumph over a charming charlatan who did not have her best interests at heart.

LM: Annabella was my first girl crush. She was my age, she had that Mohawk, she posed naked on that album cover, and in the video for "I Want Candy," her exotic, bronze skin glistened in the sun. I loved the way she emerged from the sea like a teenage Bo Derek. The guys in the group flashed a lot of skin too, but I barely noticed. Annabella was the epitome of new wave cool. In the summer of '82, "I Want Candy" was an anthem for being young and carefree. It captured the singer at her sassiest; she was provocative without being skanky. Naked, she exuded more innocence than a fully buttoned-up Rihanna. There were other female pop stars I admired—Olivia Newton-John, Pat Benatar, Annie Lennox—but none I could relate to as a teen. And now, three decades on, when I'm a mature, married woman, with all the responsibility that entails . . . I'd still do her.

LEIGH GORMAN: I'd just joined Adam and the Ants, and Malcolm comes along and he goes, "Well, Adam, your music is rubbish." He had us spellbound in the rehearsal room, just sitting there smoking Marlboros and intimidating us. Malcolm didn't like me. He said, "He's too much of a muso; he's not a punk. You need to find some kid in a club who can't really play." Adam said, "No, this guy's good. He might come up with something." So they put me to one side and said, "If you want to stay in this band, you're gonna have to come up with some good ideas."

[Malcolm and Adam] put [drummer Dave Barbarossa, guitarist Matthew Ashman, and me] in the rehearsal room and said, "We want you to reinterpret these songs." There were 23 songs on a cassette that Adam put together. One was "Rave On," another was "Mystery Train," another was "Hello Hello" by Gary Glitter. There was some Turkish belly dance music, and there was a song called "Burundi Black," this drum record that was out in the seventies. I played a little African drum to it, and I thought, *Sounds like the little legs of ants going.* I drew a mind map of what I thought "Antmusic" [might sound] like. When Malcolm and Adam came down to the rehearsal room, we played "Hello Hello" and "Rave On," and Malcolm looked at us and said, "Your band's rubbish. You should fire them." Then someone said, "We've got one more song." It was the African thing.

Malcolm went, "Right, that's your ticket."

Turns out Dave Barb was into Latin music, and he found he had a flair for coming up with all these different Latin roots. So we had the African and the Latin thing, and we combined them. Malcolm and Adam would give us a yay or nay. We all thought any one of us was going to get fired any minute if we didn't come up with the goods. But Adam wasn't getting in on our groove. His lyrics and vocals weren't fitting on top of the music. Malcolm has a cruel sense of humor. He would push us to one side and say to Adam, "You stand over there." He would look at us and go, "Yeah that's really good," and look at Adam and shake his head.

Then Malcolm brought someone who he said was an engineer and had a studio that we could record in. He listened to us play, then they took me and Dave to a pub, and Malcolm said, "This guy is not an engineer. He's a musical arranger from the West End, and I brought him down to evaluate you. He said you two are great, the guitar player is OK, but the singer is crap." He has no idea about punk rock or Adam's history. Then [McLaren] said, "I'm going to give you this option: You can be your own band and not just an employee of Adam. You find a new singer, you've got this sound, and I'll be your manager."

I wasn't happy. I thought, *Adam sup-*

"Malcolm had a saying: 'If you want to have a successful band, you have to have sex, style, and subversion.'"

▮▮▮▮▮

Then Adam said, "What about you, Leigh?" And I went, "Well, actually, I'm with Dave." So Adam went, "I suppose it's just going to be me and Matt." And Matthew said, "Well, actually, Adam . . ." And Adam went, "Oh my God! I'm getting kicked out of my own band!"

I could see Malcolm sitting at the back, smoking his Marlboro like a little Mephistophelian, a little devil smiling as all the smoke rose above him. I thought, *This isn't funny. It's cruel.* Adam was very, very upset. Then Malcolm said, "Okay, Adam. Let's go upstairs and have a cup of tea." I thought, *Well, good luck to him. I hope he does well.* I didn't realize he'd do that well!

When we were looking for a new singer, we didn't care whether it was male, female, black, white, Chinese. We wanted the band to be multicultural. We were looking for something like Frankie Lymon, like a black 13-year-old. We wanted someone special, someone who was different in some way. Annabella's being young, female, and Asian was different. She had a certain naïveté, and when she got on the mic, she just blasted it out.

ANNABELLA LWIN: I never wanted to be famous. I never had any of those aspirations. I wanted to be an air stewardess. I used to sing along to records and to Cliff Richard when he was on TV. I thought he could see me. The

ported me when Malcolm tried to get rid of me. But we also thought, *Malcolm must know what he's talking about.* But I didn't feel it was right, going behind someone's back. And I didn't think Adam was that bad, but I did feel that he wasn't fitting in with our music. But I thought that it would come in time. But I also thought maybe Adam wouldn't like me in a month and would fire me. So we decided to go with our own band. Looking back, though, it was a mistake to get rid of Adam. 'Cause Adam was definitely a star.

The next day, we came to rehearsals, and Adam knew something was up. Dave—he'd been with him for three or four years in Adam and the Ants—said, "Adam, I want to leave the band. We've got something special going on here, and it seems like you're not into it."

day I was discovered, I was working at my Saturday job [at Shamrock Express, a dry cleaner in North West London] and singing along to the radio. I was very, very shy, so why I was chosen to be in the band, I don't know. You'd have to ask Malcolm McLaren, but, God rest his soul, he's no longer here. I think he found my background interesting, because I am half Burmese, half English. I was a girl who was at school one day and, after the audition for Malcolm, I joined the band and was told I'd have to leave school.

My relationship with Malcolm was pretty good. I got on as well with him as any person could. I think he was 50 at the time. I was 14. He was in the studio when I was recording the early stuff, and he inspired me just by talking to me. I had a fondness for the English countryside; it was the most beautiful place to visit when I was a child. Malcolm heard me talking about the country, and that's where "Go Wild in the Country" came from. He told me, "This is you going down to the country, and how do you feel about that?" He really made me use

my imagination. The only thing I didn't like about the lyrics to that song were the lines, "I don't like you / I don't like your town." I said to Malcolm, "Why would I say that? It makes no sense." He said, "You're talking about going from London to the countryside, where snakes in the grass are absolutely free." Some of the songs were written before I even came on board, like "Sexy Eiffel Towers." When Malcolm told me it was about falling off the Eiffel Tower, I believed it. Later, I found out it was from a French porno film. He was a great storyteller.

GORMAN: Malcolm had a saying: "If you want to have a successful band, you have to have sex, style, and subversion." That was his formula, and he tried to introduce that with Annabella. We rebelled against that a bit because she was too young. But a little didn't hurt. I thought [the 1981 *See Jungle! See Jungle! Go Join Your Gang Yeah. City All Over! Go Ape Crazy!* album cover, where Lwin is sitting naked on a picnic blanket next to her fully clothed male bandmates] was

MIXTAPE: 5 More New Wave Cover Versions

1. "Always Something There to Remind Me," Naked Eyes   2. "Rock 'N' Roll/ Nightclubbing," The Human League   3. "If You Want Me to Stay," Ronny 4. "Femme Fatale," Propaganda   5. "Memphis Tennessee," Silicon Teens

LWIN: The rest of the group were all in their 20s. I didn't really have any chemistry with them. Matthew was the only guy in the band I felt a connection with. How can I put this without it sounding really, really strange? It's like you meet people, and you either click or you don't, right? I didn't spend a lot of time with them. I got on stage, and whatever happened, happened. In those days, I didn't speak very much because I was told not to. I didn't really enjoy the experience with the guys in the band, let's put it that way. If you've seen any footage of interviews I've done back in those days, you can see I'm very short and sharp and pretty aloof. I've seen some footage, and I think I must come across like a really cocky young girl. But I was very shy, very unconfident. I had no idea what I was doing. I look at that girl now, and I don't know who she was.

GORMAN: Me and Malcolm took "Go Wild in the Country" round to the publishers, and they went, "Well, that's not quite strong enough." And the American branch of RCA said we needed a more radio-friendly song, otherwise they weren't going to give us any tour support.

So we were thinking, plotting: What could we do? I go, "Let's do a cover. What about a classic bubblegum song?" Bubblegum songs had great hooks, and we could update one with our percus-

a good, artistic idea. It wasn't too lewd; it wasn't too lascivious. You wouldn't get away with it now, 'cause standards are different. It's based on a painting by Manet called *Le déjeneur sur l'herbe—The Luncheon in the Grass*—and it was risqué, obviously. But I thought it was tasteful, and it was an artistic statement. Annabella went along with it—she was a little trouper. I think her mum objected to it. I'm a parent now; I understand. That's why we dialed down a lot of the nonsense. I'm not sure she was quite aware of it. When she wasn't around, we would say, "No, no, that's too much." I felt like we were her older brothers.

sive vibe. A guy called Steve Leeds, who worked with [Joan Jett and the Blackhearts manager-producer] Kenny Laguna, suggested "I Want Candy" by the Strangeloves. It had a fantastic hook, lots of connotations and meanings, and it's a love song about someone in a sunny way.

They flew us to Miami, put us in a posh house with a cook and a maid and a swimming pool. We'd never experienced anything like that. They'd spent a fortune—which, of course, we had to pay back over the years—and put us in a studio with Kenny, who was part of that era, so he seemed perfect for it. We hadn't actually heard it properly yet at that point, so we were given cassettes at the airport; we put 'em in our Walkman, and we were listening to it on the way to the house.

We arranged it live. We had it in an hour. It has a great rhythm, and it caught the moment of when we were recording it. It caught our performance style, our joie de vivre. We were used to working with producers in London, where it's gray and cold. And here we are, the sun is shining, we're in a big, expensive studio, we've got a funny, friendly producer who seems to manage our personalities and make us feel good. When we recorded, they had the lights, all my rig, tons of speakers all set up, Joan Jett in the control room, all their family, all the [Blackhearts]. When Annabella did her

vocals, he made her feel special, made her feel comfortable, and I think that boosted her performance.

LWIN: I can honestly say when I first heard my vocals on "I Want Candy," I was stunned. I was thinking, *Is that me? Who's that girl singing?* Because I actually sounded good. That was the first song on which I actually sounded like a singer. The way they produced it, it was brilliant. It stands the test of time. Such a shame it was the only song we ever did with them. I don't know what happened.

GORMAN: We tried to [work with Laguna again], but while we were mixing, "I Love Rock 'n' Roll" went to number one, and I think they were inundated with too much to do.

LWIN: I wasn't involved in the decision-making process. I was just told to sing the song. But it brought us a new audience, and the difference over here [in the United States] is they really appreciate if you can perform live—more than they seemed to appreciate it in the U.K.

The original Ants kicked out Adam, who was the lead singer, and history repeated itself with me. [My firing] was sprung on me. I read in the music press that apparently I'd stormed off stage, which I've never done, even to this day, with any band I've worked with. I don't understand what happened. I've worked with the bass player [Gorman] since, and he keeps telling me, "I was in the hospital." You were in the band—what do you mean you were in the hospital? Things are not clear. People are avoiding the truth, and I speak the truth. I was a young girl in a rock 'n' roll band with three guys. The next thing I know, the three guys had basically kicked me out and formed another band. I'm certainly not going to take any blame for that.

GORMAN: It's true: I was in hospital. I don't know why she doesn't believe me. Annabella's mum was a head nurse, and they put me in the ward with people with lung cancer and TB, 'cause I couldn't breathe properly. Matthew was in a bad way too. He was coming down with diabetes—he didn't know it; it was undiagnosed. He was going blind, and it was probably affecting his mental state.

I got wind of what was going on from [Barbarossa and Ashman]. We were at our height, and they were dissatisfied with her. I think they wanted a guy singer and to be less pop. I actually called Annabella and said, "They're thinking of leaving the band and doing something else." And she said, "Oh, Leigh. You're making a mountain out of a molehill." Then they decided to [fire her] without me.

LWIN: Why would anyone break up a band that was doing well? Nobody at any record company wanted that to happen. I think the mistake that's made is when bands have a lead singer, they seem to get upset or, dare I say, jealous that the lead singer gets all the attention. The truth is, of course the lead singer will get a degree of attention, because that's who connects with the audience. It's the only human element in the equation. The bass player plugs in his bass; the drummer bashes away on the drums. With all due respect, I'm not demeaning them; I'm just stating a fact. Every lead singer since time immemorial will always get more attention. You need to understand this. If you cannot have that kind of relationship within a band, the band will split up, which is obviously what happened. I was in the band three years. I gave up school and my friends to be able to work on the road and sell the band and perform as lead singer as well as write songs, and I have to read they're getting rid of me in the *NME*? It was a huge blow at the time—a huge blow. It's a shock for anyone to realize the people they're working with don't have the courtesy to let you know. How would you take it if you were told, "Tomorrow, the job's finished," and you've got no money? And I was 17.

THAT WAS THEN BUT THIS IS NOW

Gorman, Barbarossa, and Ashman spent a brief time playing together as Chiefs of Relief. Ashman died in 1995. Gorman reunited with Lwin, first in an attempt to launch her as a solo star, then as part of a rebooted Bow Wow Wow. The two recorded and toured together until December 2012, when Lwin suddenly departed mid-tour. In January 2013, Lwin appeared as the opening act—billed as Annabella Lwin of Bow Wow Wow—on Midge Ure's U.S. tour. The band's version of "I Want Candy" has become the blueprint for terrible punk bands and awful teen acts to record. Among those failing to reach the heights of the '82 version: Good Charlotte, Bouncing Souls, Aaron Carter, Westlife, Melanie C, Cody Simpson, and Jedward. Among those succeeding: potato chip giant Pringles and its "I Want Pringles" jingle.

GORMAN: Chiefs of Relief was a good band but nothing like Bow Wow Wow. We put out a single called "Holiday." They had a roundtable on BBC Radio on the new singles released, and on the panel was Adam Ant. Adam says, "God, is that what they're doing now? That's terrible." Then my mum called me: "What the hell are you doing? You had that great band—why have you faded?" I should have stuck with Annabella and carried on Bow Wow Wow without them.

LWIN: People tell me I was ahead of my time. I still get that today. And they seem to be getting younger. They have all-ages shows where I have these young girls, five- to eight-year-olds, looking at me.

I always sound like I was this bitchy, angry, attitudinal young girl when I was in my teens, and God knows, I was none of that. It's all down to collaboration and who you're working with. It doesn't always work out in bands. Our career was only three years. I hope I can continue to sing and write songs and perform. I went on to try and pursue a career in music in the U.K., but unfortunately they said I was too old. I really think that if the music industry is to survive, they need to get rid of this ageist thing. You can't package a human being to the extent where they become unreal. When you get on stage in front of 1,000 people, they just want to feel something, and that's where I come from.

"I KNOW WHAT BOYS LIKE"

New York's achingly hip ZE Records was dubbed "the world's most fashionable record label" by the *Face*, whose contributors knew of which they spoke. ZE's catalog was adored by tastemakers, critics, and DJs. It released smart, witty, cynical, self-satisfied dance records by the untouchably cool likes of Cristina, Kid Creole and the Coconuts, Was (Not Was), Lizzy Mercier Descloux, and Material. ZE never courted mainstream success and would've professed to have been appalled had they achieved it. Fittingly, the closest ZE came to connecting with a popular audience was with a band that didn't exist—at least, not at first. An Akron, Ohio, art-pop outfit, the Waitresses were dreamed up by Chris Butler as a vehicle for a scratchy, stuttering, put-down song crying out for a female vocal. Butler would eventually find his voice and his muse in Clevelander Patty Donahue, who delivered his words with the sass and gum-chewing snap of a screwball-comedy heroine. As the Waitresses gradually evolved into an actual band, they occupied a unique position somewhere between the honking, atonal jittery rhythms of New York's no wave scene and the pop star allure of Donahue's trash-talking, tough chick. While ZE's back catalog is still adored by tastemakers, critics, and DJs, the Waitresses, almost by accident, are responsible for two of the label's best-known records—one a novelty hit, the other a Christmas song—which are kept alive by the love of the unhip.

THE WAITRESSES

JB: There was a time I would leave the house. I would willingly go and see bands, and I would harbor the hope that they would be good. During this uncharacteristic period, I suffered through what seemed like a lifetime of bands who just stood there. The visiting American bands did not just stand there. The B-52s didn't just stand there. The Cramps didn't just stand there. And neither did the Waitresses. All I knew of them when I went to see them play Glasgow's Satellite City was that one taunting single. It's possible I caught them on an exceptionally good night, but what I saw was a very tight but also very chaotic group (like the Muppet Show band, in that respect) with a set list so preoccupied by the romantic misadventures of its wisecracking chick singer that it was almost like being at a musical—only without the terrible music. It's one of the few times seeing a band live persuaded me to purchase their album, and the only time it didn't turn out to be a huge mistake.

LM: Before *Valley Girl*, before John Hughes's Molly Ringwald trilogy, there was *Square Pegs*. It aired for just one prime-time TV season, from 1982 to '83, but, *omigod*, it was, like, the best show ever. Its cast of characters was awash in cool coifs and lurid new wave attire, their bedrooms were festooned with Berlin and Missing Persons posters. There was also a bat mitzvah performance by Devo, and of course, that catchy, singsongy theme tune by the Waitresses: "Square pegs, square pegs / Square, square." Head Waitress Donahue was like a real-life version of the show's Jennifer DeNuccio: aloof, scary, and seemingly slutty, but not really. Sure, she knew what boys liked, she knew what guys wanted, but she didn't let them have it. ("Sucker. Ha ha ha!")

CHRIS BUTLER: Women's sexual power is pretty obvious. In this case, I was living in Akron, and there was a bar on our high street called the Bucket Street. It was our local watering hole, and it was an interesting mix of bohemians and lawyers and politicians and artists. At the time, I had a record deal, I didn't have a girlfriend, and all these lawyers were going home with hotties up the ying-yang, while I'm going home alone. I was getting a little bitter about that. The song is not polite, although it does seem to capture the empowering of women. The dirty little secret about "I Know What Boys Like" is that it's me going, "What's wrong with me? Go home with me! I'm horny!"

I liked Patty Donahue's deadpan delivery. She was a girl about town, and she was a firecracker and a fun person. She was willing to give it a try on my demo. I guess I can claim that I had a little bit of an idea what I wanted, but it wasn't that calculated. She could play that role really easily; she was a tough party girl. I was like, "Just do that thing where the guy comes up to you at the bar who you don't want to do the deal with," and she goes, "Oh yeah, I know how to do that." She brought a nonthreatening kind of puckish manner. The idea was "I'm gonna be playful here, but in the end I'm gonna say no. I'm gonna toy with you a little bit, but in the end, sorry. No score."

I was in a band from Akron called Tin Huey—very influenced by Kraftwerk, Matching Mole, anything with Robert Wyatt. As a song, ["I Know What Boys Like"] was the complete opposite of what I thought I wanted to do and nothing that Tin Huey would think was aesthetically correct. I presented the song to them as a goof—maybe Tin Huey should have a side project that does pop stuff—and they all just thought it was crap. But they were generous enough that, after a Tin Huey show, [Patty and I] would do it for an encore. We would put on these T-shirts that a wonderful diner in the town of Kent gave us that said "Waitresses Unite." It wasn't a real band. It was a fake name, and Patty would come up and Tin Huey would do a "Waitresses" set, two or three numbers, and have a laugh.

Tin Huey ran its course. We got dropped from Warner Bros. We had two records left in our contract, and they gave us a butt-load of money to go away, and we did. We split up the money and moved to the New York area. Tin Huey had done very well in New York. It was the only place we had done well. I had that version of "I Know What Boys Like," and I played it to a couple of people, and they thought it was a hit. This guy named Mark Kamins, who was a DJ at Danceteria, flipped over it. He played it a couple of times one night, then the next day he took it up to Island Records and said, "I want a job as an A&R man, because I can sign stuff like this." And they wanted to sign it. They said, "Where's the band?" I lied and said, "They're back in Ohio." Island said they wanted to sign the Waitresses for a single, and they needed a B-side. So I got some folks together. I convinced Patty. I sent her my last 50 bucks to come to New York. Her boyfriend drove her to the bus terminal, and she went off to the big city. She flew from Boston to New York, and we put a band together. I was able to cobble together some of the Contortions, and we recorded the B-side, "No Guilt." Then Island had its first number one, "Video Killed the Radio Star." The A&R guy in the U.K. did not like "I Know What Boys Like," and it got bumped down to Antilles, their sublabel. It did well enough to where they were thinking about putting out an album, and I thought, *Okay, maybe I should put together a real band.*

Our contract was traded like a football star over to ZE Records, and we recorded our album [*Wasn't Tomorrow Wonderful*, 1982], but "I Know What Boys Like" continued to crawl along. It never hit number one, but it got caught in the hierarchy of the social consciousness, and it stayed there.

With the Waitresses, there's a veneer of pop, but if you try to dissect the music, I think the musicians flatter the hell out of me. It's pretty fucking complicated and sophisticated for a "pop" band, but that was a bit of a sleight of hand I was trying to achieve because I wanted to keep my job and feed everybody, do something the record company liked and something Patty could handle. She was a great actress, but she didn't have great pipes. She wasn't a full-throated singer. She was great with character and story lines.

We talked a lot [about a male writing lyrics for a woman to sing]. It wasn't any big deal that there were once no women in Shakespeare's plays, but this was a little different because I came up with a character who was half based on the wisecracking

MIXTAPE: 5 More Quirky, Female-Fronted Songs
1. "Give Me Back My Man," The B-52s 2. "How to Pick Up Girls," The Little Girls 3. "Who Does Lisa Like?," Rachel Sweet 4. "Lucky Number," Lene Lovich 5. "Call Me Every Night," Jane Aire and the Belvederes

school of comedy from the 1930s and half on me kind of wanting a big sister to explain what's going on. I wanted to—how shall I say this politely?—know the enemy. I tried to get it right as much as a man could. In hindsight, I didn't think there was anybody writing that type of character. I loved the confessional side of the stuff that Marianne Faithfull was doing. That was brutal in its honesty. I thought, *Gee, how come nobody else is doing that in the mainstream? How come it's either a rock tart or a party girl or a sensitive folk singer?* How come there's no sort of manic pixie with a feminist streak who's just trying to get through life? It was part of my modus operandi.

THAT WAS THEN
BUT THIS IS NOW

The Waitresses released an EP, *I Could Rule the World If I Could Only Get the Part***s, and their final album, 1983's** *Bruiseology***. The group disbanded in 1984. Donahue died of lung cancer in 1996. "I Know What Boys Like" has been covered many, many times, mostly poorly. Among the culprits: Tracey Ullman, Shampoo, Vitamin C, the Bouncing Souls (also responsible for roughing up the Bow Wow Wow version of "I Want Candy"). It was performed on** *Glee***—by that show's worst-ever**

character (and it sets a sky-high bar!), the overconfident Lauren Zizes. And Katharine McPhee sucked all the fun out of the song when she performed it in *The House Bunny***.**

The Waitresses recorded another song that never went away: 1981's seasonal classic "Christmas Wrapping," which was also performed on *Glee***, this time by that show's best-ever character, Brittany S. Pierce.**

BUTLER: "I Know What Boys Like" is a period piece now, and I'm amazed. I thought it was a novelty record. It seems to make people laugh. It makes women feel sexy when they sing it. It's a gay anthem. It's a gift. I'm not living on the Riviera, and I'm not driving a Maserati. Harvard? Forget it. But my kid will be able to go to the finest trade school in America. I did hold on to my publishing. It goes up and down over the years, but I am very grateful that [the song's] stuck to the culture. It's evocative of an era. It's turned out to be utilitarian for sampling or setting the musical theme to supplement a movie scene or TV show.

I have two half-hits. I'm as flabbergasted about "Christmas Wrapping" as I am about "I Know What Boys Like." Thank you, world. Even the Spice Girls couldn't ruin it.

MUTE
RECORDS

©1978
mute records

45 rpm
MUTE 001B*
stereo

warm leatherette
(MILLER)

the normal

"WARM LEATHERETTE"

In the same way that we put blind faith in fresh offerings from HBO, AMC, FX, and occasionally Showtime, based on their previous output, we used to put trust in record labels. We bought releases from Rough Trade because its zero-budget track record was incredibly consistent, from ZTT because of the grandiosity of Trevor Horn's production and Paul Morley's bombard-and-confuse approach to marketing, and from Factory Records because of Peter Saville's iconic sleeves. And we purchased whatever Mute Records put out because of Daniel Miller's taste in electronic music. He brought us tunes that popped like bubbles; he brought us painful, dark industrial noise; he brought us groups who passed the test of time and continue to thrive—and he brought us groups who didn't. (We don't mean you, I Start Counting.) But before he did any of that, he put out a track under the name the Normal, and that 1978 record played a big part in changing music for the next few decades.

JB: "Warm Leatherette" and "T.V.O.D." couldn't have come at a better time. I was obsessed with punk, but I hadn't realized there would be so many Cockneys—so many phlegmy, shouty Cockneys fronting what were little better than the boogie outfits they'd displaced. As Sham 69 supplanted the Sex Pistols and punk lost the power to shock, the Normal released a record that was genuinely disconcerting. I was the type of teenager who memorized record reviews, which meant I could drop J. G. Ballard's name as the lyrical inspiration of "Warm Leatherette" without having read a word he'd written. I responded to the noise. I liked the machines; it sounded like the lead instrument was a dentist's drill. And I liked Miller's dead, detached delivery.

 Several formative electronic tracks were released in 1978: the Human League's "Being Boiled," Cabaret Voltaire's "Nag Nag Nag," Dr. Mix and the Remix's version of "No Fun." "Warm Leatherette" was the one that pointed me in the direction of the others—and away from the Boomtown Rats.

LM: Whenever Dave Kendall would spin "Warm Leatherette" at Communion, the weekly freak fest at New York's infamous Limelight, every punk, skin, goth, drag queen, and collegiate would assemble on the dance floor. Madonna and her voguing had nothing on us. We'd strike and alter our poses in time to the whirring of the power-drill effect, miming every word and taking particular pleasure when pointing to the "tear of petrol" in our eye. "Warm Leatherette" has no intro and no outro, and there's barely a bridge—just a few droning verses and a highly repetitive chorus courtesy of an anonymous male voice. Yet, it was our new wave rave's version of Kool and the Gang's "Celebration," inviting even those not outfitted in skin-tight PVC to join . . . the car crash set.

DANIEL MILLER: Punk rock inspired me because it was a real kick in the teeth to all the shit that I already hated. It wasn't an awakening for me, because I'd had that years before. By 1970, I'd already rejected most Anglo-American music. I only listened to Krautrock and electronic music. I think Krautrock actually inspired a lot of punk. The very first time I heard the Ramones on *John Peel*, I thought it was Neu!.

I made music from the age of 12—very bad music. I had a lot of ideas; I just couldn't express them at all. I was making music in a very frustrated way for many years before I got my first synthesizer, which is what turned a corner for me. I'd figured out that electronic music was actually pure punk music. Not punk rock but punk music—that's two different things. Punk rock was a type of music that was very important for a short period of time: '76 to '77. The punk aesthetic or ideal, which is the same as the hippie ideal—that do-it-yourself thing—does things that will change people's perceptions. I was already in my mid-20s. I said, "This is my moment to do something. If I'm going to do anything, this is the climate, the atmosphere, in which to do it." I started mucking around and realized that I could do a lot of the ideas that I couldn't with conventional instruments.

I was able to make the sounds that were in my head, and that was a big moment for me. I had a synthesizer and a tape recorder, and I had to hire a couple of extra things to make it into a record. I could only afford to hire those things for a day, so I cut both ["Warm Leatherette" and "T.V.O.D."] in a day. I just came up with these songs out of the blue. Well, not really out of the blue: "Warm Leatherette" was very deliberate lyrically. I was a big fan of J. G. Ballard. I'd been working on a film script for *Crash* with a friend. Nothing came of it, but through working on that, I had a lot of visual ideas, and I condensed what was in my head into that song.

Most people, when they sing, put on a voice, either an American accent or some drawl or some acting thing. One of the ideas of it was that I didn't really put on a voice. I wanted it to be as dispassionate as possible.

When I decided to do this project, I went back to film editing. That had been my job. I can't remember sleeping; I was either working overtime in the cutting room or I was working at home on music. I earned as much money as I could [so that I could get] some test pressings made. I was going to press 500 copies, because that was the minimum. I went to a couple of shops to see if they wanted to buy any of them. I went to Rough Trade, and they loved it and said they'd like to distribute it. They gave me some money to press up 2,000 copies.

„the normal"

I think I did that. I didn't really plan to have a recording career. I didn't have songs pouring out of me. It was just one moment in time, which happened to work, and I didn't really know what I was going to do next.

The single sleeve had my address on it, so I was getting sent demo tapes because people thought I was a proper record label. Then a friend introduced me to his flatmate, Frank Tovey— Fad Gadget—and his were the first demos I really liked. He was 21 at the time; I was 25. We met up and found we shared a similar aesthetic, and there was humor in what we were doing. So I said, "Let's make a record."

We went into the studio. I had no experience; he had less than me. He made the first single [1980's "Back to Nature"] and that was *Mute 002*, which was the first non-me release. That was the start of Mute Records as a label for other artists. It was very day-to-day. I didn't have any contracts with any of the artists—it was like, "Let's see how this goes." I quite liked being the person in the background helping the artist realize their vision. I actually enjoyed that more than making music, and I realized that's what I should be doing.

I left a couple of test pressings at Rough Trade, and they played it to a journalist called Jane Suck, who worked at Sounds. She had a pretty vitriolic tone and didn't suffer any fools. She gave it an amazing review— called it "single of the century." Then John Peel played it, and that made everything worthwhile.

I wanted to make a statement with that record about the possibilities of electronic music—how I felt it was the most accessible, democratic music, except for punk—and

THAT WAS THEN BUT THIS IS NOW

Mute was founded in 1978. Over the years, the label's roster has included Depeche Mode, Yaz, D.A.F., Moby, Goldfrapp, the Birthday Party, Einstürzende Neubauten, Laibach, Nitzer Ebb, and Erasure. Although Miller never subsequently recorded as the Normal, he found further pseudonymous success as Silicon Teens, a fictional teen-synth band best known for their cover of Chuck Berry's "Memphis, Tennessee." "Warm Leatherette" also lives on as the title track of Grace Jones's 1980 album. "I thought it was so funny," Miller says of the first time he heard the cover. "The title was appropriate for her, maybe not the lyrics. Her voice suited the song, even though she overacted it slightly."

MILLER: Bands like Depeche or Soft Cell, Blancmange, Human League, OMD, Cabaret Voltaire—we were creating something new. You look at some of the big dance techno artists or whatever you want to call it—EDM; I hate that term—they're all super-influenced by Depeche and Yazoo and Human League and OMD. The number of people who say, "We heard Depeche, and that's what got us started"—it makes me cry almost, it moves me so much. You speak to Richie Hawtin [Plastikman], and he says, "The reason I'm making music is because of Depeche and Nitzer Ebb." We did our job. We brought electronic music to a much broader audience.

MIXTAPE 5 More Songs from This Month's Labels

1. "Is That All There Is?," Cristina (ZE) 2. "Moments in Love," Art of Noise (ZTT) "The 'Sweetest' Girl," Scritti Politti (Rough Trade) 4. "You're No Good," ESG (Factory) 5. "Song to the Siren," This Mortal Coil (4AD)

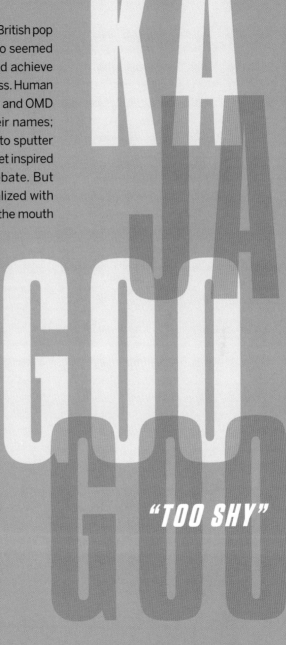

Kajagoogoo were the first British pop band of the eighties who seemed to fall out of the sky and achieve instant worldwide success. Human League, Depeche Mode, and OMD had indie singles to their names; Duran Duran took a little while to sputter off the launchpad; Spandau Ballet inspired months of discussion and debate. But Kajagoogoo suddenly materialized with a name that sloshed around in the mouth like molasses, a singer with a mass of two-tone hair, and a bass-dominated debut single produced by Nick Rhodes and Duran knob-manipulator Colin Thurston. Kajagoogoo's success was massive, mocked, and brief. Few mourned their loss. But Kajagoogoo were also a bellwether for what was to come: pop bands without a past, that didn't look back any further than 1978, and pop bands that wanted to look weird and shocking without actually being weird and shocking.

KAJAGOOGOO

"TOO SHY"

JB: Here's one of the core differences between me and my co-author: She's a people person. In fact, she's a "People Are People" person. I'm neither. But I sort of enjoyed talking to Kajagoogoo singer Limahl. He was fairly candid and had a wry sense of humor and a degree of self-awareness. Which makes it harder for me to act on my natural impulse and shit on his band. So I'll briefly channel Teen Me, who found "Too Shy" both tedious and grating, and that "Hey girl, move a little closer" bit especially murderous. Older, Decrepit Me is slightly more diplomatic. Yes, that "Hey, girl" line is shameful, but it scored a direct hit on the pleasure zones of the audiences it was aimed at. And one thing I will say in the song's favor: Along with Gary Numan's "Music for Chameleons," Japan's "Visions of China," and Visage's "Night Train," "Too Shy" is one of the decade's best bass records.

LM: Don't forget "Rio"! As for "Too Shy," I'd forgotten just how funky it is. Credit the greatness of bassist Nick Beggs. I can still recall Zappa/Duran guitarist Warren Cuccurullo going on at length about Beggs's ability. Of course, as a young, obsessive Duranie, I was preoccupied with the fact that "Too Shy" was produced by Nick Rhodes, garnering him his first U.K. number one a couple of months ahead of his own band's inaugural chart–topper, "Is There Something I Should Know?" Oh, and the lyrics, "Moving in circles / Won't you dilate." So dirty!

LIMAHL: I was raised in Wigan [on the outskirts of Manchester]. My dad was a miner. My two brothers went down the mines. I was expected to do the same. You got a job, you got married, you had kids, and then you're trapped. Nobody went to college where I lived; there were no aspirations. I was obsessed with music—that's how I escaped. I'd do anything to get money when I was younger. I had a paper round, I used to deliver bread, I'd clip people's hedges. It would take me all day to earn 50p. At the end of the day, I'd go straight down to the record shop with my 50p and buy a vinyl single. My dad thought I was completely deluded. He used to say, "Why have you gone out all day working for that money and then you wasted it on that one record?" And I was going, "But I like music, Dad."

I'd auditioned for bands looking for singers. I was really into everything that was synthesizer-based—Depeche Mode, Soft Cell, Human League, Kraftwerk—but every band I went to meet was just thrashing guitars. So I put an ad in *Melody Maker* looking for musicians, and I got a call from Nick Beggs. He was in a band called Art Nouveau. He said, "I know you're looking to form your own band, but do you want to come up anyway?" I said sure and hopped on a train to Leighton Buzzard.

They were very welcoming, and they had a synthesizer: a Korg Pro 1. It was making all these weeee-ooooh-oooh sounds, and it made the band sound modern. The energy was good, everybody was superfriendly, and there was a general desire to make it work.

At the time, Nick was a dustbin man [garbageman], and over the next year everybody left their jobs. It's that age when you can take chances like that. It was a lovely period when you've got no deadlines, no record company breathing down your neck, saying, "Where's the album?" I've still got a little cassette of when we were writing "Too Shy" in Nick's living room. It didn't seem that special. We had this beautiful intro, and then it got to the verse, and it just went off on a tangent. I said to Stuart [Neale], the keyboard player, "You've got to keep that

going." That was the bed, the cushion, the lace on the bed. Thankfully, we got it right.

The name Kajagoogoo shocked people a bit, but we loved to shock. I was quite theatrical. I'd go out to nightclubs in London with a spaceman's outfit on and weird oil paint over my face, which was a bit punk/Toyah/Adam and the Ants. I'd spend two and a half hours getting ready. Choosing the name was an extension of that. I remember I'd been to see an Agatha Christie movie called *The Mirror Crack'd*, and I said we should call ourselves the Mirror Crack'd. But when Nick walked in one day—and Nick's really left of center, very bright, really out-there—he said, "What do you think of 'Kajagoogoo'?" I immediately loved it. The other three looked puzzled, but they came round over a few days.

My name was Chris Hamill when I met the band. About six months into our relationship, I decided I wanted a stage name. I thought Sting was cool, because it was one word and nobody else had that name. Because I'd come from acting, I knew that Judy Garland was Frances Gumm, and I worked with actors who had stage names and they weren't even famous. I was a big fan of ABBA, and we all know now that they got their name from the first letters of everyone's Christian names. So I started thinking about letters, and I thought, Limahl. *Limahl*. I kept on saying it, and I thought, *That's clever that it's from my surname.* So I turned up to the band one day and said, "You've all got to call me 'Limahl' from now on." There was definitely a bit of sniggering, but, thankfully, they were respectful.

I worked at the Embassy Club in London. One night, Nick Rhodes came in. That changed everything. I was so tenacious; I always carried our demos around with me in case I met anybody. I said, "I'm such a big fan, and I'm also a singer, and I've done some demos of my band. Could I persuade you to have a listen?" And of course I was incredibly cute at 19. No, I was! I had this amazing energy, this wild look, perfect for London: all this hair with black bits here and there and this pretty face I'd inherited from my mum. He later said in an interview that he was very charmed by me. Of course, he could have just been blowing smoke up my

arse, and I'd never hear from him again. But he was already thinking outside the Duran Duran box. He wanted to be a Svengali music character. I didn't find out till many years later that Nick had a family relation who worked on the board of EMI. And when he called his uncle, or whomever it was, and said, "I want to sign Kajagoogoo," somebody at the top said, "You better sign them." It isn't always just about talent.

I was in a gay nightclub in London called Heaven. I used to see Freddie Mercury in there, and nobody batted an eyelid. I went up to [expatriate American BBC DJ] Paul Gambaccini, gave him a cassette, and said, "Hello, I'm Limahl. I'm in a band, we've just been signed by EMI, and we've been produced by Nick Rhodes. Would you have a listen?" He was working at Radio 1 at the time. Paul fancied me. He was round there like a shot, mate—phoned me the next day

STYLE COUNCIL

"The hair wasn't a calculated thing," Limahl says. "I didn't sit down and think, *In six months, I'll change everybody's hair.* But we were very image-conscious. I started messing around with the band's hair, and Nick went out and got the beads. They looked fantastic, but they were hard work. He said they were difficult to sleep on. Suffering for his art."

and said, "I loooove your tape. Let's have dinner." Paul went to EMI and said, "I'm making a new TV show, and I'd like to include Kajagoogoo." And then he was telling Radio 1 about "Too Shy," and then the Duran Duran fans were interested in what Nick was doing. You know how fans are in that obsessive way.

In the U.K., "Too Shy" went in at 33. The phone call came through on Tuesday: "You're going to do *Top of the Pops*." Everybody got straight on the phone to their mum and dad. It was like Christmas morning. It went from 33 to 17, then to 5, then to 2, then to 1. They couldn't press enough to sell them—30,000 copies a day. What a feeling to know you're number one. It's every orgasm rolled into one.

I was very androgynous. I was pretty. I wore makeup. To my family and the band, I was out. I did date a girl, briefly, in Leighton Buzzard, pretty much because there were no gay guys and I had to get some action somewhere. I hadn't decided if I was 100 percent gay, and it wasn't an issue. When you're that age, you love anybody playing with your cock. I wasn't embarrassed about being gay, but my role as Limahl, my pop star role, had to be more enigmatic. I didn't want to start talking about gay sex and gays in 1983 when most of our following was teenage girls. It didn't seem right. They were into our music. They were into our fashion. I don't think teenage girls really want to fuck you—they just want to love you. Our whole thing was very innocent. Maybe if the band had stayed together, if we'd been in the public eye a little longer, certainly the issue would have come up. But, also, I didn't feel equipped at 23. I think I would have been terrified if I'd started getting the third degree from journalists about "How can you be gay and be in this band that thousands of teenage girls love?" But nobody talked about it. Of course, looking back, I can realize anybody with a modicum of life experience would have said, "He's gay—he just doesn't know it yet."

For six months it became like Beatlemania: girls fainting at the front of the concerts; you couldn't hear the music for

MIXTAPE: 5 More Songs by Bands with Interesting Names

1. "Love Missile F1-11," Sigue Sigue Sputnik   2. "Papa's Got a Brand-New Pigbag," Pigbag   3. "The Smile and the Kiss," Bonk   4. "I Eat Cannibals," Total Coelo   5. "Doot Doot," Freur

"They thought, We've got this pretty-boy lead singer, and if we get rid of him, we can gain a new audience; we can be a bit more credible and change our direction."

the screaming. That's when it all started to go wrong. The band considered themselves very credible, serious musicians, which they are. Nick didn't want to be a teen idol. I don't think they had any idea they would become teeny idols but, looking back, it's such a fucking cute bunch it was bound to happen. Of course, being naive and not having strong management, they made that fatal mistake to get rid of me, because they thought, *We've got this pretty-boy lead singer, and if we get rid of him, we can gain a new audience; we can be a bit more credible and change our direction.* They just fractured the whole thing, and it imploded.

I was living at Paul Gambaccini's house in North London. It was Monday morning, and I got the call. It was Paul, the manager:

"Hi, Limahl. Having a meeting with the band—we're all here." I remember thinking, *Why are they having a meeting without me?* And he said, "We've decided we're going to let you go, and we're going to do the next album without you." You could have knocked me down with a feather. My jaw just hit the floor. I had no idea it was coming. My diary for the next 12 months was full of Kajagoogoo events. I'd just played a huge festival in Finland—40,000 people. We were laughing, and they'd already decided before the festival to get rid of me, so they were backstabbing me.

EMI tried everything [to stop the split]. They tried to get Duran Duran to stop it. They tried to bring in Duran Duran's managers, the Berrow brothers. In the end, they called Paul Gambaccini and—he told me this only three years ago—said, "EMI called and said, 'Can you please step in and somehow save this band?'" To them, this was a major investment, an act that was making them lots of money. Paul said he managed to persuade everybody except the bass player. He wouldn't do it. Nick was the leader, and the others jumped like poodles when he said "Jump."

I was just, "Oh, fuck them. I'll go solo. I'll show them." Little did I know that when you lose your creative team, you lose your sound, you lose your direction. That's why my first solo album sounded nothing like

Kajagoogoo. I didn't have that bass funk from Nick. You can have a great look and you can have a great voice, but you need all the other ingredients. That's why we were successful in the first place. And when they lost me as lead singer, they lost something as well.

NICK BEGGS: The elephant in the room here is the fact that Limahl never has and never will take responsibility for the way he behaved. If he had not treated us all like shit, we would not have fired him. Why would a band at the top of their success do that without good reason? None of us could bear to be around him at that point because he was impos-sible. I'm very disappointed he found it necessary to bring it up. I'd hoped he would have squared this away with himself by now. But...here it is again. He does himself no favors by raising this point ad nauseam.

As with so much music from that period, "Too Shy" sounds like the eighties. I think the Jupiter-8 synth and the production is what made it work in the end. It's not a great song; it's just a reasonable pop tune.

I remember [Gambaccini attempting to salvage the band]. However, I believe if we had worked with Limahl again at that time, it would have resulted in at least three of us serving custodial sentences and not just me.

THAT WAS THEN *BUT THIS IS NOW*

 A Limahl-less Kajagoogoo had several more British hits before truncating their name to Kaja and calling it a day. Beggs formed a few more groups before becoming a freelance bassist for hire and working with everybody. Literally everybody. Limahl had an international hit with the Giorgio Moroder–produced theme from the nightmarish children's fantasy movie *The Never Ending Story*. He has popped up on numerous reality shows including *I'm a Celebrity...Get Me Out of Here*. The band re-formed in 2008.

LIMAHL: They gave me a lump sum to leave. This was all very skillfully negotiated by their lawyer. In return, I would take a reduced royalty on the first album. I remember thinking, *Why the fuck would I do that? I've been fired!* But the lawyer had negotiated the split for Haircut 100, and he told me it was quite normal. And I didn't know what I was doing at 24. So instead of being an equal fifth, 20 percent, I was 6 percent. It didn't matter until 1998. The eighties revival started, and "Too Shy" was on every compilation in the world, and it was used in *The Wedding Singer*. Every time I got my royalties, I'd think, *Oh God*. It was quite painful, and I lost out financially for quite a few years. That's why our reunion didn't happen sooner. They approached me to reunite twice, once in 1998 and once in 2000. Twice I said, "Yes, but I want my royalties reinstated to the full equal." And twice they said no. The third time—this was 2008—they said okay. So I got my royalties back. I'm so happy I held out. I can die happy now.

We all knew why we were doing the reunion. None of us had repeated even remotely the success we'd had as Kajagoogoo. It seemed like a lot of bands were reuniting. And, a bit like a vase from the sixties, it's now got this antique value. We never really discussed the past, because we all knew we can't undo it. All the emotion shit was stuffed in a big closet and a big padlock put on it. We didn't talk about anything. A lot of people have said, "They were their own worst enemies," but I would say, "They just made some mistakes."

And then Nick buggered off, which is why we're not working together again. After three years, he said, "I don't know what I want to do." We'd all worked so hard, made a new video, made a new EP, did a load of gigs trying to get the momentum going and telling everybody we're back together, and he just went off. I think he thought it was going to be bigger, and it may have been if we'd stuck at it.

BEGGS: Wow! He's gonna develop an ulcer if he's not careful. I'm sorry to say that, once again, that is not quite accurate.

Limahl had a list of demands that had to be met before he would agree to work with us again—top of the list related to money. We agreed to give him what he wanted. I'd just bought a new house and felt that, by giving him what he wished for, we would all make enough to justify the shortfall. It worked. And I'm glad we did it. I also think it brought us together as friends again.

We all discovered that, after 30 years, not a lot had changed. Subsequently, it resulted in us losing three managers and a lot of work. Where do you go after that? Truth is, I've had too many offers of other work to waste my time on continuing with something that is destined to fail. We should all look back on that period of our lives and remember it for the good times. Other than that, I'm over it. I also think Limahl should stop bitching about us in the media because it makes him look tragic, and the truth is even less palatable. I wish Limahl well, but he needs to take a long, hard look at himself.

"Too Shy" has stood the test of time for no other reason than, like perfume, music can transport us across the years to where we once stood. It had the x-factor for a few seconds back in 1983. Like the big bang, the background noise is still all around us. You can also see the debris if you look hard enough.

 you're a music consumer of a certain age—i.e., old—you heard Thomas Dolby long before you knew his name. That ethereal, lengthily gestating introduction to Foreigner's "Waiting for a Girl Like You"? That's him. That defibrillator of an intro to the same band's "Urgent"? Him as well. The vocoder and synths on Whodini's "Magic's Wand"? Same dude. Dolby also co-wrote Lene Lovich's hyper-caffeinated "New Toy" and was an early keyboard player with the Thompson Twins. But if you know his name as a solo artist, chances are it's for his 1982 Top 5 song "She Blinded Me with Science." Though Dolby isn't technically a one-hit wonder—the follow-up to "Science," 1984's "Hyperactive," went to number 17 in the U.K. but only 62 in the United States—the combination of a song about science, a tweedy, academic image, and an indelibly goofy video, featuring real-life eccentric boffin and British TV personality Dr. Magnus Pyke, tied a bit of an anchor around him. He would go on to dabble in many genres of music, but to the audience who first experienced Dolby through that video, he would forever be the guy who was to MTV what Dr. Bunsen Honeydew was to the Muppets.

"SHE BLINDED ME WITH SCIENCE"

THOMAS DOLBY

JB: One of the hallmarks of the decade was the willingness of artists to blow up the formula that had brought them success. I applaud Thomas Dolby's disinclination to stand still and repeat himself. I just like his earlier stuff better. "Europa and the Pirate Twins," that headlong propulsive rush set against nostalgic imagery of an idyllic childhood, is still thrilling.

 "Airwaves" is one of the great heartsick, paranoid laments of the era. "Radio Silence," "One of Our Submarines," "Urges"—I have warm feelings for them all. "She Blinded Me with Science" was a great leap forward: way more of a jam than anything else he'd done—hilarious concept, deranged vocal. And I appreciate someone selling himself as cerebral at a time when his contemporaries were unabashed in their superficiality.

LM: Science was never my favorite subject.

THOMAS DOLBY: I left school at 16, and I sat in my bedsitter [studio apartment] in South London with my one synthesizer and two-track tape recorder trying to express myself. I'd program a kick-drum sound, then rewind it and program a bass-drum sound, and ping-pong back and forth. If you made a mistake, there was no unraveling it.

I needed to get out [so] I joined bands and got invited to do sessions. I got invited to do Foreigner's *4*, and at the time, I was living in Paris, trying to make a few centimes on the Metro with my guitar, playing Dylan songs to Japanese tourists. Foreigner rescued me from that and got me to New York. I played on that album and earned enough money working in a month to go back to England and record my first album [*The Golden Age of Wireless*, 1982].

I had no idea about image at all. My very first appearances were with Bruce Woolley and the Camera Club, who were at the very early days of the New Romantic period, and we had outfits that made us look like we were in *Barbarella*. It became clear to me, seeing myself on TV or in the music papers, that I was not a pinup boy like Adam Ant or Simon Le Bon or Sting, and I thought, *There's no point in trying to be something you're not. I should go back and look at my background.* My father was an Oxford professor, and most of my siblings are teachers—there's no showbiz at all. So I came up with the idea of the mad professor character, this young scientist. I explored it a bit in my early photo sessions. Music videos were just starting to come in, and I talked my record company into giving me a budget for a day's worth of shooting. So I came up with a storyboard, which was "She Blinded Me with Science," before I had a song. I had the title. I very often come up with the title first—I have a notebook filled with potential song titles and I work backwards from there. I visualize an empty stage with a spotlight, and a guy walks into the spotlight and starts to sing a song called "She Blinded Me with Science": What does it sound like? What's the groove, what are the words, what's the chord sequence? I fill in the blanks from there, and it becomes like a crossword puzzle.

The song was like a soundtrack for the film. I viewed videos as silent movies with soundtracks and, in silent movie terms, my heroes were always the underdogs—Buster Keaton, Harold Lloyd, and Charlie Chaplin. These were not romantic heroes, but they were the underdogs you sympathized with, so that was the character I created for myself.

It was very easy getting Dr. Magnus Pyke to be in the video. I told him the concept, we agreed on a fee with his agent, and then he showed up on set and refused to do most of what was on the storyboard. I wanted him to wear a white lab coat, and he refused point-blank because that wasn't the way his audience saw him. I asked him to say, "She blinded me with science!" But he did it like a question, not a statement: "She blinded me with science?" I was like, "It's really more of a statement, Dr. Pyke," and he was like, "Yes, but it would be a bit surprising if a girl blinded *me* with science." He was very concerned about whether his car would be there to take him off to his next appointment. He didn't exactly get in the spirit of it. The last time I saw him alive, he'd just come back from a lecture tour of the U.S., and I asked him how it went. He said, "Badly, Dolby." I asked why, and he said, "Every time I walked down the street, someone would come up behind me and shout, 'SCIENCE!' It frightened me out of my skin. Your MTV video is better known than my body of academic work."

Most of my first album was definitely new wave electronic rock, definitely pretty white. So why was "She Blinded Me with Science" a bit funkier? Maybe because it juxtaposes the geeky bookworm character with the funky dance groove. Also, this was after "Planet Rock." It was the time of DJs taking elements and turning them into different styles, so the groundwork was laid. It was an R&B hit, but I'm sure most of the R&B audience had no idea who I was. Michael Jackson thought I was black. I'm not sure whether that should be flattering or not.

"She Blinded Me with Science" was a one-off for the film that I made but, very much to my surprise and most other people's surprise too, it took off commercially. Suddenly the media and the industry were expecting the Dolby formula trotted out over the course of multiple hits and albums and tours and videos, and that was never really the intention. The record company wrang their hands when they heard *The Flat Earth*, which I think is one of my best albums. Their point of view is, it takes so much hard work and effort to break somebody—once you're there, you've got to do a few more copycat hits. They said, "Look, Thomas, when you're on your third or fourth album, maybe you can start experimenting with jazz instrumenta-tion and brushes on the cymbals and trombones. But, for heaven's sake, let's make hay while the sun shines." I think the middle-aged me with a mortgage to pay might think they have a point, but when I was 24, it was like, "Forget it." I will tap into different genres of music in order to help tell a story and set the scene. I've always been jealous of novelists who, with each book they write, get to pick a period of history or geographical location and a new cast of characters. It's like a dirty word in music, though. People get suspicious if you're too free with your leaping between genres—they think there's something fake about it.

I don't feel the boffin image encroached, but I do feel that if people only know one thing about me, it's the wacky boffin image, and maybe that was a turnoff for people if they couldn't see past it into the more organic and emotional side of my music. But the really loyal, long-term, hard-core fans don't talk about "Science" or "Hyperactive." They talk about "Screen Kiss" or "Budapest by Blimp," and those are the songs that mean the most to me. You sit at a piano and you come up with a chord change, and it melts your heart. And you just hope if you put it out there, it's going to melt a few other hearts as well. The difference between a few thousand and a few million is not apparent from the artist's point of view. The main thing is, you've made the connection.

THAT WAS THEN BUT THIS IS NOW

It's easier to make a list of what Dolby hasn't been doing. But that's another book. He led David Bowie's Live Aid band. He has produced records by Joni Mitchell and Prefab Sprout. He has composed scores for video games and movies, most notoriously George Lucas's *Howard the Duck*. He's worked extensively in Silicon Valley. He has been the musical director of the TED conferences, and he helped create the polyphonic technology that brought ringtones to the world. In 2011, he returned to music as a solo artist with the three-part album *A Map of the Floating City*, the third section of which was available only as part of the accompanying video game.

DOLBY: The record companies made themselves virtually extinct. The industry is now a cottage industry, and people are trying out all sorts of alternatives. It's like Detroit in the 1920s when there were 125 automobile companies. Stamping out records and putting them in trucks and shipping them across the country, that's a pretty hard thing to do. But making an album on a laptop from home and uploading it to YouTube or SoundCloud is something tens of thousands of people can do, which is fantastic. But then you have this sea of white noise. How do you rise above that? None of the old formulas apply anymore. It's like the Wild West. What I'm doing now is contrarian, which is what I love. You can argue, "Doesn't that make it hard to promote? Isn't it like pushing a rope or swimming against the current?" It certainly does. But just making an album with a cover and lyrics and getting it on the radio weren't going to work for *The Floating City*. That's why I came up with a multiuser game; that's why I came up with *The Invisible Lighthouse* film that I'm doing now. These are all areas where I get to learn new skills and try out new forms of expression for myself, which is what keeps my creative juices flowing.

MIXTAPE: 5 More Songs About Science, Technology, and Robots
1. "Video Killed the Radio Star," The Buggles   2. "I Dream of Wires," Gary Numan   3. "Weird Science," Oingo Boingo   4. "E=MC2," Big Audio Dynamite   5. "Science," Berlin Blondes

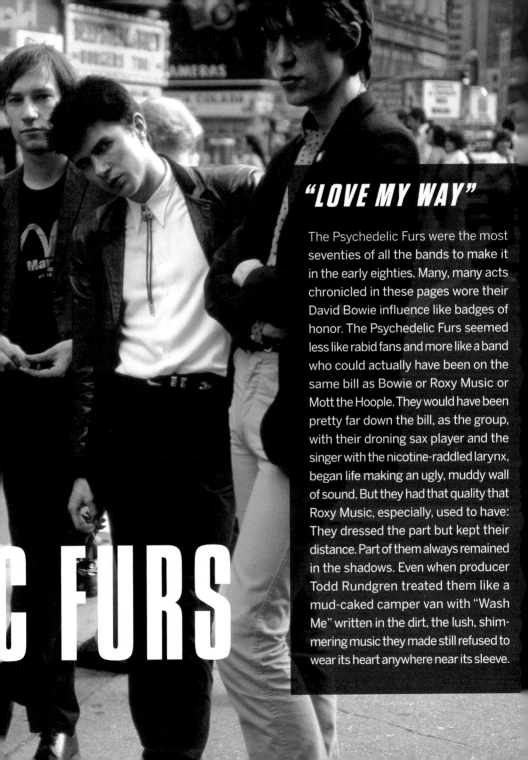

C FURS

"LOVE MY WAY"

The Psychedelic Furs were the most seventies of all the bands to make it in the early eighties. Many, many acts chronicled in these pages wore their David Bowie influence like badges of honor. The Psychedelic Furs seemed less like rabid fans and more like a band who could actually have been on the same bill as Bowie or Roxy Music or Mott the Hoople. They would have been pretty far down the bill, as the group, with their droning sax player and the singer with the nicotine-raddled larynx, began life making an ugly, muddy wall of sound. But they had that quality that Roxy Music, especially, used to have: They dressed the part but kept their distance. Part of them always remained in the shadows. Even when producer Todd Rundgren treated them like a mud-caked camper van with "Wash Me" written in the dirt, the lush, shimmering music they made still refused to wear its heart anywhere near its sleeve.

LM: "Love My Way" and "The Ghost in You" are two of the most transformative, hypnotizing tracks in my record collection. "Love My Way" is the darker of the pair, but both radiate all the hope and optimism of a young girl who's yet to have her heart broken. Whenever I hear "The Ghost in You," I become that girl all over again. Richard Butler may look and, certainly on the first two Furs albums, sound like a more mature John Lydon, but after Todd Rundgren got a hold of him, the singer-songwriter parted ways with the petulance and morphed into one of the most romantic figures in music.

JB: If I can indulge in a new wave career-trajectory version of Fantasy Baseball, I would liked to have seen the Furs continue in that wistful, vulnerable direction that so suited Butler's phlegmy tones. I would like to have seen them follow the path of latter-day Roxy Music, where they faded into tasteful anonymity and the music became almost mouth-watering in its sophistication (*Flesh + Blood* = awesome, underrated record. Reappraise!) until ultimately they made the Most Beautiful Album Ever (*Avalon*—no reappraisal needed). The Psychedelic Furs took another route, but in a parallel universe, "Love My Way" was just the first step to a glorious future.

RICHARD BUTLER: The songs that were really important are the ones that changed the course of our careers, and that would be "Pretty in Pink" and "Love My Way." "Love My Way" turned things around a lot more than "Pretty in Pink" did, and that's why we went on to do songs like "Ghost in You."

I was working with [ex-Furs guitarist] John Ashton on the third album [1982's *Forever Now*]. I was supposed to have written some ideas before I went over, but I'd been out carousing instead. The next morning, I had one of those little xylophone things, and I picked out these three notes and made this little melody [sings the opening notes of "Love My Way"]. It was all done in about 10 minutes, and I thought, *That's good. I can go to John's now.* I loved the song; John wasn't so struck by it. Then Ed Buller, a keyboardist who was working with us at the time, put this marimba part on it, which became the bulk of the song.

I enjoyed the direction "Love My Way" took the band. We wanted cellos—I'd listened to Stravinsky's *The Rite of Spring*—we wanted horns; we were using more keyboard-y sounds, and we looked for a producer who would be good at that kind of thing. Todd Rundgren came to mind because he had just done *Deface the Music*, sounding like the Beatles, and I thought, *He's using those instruments. He knows what he's doing.*

When we went to work with Todd, "Love My Way" wasn't the song you hear today. He said, "This song could be a great song, Richard, if you try and be less aggressive with it." The idea of singing had been anathema to me. Then he came up with the idea of using Flo and Eddie. Even though I liked Marc Bolan and T. Rex [to whom Flo and Eddie lent their trademark harmonies], I didn't know whether I loved the idea of these backup singers on the song. But [Rundgren] said, "If you don't like them, we'll take them off, I promise." So we recorded it with Flo and Eddie, and it sounded great.

I loved [working with Rundgren]. It's funny, because Andy Partridge apparently hated it. He came up to me in a coffee shop in New York and said, "How was your experience with Todd then?" Andy Partridge thought he was overcontrolling, but Todd consulted us every step of the way. He said, "What kind of sound do you want? Imagine for a minute you're playing in a room: What kind of room do you want it to be? A club? A theater?" We decided on a theater. We wanted it to be intimate and warm, of a certain size but not overblown.

We've always been a band that pulls people in. You won't see me stomping up and down saying, "Can you hear me at the back?!" and "Hello, Chattanooga! It's great to be here!" The amount of words I will say to an audience during a tour is a page of a notebook, and they would mostly be "Thank you." I don't like talking much between songs. It's a degree of shyness and a degree of not seeing the point in saying any of those things. I don't feel the need to go, "Are you having a good time, fill in the name of the city." I first noticed a difference [in the Furs' core fan base] when "Love My Way" became a radio hit in America on the West Coast. We did an in-store in Seattle, and the place was absolutely mobbed. We had to go out the back entrance and get in this car, and it was like being in the Beatles. Up until then we hadn't really experienced that. It was more like being in a pop band rather than the rock band we'd been in before. There were a lot more girls down at the front of the stage. You have to be careful of that kind of popularity. We had had a very cool type of popularity, and "Love My Way" threatened that to a degree.

I was a big Dylan fan until art school. That's where I discovered the Velvet Underground, Bowie, and Roxy Music. [The Epsom School of Art and Design in Surrey, England] was a very old-fashioned type of art school—quite academic. In the last years, I got into Warhol and doing prints. Two years later, I was working in a screen-printing place doing prints of my own, and punk rock came along with the Sex Pistols. I got to see them at the 100 Club [in London]. The place was packed, even though punk hadn't quite caught on at that point. I formed a band and started to print the posters for the shows we were doing. I don't know how I ended up being the singer—probably because it was my big idea to form a band. [Our first gig] was at somebody's party in Leatherhead. We just decided we were going to play. We played about two songs, then everybody left and shut the door. They were hippies—they didn't know what was happening.

Eventually we were playing clubs [in London] like the Roxy, the Africa Centre, the Lyceum, Music Machine. Early on, our music was jaded and angry. It was the mood in England around that time: Margaret Thatcher, garbage strikes, the IRA bombing in Guildford, my hometown. It was an easy time to be jaded in. I used that feeling but didn't use the obvious political words. I always found obvious political songs don't ever seem to work. I was more into the poetry of lyric writing. I was inspired by T. S. Eliot, Dylan Thomas, the Velvet Underground, David Bowie, and certainly Bob Dylan.

For the first album [1980's *Psychedelic Furs*], we worked with [producer] Steve Lillywhite. Steve had done the first Banshees record. He said that he would like to record us not using very many tricks, just make it sound how an amazing live show would sound. It was recorded very quickly—a lot of it was live—and I think the whole thing might have been done in a week or 10 days. I loved it!

While we were writing songs for the second album [1981's *Talk Talk Talk*], we improved as songwriters. "Pretty in Pink" just came to me, and I built the song around what that phrase conjured up. I always thought "Pretty in Pink" was a song about a girl who sleeps around a lot and thinks she's very clever for doing it and feels very desired, but people are laughing at her behind her back. I don't think the movie *Pretty in Pink* did us any favors. It made light of and put a different spin on a song that actually had more to say than what the movie did. It's certainly less fluffy.

The story I heard [about how the song came to be the title of and theme song for the 1986 film] was that Molly Ringwald went up to John Hughes and said, "You've got to listen to this song. You've got to write something about this." Hughes [supposedly] loved it and went on to write the movie. The original version came out in 1981. It was a fairly well-known song, but in a college-radio situation. We rerecorded it for the movie. It was our idea. The record company was perfectly willing to go with the original version, which we should have. The original is better. It's not radically different, but I don't think it has the same rawness as the original.

THAT WAS THEN BUT THIS IS NOW

"Love My Way," a cover favorite for artists as disparate as Live and Korn, was the first in a U.S. hit parade that also included "Heaven," "The Ghost in You," the rerecorded "Pretty in Pink," and "Heartbreak Beat." In 1992 Butler and brother/fellow Fur Tim started Love Spit Love, which recorded a popular rendition of the Smiths' "How Soon Is Now?" (see page 234) for the film _The Craft_. It was later repurposed as the theme for a TV show with a similar hot-young-witches approach, _Charmed_. The Furs re-formed in

2000 and continue to tour. Meanwhile, Butler has also returned to his first love, painting, with his 2013 *ahatfulofrain* show at a Chelsea gallery in Manhattan earning rave reviews, like this one: "Unlike the Ronnie Woods and Bob Dylans of the music-to-art crossover world, Butler actually has real talent for creating captivating artwork."

BUTLER: We'd made [the Furs' fifth album, 1987's] *Midnight to Midnight*, which I absolutely hated. We were very dry of ideas and under a great deal of pressure from the record company and ourselves. We were recording in Europe. It was a hellish adventure just to get it done. I felt it was a really subpar album that really didn't have that much direction to it, and that took a lot of the wind out of my sails as far as belief in the direction that we were going in. After that, we'd made a couple of records [1989's *Book of Days* and 1991's *World Outside*] that were consciously very uncommercial to redress the balance to some degree, but then I felt I'd needed a break.

MIXTAPE: 5 More Love Songs with Ice in Their Veins 1. "I'm in Love with a German Film Star," The Passions 2. "Love Shadow," Fashion 3. "Another Girl, Another Planet," The Only Ones 4. "The Last Beat of My Heart," Siouxsie and the Banshees 5. "You Have Placed a Chill in My Heart," Eurythmics

In their earliest incarnations, the synth-pop stars of the eighties lived in a bleak, oppressive, futuristic netherworld where emotions were forbidden and humanity was a faintly flickering memory. Gary Numan, the Human League, OMD, Ultravox, Soft Cell, the Normal—none of them were having much fun. But there was one group of electronic artists who were not crushed under the heel of robot overlords, who were not afraid of being assimilated into a giant hive mind, who were, if anything, uncomplicated and optimistic: Depeche Mode. Vince Clarke's Depeche Mode. Where their contemporaries shuddered in fear and lurked in the shadows like a doomed platoon of Winston Smiths, Depeche Mode were cheerful, wholesome boys, happy to have hatched an escape route out of the unpromising environs of Basildon, England. Depeche's single "New Life" was innocent, awkward, and eager to please. Their other Clarke-penned hits, "Just Can't Get Enough" and "Dreaming of Me," gleamed with confidence and charm. But exhilarating as it was, this iteration had a limited shelf life. Clarke chose to stay positive and, for the remaining members of the group, his departure signaled the end of the innocence.

"NEW LIFE"

DEPECHE

JB: The bald musician Moby wrote a witty and affectionate afterword for this book in which he—spoiler alert!—describes the music and artists of the new wave era under discussion as not alluding to "anything even remotely sexual." Being an argumentative sort, I took issue with that blanket dismissal, and my prime example was latter-day Depeche Mode and their S&M leanings. He replied to the effect that all the Mode really wanted was to cuddle. In retrospect, I think he's right, and that's why I've always found them a little bit laughable. No matter how much Martin L. Gore bares his diseased soul, no matter how dank and deviant their material, no matter how brooding and perverse Dave Gahan gets, I never quite got past my initial perception of them as clean-cut, obedient purveyors of chirpy electro-pop. The "Personal Jesus" video—the one where they're supposed to be snarling, smoldering gunslingers getting ready to 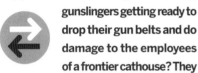 drop their gun belts and do damage to the employees of a frontier cathouse? They looked more like pale, malnourished, middle-management types heading off to a sales conference. They may see themselves as debauched outlaws with insatiable appetites for the forbidden, but for me, Depeche Mode will always be the sound of the suburbs.

LM: If Duran Duran were my first crush and the Smiths wrote the soundtrack of my soul, then Depeche Mode provided the playlist for my sex life—or at least the one I'd imagined myself having. "Master and Servant." "A Question of Lust." "Strangelove." "In Your Room." But I wouldn't even have an imaginary sex life if it weren't for Vince Clarke. He built the foundation on which the mighty edifice of Depeche would flourish. A few months back, I bumped into Gahan at my Manhattan hair salon, where the smock-clad singer was about to have his grays covered before Depeche's upcoming international arena tour, and he and I reflected on how far they've come. Decades on, the band is the biggest electronic music act of all time. They're still making new music that sends albums up the charts, and still an influence on contemporary musicians and dance culture. They might not be the same band Clarke started all those years ago, but if it wasn't for him, Gahan might be the proud proprietor of a nice little upholstery business in Basildon.

VINCE CLARKE: "New Life" was the first song that was played on the radio, and the first one that went into the charts in the U.K. That was a game changer. The first time we heard it on the radio, we were all in Danny's [Mute Records founder Daniel Miller's] car. It was the band, Daniel driving, and the synths in the back. We were going to get a train to Newcastle, where we were to do one of the first TV shows we'd ever done, a Saturday-morning kids show, and it just came on the radio. I think it was Radio 1, which is the most important radio station in the U.K. It was a great feeling.

Around the same time, we did our first appearance on *Top of the Pops*. The charts would be released on Sunday, and we got the call from Daniel that night saying we'd be on. We'd all grown up on *Top of the Pops*. I was 19 and wasn't living with my mum at the time. We had fallen out. But I decided to go round to her house and tell her. I don't think she believed me.

We lived in Basildon.✻ Basildon is a town that was built after the Second World War to house all the people who were bombed out of the East End of London, so it was a new town. It was built in the fifties, and

it was built so quickly that they didn't bother to build anything kids could do—it was just housing. When I moved there, there was no grass, no gardens—there was just mud. You spent a lot of time being bored. There was no TV. So we started a band.

When Depeche Mode started, when it was just me and [Andy] Fletcher, we were playing guitars. The band that really influenced us the most, that we wanted to be, was the Cure. We'd play their first album, [1979's] *Three Imaginary Boys*. It's incredibly minimal. There were only three players on it. There was hardly any overdub, I think, just a single voice. We felt that we could do that sound because Fletch played guitar and I had a drum machine. We weren't really interested in synths until Martin, who was a friend of Fletch's from school, bought a synthesizer and decided to join the band. Martin joined two bands, actually: my band and my best friend's band. That caused a bit of a rift. Martin was hedging his bets. Anyway, when Martin chose the synth, we were super impressed. It seemed to be really easy to play, unlike guitar. It wasn't expensive, particularly because you didn't have to buy an

---

✻ **ALISON MOYET:** The Depeche boys, Fletcher and Martin, and I were in the same class. Perry Bamonte, who was in the Cure, was there as well. They were from the right side of the street in our town: They were all studious, they did their homework, they had blazers and briefcases when the rest of us had plastic bags. I remember being bemused when they got together with Dave Gahan. He was one of the punks who was in Southend College with me. We were mates, and he was a bit more lairy [British slang for aggressive, confrontational; master rather than servant].

expensive amp. We never could afford amps for our guitars, so we all bought synths.

Synth music was really homemade. I don't think punk was as liberating as people make it out to be. They still needed to know how to play instruments. Synth music is more accessible 'cause you don't have to learn your three chords. On our first album [1981's *Speak & Spell*], no one played anything. It was all done on sequencers.

The synths gave us credibility. All the cool, alternative records—the ones that weren't charting—were all done with people messing about with synths: "T.V.O.D."/"Warm Leatherette" by the Normal, the first Silicon Teens album. They were breaking new ground. Those songs were an influence on "New Life" and "Just Can't Get Enough." Obviously there was Gary Numan too, but we didn't want to sound like Gary Numan because he was a sellout. You know what it's like when you're younger: Anyone who succeeds is no longer credible. Whereas, we thought the first two Human League albums were

amazing records [in part because] they were commercially unsuccessful. Of course, way before any of that was Kraftwerk, but the thing that changed in the eighties was that people used synthesizers to make pop records rather than concept records. I'm a fan of Kraftwerk, but I'm more of a fan of people like OMD, because I like emotional records. Music affects me, changes my insides—it really does. The thing that really turned me on to synths was "Almost," the B-side to OMD's "Electricity." That was when I connected synthesizers with folk music. I'd realized that I wanted to play guitar when I heard Simon and Garfunkel singing on the soundtrack for *The Graduate*. That's what made me realize the power of songwriting. The next day I bought the songbook and learned how to play every song. Suddenly, music wasn't just a bunch of people doing it on TV—you could do it yourself.

We'd started a band, but we didn't really have aspirations to make a record. We had aspirations to play in the pub, and it went from there. Eventually we were playing a

MIXTAPE: 5 Favorite Synth Songs of Vince Clarke (in no particular order)
1. "Almost," OMD 2. "Dreams of Leaving," The Human League 3. "Cars," Gary Numan 4. "Warm Leatherette," The Normal 5. "Back to Nature," Fad Gadget

pub in London, and we met Daniel, and he offered for us to make a single. That was probably the happiest day of my life. If we had made that single and I died, I would have died in heaven.

The first time we met Daniel, though, he didn't want to sign us. We had made a demo, and because Dave and I were both unemployed at the time, or Dave was in college, which is the same thing, really— I'm kidding—we got dressed in our best futurist clothes and got the train down to London. I think Dave had on leather trousers. He was studying fashion in college. (Our name was his idea; it was from a magazine he was reading.) Maybe mum had made me something—my mum was a seamstress. So we went to all these companies: Island, Virgin, all those people. In those days you could actually knock on the door, go into the office, and play them a cassette. When we went to the Rough Trade office, they said, "It's not really our cup of tea, but this bloke might be interested," and there was Daniel. And Daniel said no. Then we supported Fad Gadget at a gig in East London, and Daniel was there again. There were two guys who wanted us: Daniel and this guy Stevo, who used to manage Soft Cell. Stevo said, "If you sign with me, I'll get you on the next Ultravox tour." Daniel says, "We never sign anything, but I'm offering for you to make a single." We decided in about five minutes to go with

> **"The synths gave us credibility. All the cool, alternative records … were all done with people messing about with synths."**

Daniel and Mute. We knew the records he had made: both the Silicon Teens and the Normal. We knew his label because of Fad Gadget.

The first track we recorded with Daniel was "Photographic." It was for an album called *Some Bizarre*, a compilation record [from Stevo], which was a fantastic record. Then we did the single, which was "Dreaming of Me." Because that did fairly well, Daniel said, "Let's make an album."

"Just Can't Get Enough" I had written ages ago. We were performing it for a long time before we met Daniel. It was written on guitar. We could do harmonies because Martin is quite a good singer. That made us a little more interesting for Daniel. It's certainly gotten more exposure [than other songs on the first album] because of commercials, and because Depeche has been performing it for years and years in concert.

THAT WAS THEN BUT THIS IS NOW

Clarke departed Depeche after only one album. After a shaky start, Martin Gore grew into one of the era's most celebrated songwriters and oversaw his group's metamorphosis into Depressed Mode, the black-celebrating dance-floor juggernaut that's moved more than 100 million records. Clarke went on to form Yaz with Alison Moyet (see page 166), then the Assembly, which produced one single. In 1985 Clarke finally found a permanent situation with singer Andy Bell: 30 years and 30 hit U.K. singles later, Erasure are still a functioning duo. In 2012, Clarke reunited with Gore as VCMG and made the instrumental techno record *Ssss*.

CLARKE: When I decided to leave, it wasn't for another music band or to form Yaz—I just decided to leave.✱ We were just young, and things happened quite quickly for us, and there were a lot of egos flying around. I was just fed up. In retrospect, I'm really glad [I left]. No regrets at all, because I've worked with some really brilliant artists.

I did a single, [the Assembly's] "Never Never," with Feargal Sharkey. I was thinking that since I'd had the personality clashes with Alison I would move on with working with different singers instead [of being in a permanent group]. Then I met Andy. We had auditions. He came alone, and he was there for about 20 minutes and sang two songs I had written: "Who Needs Love Like That" and "My Heart So Blue." We had been through 39 or 40 singers by that time. They were really good, but the moment he opened his mouth and started singing, we knew it.

We had discussions about making dance-type music. He took me to a lot of clubs—the first time I had ever been to a gay club. These gay clubs were playing high-energy music. We were into the idea of making music like that so we could perform it live. But it wasn't really until the second album [1987's *Circus*] that we became

---

✱ **DANIEL MILLER:** Creatively, could they have done more together? Yes. But the band started to change almost as soon as I started working with them. Vince was a restless soul. You could see that during the making of *Speak & Spell*. Vince was the leader: He was the songwriter, he organized the band, he was the one getting the gigs, he pretty much made all the records. Obviously Dave sang and Martin did some melody lines, but Vince led, he produced. I was credited as co-producer, but most of the big ideas came from Vince. I think the other members of the group were very happy for that to continue. I don't know for how long they would have been happy, but there was more to do if they wanted to do it. But Vince decided he didn't want to be in the band anymore. The touring, he felt there were limitations—there were lots of different reasons and those reasons were very fixed in his mind, so I don't think there could have been another Depeche Mode album from those four people.

friends, because then we started writing songs together. You can't write a song with somebody you don't trust. And we went through a lot together. We played some really shitty clubs, traveled in some shitty vans, we had a car crash once. We really were a band.

[Regarding reuniting with Gore for *Ssss*,] I've never really been interested in techno. I didn't know anything about it. But after I did a remix for Plastikman, I started to get interested in the genre. I did two or three tracks and got a bit bored, so I emailed Martin. That email that I sent him was the first I ever sent him. So we started exchanging files: I'd send

him a written track, he'd send me a bass part....We did that over the course of a year. We didn't even talk at all until the very end, when we had a conference call with Daniel. Just before it was released, I went to L.A. to do some promotion. I had spoken more words to Martin in that meeting than I had when I was in Depeche Mode! Martin's really shy.

I love making music. It's the best job in the world. When you start making something from nothing, it's just an incredible feeling. Even now, with Erasure, it's always about the next record, the next song you're gonna write. I never stop.

he rich pageant of pop has no shortage of slight, sinister, Machiavellian male figures who made their millions ruthlessly manipulating the talents and emotions of the powerhouse women in their lives. Phil Spector had Ronnie, Sonny had Cher, Ike had Tina—the list is long and grim. But Vince Clarke was no master puppeteer and Alison Moyet far from his docile discovery. No romantic feelings fueled their relationship. Of the many duos littering the new wave landscape, Yaz (short for "Yazoo," a name already taken by an American rock band that filed suit and were never heard from again) were the most like complete strangers who had accidentally wandered into each other's personal space. And yet Moyet's malleable vocals—as impressive when they were angelic and intimate as when she was unleashing her trademark bellow of bluesy rage—caused blood to pump furiously through Clarke's airy, catchy compositions. Though he'd started his career with Depeche Mode and would go on to form Erasure—another duo, with a singer with whom he'd feel a far stronger connection—Clarke's best coupling was his brief, two-album (mis)matchup with Moyet.

"ONLY YOU"

JB: Like Clarke, I was the male half of a boy-girl pop duo at the start of the eighties. Like Yaz, my group (April Showers—Google us!) demoed a song that was swiftly snapped up and released by a label. We, too, had insurmountable communication problems and couldn't cope with instant success…and the way it completely evaded us. And like Moyet and Clarke, my ex-bandmate, Beatrice Colin, and I are now good friends and comfortable enough to indulge in the occasional bout of "You were the bigger asshole" / "No, you were the bigger asshole!" without tears being shed. (Let's hope my current boy-girl duo—in which I'm clearly the bigger asshole—manages a similarly happy ending.) So I don't find it particularly surprising that Yaz didn't endure past two albums, but the amount of leeway they allowed each other is kind of amazing. Pre- and post-Yaz, Clarke was all hyper-caffeinated pop, all the time. While in the environs of Yaz, he was amenable to Moyet's goth fantasies and her penchant for moody balladeering. But Clarke's "Only You" is their song for all seasons.

LM: When I went to Clarke's Brooklyn brownstone for our interview, I didn't know what to expect. Although he set the agendas for his various groups, Clarke has always seemed to avoid the spotlight, both on stage and in the press. His manager warned he'd be shy, but as Clarke followed close behind me while we descended the two flights to his sub-basement, I wondered if I was being led into the lair of a synth-pop serial killer. Even more disconcerting, Clarke refers to his studio as…the Cabin. (I've watched enough horror films to know that girls don't come back from places called the Cabin.) As I passed the snaking tangles of wires hanging from the walls, my mind started to race: strangulation at worse, electrocution at best? Finally, we arrived, and there they were: the cold, inert bodies of his keyboard collection. The man loves his machines—maybe more than he likes people? Which is why it's so reassuring that he's capable of writing such a plaintive little lullaby like "Only You."

VINCE CLARKE: When I left Depeche Mode, I wrote "Only You." It's like a folk record with synths. The actual implement was a guitar; I transposed the riff into synth notes. It was a very simple arrangement. For the lyrics, I just formed words on a piece of paper. I was just hoping that Daniel [Miller, Mute Records founder] would like it.

ALISON MOYET: "Only You" has a nursery rhyme simplicity and a lack of pretension. You don't need to be a great singer to sing it; you don't need to be a great instrumentalist to play it. It's a universal, everyman song.

CLARKE: I kind of knew Alison. I'd seen her perform locally. She was in a punk band with my best friend, and she'd been in a couple of blues bands. I knew that she could sing with a huge amount of emotion, and "Only You" was supposed to be a ballad, so I asked her to demo it on a four-track tape recorder.

MOYET: I never intended to be in a band with Vince. I was hanging around on Canvey Island [in Essex, England] with the Dr. Feelgood lot doing the pub-rock thing, which seemed like a more natural progression for me to go from punk than New Romantic. I never aspired to be a pop star or to have a mainstream hit. I never listened to pop music. Basildon was a new town with no culture, and we had no money. Punk was an ethos that we could relate to because it didn't matter if you had money, education, or social standing. It belonged to us. I bought into that, but there was a time when I realized for a lot of people it was all about fashion and clothes. A lot of my friends who would have been wearing dishcloths the same as I was were then spending a lot of money when the New Romantics came out, and I felt quite betrayed by that. My ambition was to be part of the London pub circuit. When you say that now, it makes you think of some kind of nasty, gnarly old singer, but in the seventies, the pub-rock scene was really interesting. You had Elvis Costello, Ian Dury, and the Stranglers. I wanted to headline the places they played. So a part of me was thinking, *I'll never hear the end of it if I go and sing with this pretty boy*. But I had no money, no tape recorder, no way of making a demo, so I thought, *Okay, I'll use this as a demo.*

CLARKE: I took the demo to Daniel. He seemed completely not interested. I thought I was going to have to go back to working in factories. Fortunately, there were four associates from Norway, Denmark, and Sweden [in the Mute offices] at the time. They got to hear the song and really liked it. That made Daniel pay attention.

> **"A part of me was thinking, I'll never hear the end of it if I go and sing with this pretty boy. But I had no money, no tape recorder, no way of making a demo, so I thought, *Okay, I'll use this as a demo.*"**

MOYET: Vince called and said, "The record company thinks we should record an album together," and two months later I was a pop star.

CLARKE: Alison and I weren't a real band. We barely knew each other. We wanted to use Black Studios, but Fad Gadget was recording their second album. [Frank "Fad Gadget" Tovey] would be in there from 11 a.m. to 11 p.m., so Alison and I would go in around six in the morning and record from 6 to 10 a.m. That was quite stressful because we had to commute to London.

MOYET: The first thing Vince said to me was, "You got any songs?" He'd written

"Only You," and we were going to release that as a single. He wrote "Don't Go" for the B-side, and that was obviously too good for a B-side, so we wrote "Situation" together, which ended up being flipped over [released as the A-side] in America. From that point, the songwriting was completely equitable. I wrote half of the material in Yaz. But Vince is a famous songwriter, so the assumption was that I was the voice and he was the creator. It wasn't the case, but you get tired of trying to explain. You just have to look at the difference between Yaz and Erasure to see what my input in the band was compared to what Andy [Bell's] influence is. I am very aware that the assumption is the female voice is the mouthpiece of the male creator. I was talking about "Nobody's Diary" to someone the other day, and he said, "You really interpreted that song well." I said, "No, I wrote that song when I was 16." Even with all the credits on the album sleeve, even now when it's on Google for anyone to see, the assumption is always that the vocalist is not the creative influence.

CLARKE: We fell out pretty fast. We just didn't know what to say to each other. We never went out for a drink—not one drink. We were quite different. We weren't in the same school. We didn't have anything in common. She was a bit younger than me. Alison was incredibly lacking in self-confidence. I think she felt a bit put out because I knew my way around the studio by then. I knew the record company. I don't think she felt like a part of the camp. I'm sure that was something she went through, that she was in "the boys club." We did the first record and a tour in the U.K., and by the end, we had pretty much fallen out, so the second album was really thrown together. We weren't even in the studio together.

MOYET: We always worked separately. He would play me a song on the guitar, and I would sing it in the way I chose to sing it. I would play him a song on the guitar, and he would arrange it in the way he chose to arrange it. I didn't mess with him, and he didn't mess with me. We were very different in the sense that I come from a French peasant family who have no problem expressing themselves loudly, and he was very reserved and English and was more of a passive-aggressive to my aggressive. And then we were famous, and I was getting a lot of attention. When Yaz started, there was a lot [of talk] that I was the great singer and Vince was the lightweight. Obviously, that [perception's] changed. Singers, schmingers—there's plenty of them about, and Vince is recognized as the great, consistent musical talent that he is.

The big shock was going from being a bit of a black sheep, the sort of person that people around town avoided, to being really famous. I was always remarkable, and obviously I don't mean that like, "Aren't I wonderful?" I mean it like people have always had something to say about me. You noticed me in a room, for good or bad. It was hard to get that sort of universal attention, to be recognized everywhere within a matter of weeks.

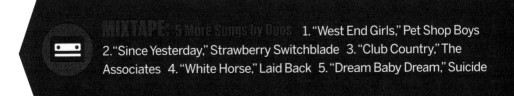

MIXTAPE: 5 More Songs by Duos   1. "West End Girls," Pet Shop Boys   2. "Since Yesterday," Strawberry Switchblade   3. "Club Country," The Associates   4. "White Horse," Laid Back   5. "Dream Baby Dream," Suicide

THAT WAS THEN BUT THIS IS NOW

 Following the dissolution of Yaz, Moyet launched a solo career in the U.K. with 1984's hugely successful *Alf*. She seemed geared for international success but instead chose a more idiosyncratic career path, recording what and when she wanted. In 2008 Moyet reunited with Clarke for a live Yaz album and tour. In 2013, after several grueling years of disinterest from British record labels that only wanted to work with her if she recorded cover versions or played the nostalgia card on reality TV, she released the critically acclaimed album *The Minutes*, her highest U.K.-charting album in 25 years. Almost as much attention was paid to her weight loss, which saw her dwindle from an English size 22 to a 10. Meanwhile, Clarke started another duo, Erasure, which to date has sold 25 million albums—spawning the 1988 U.S. hits "Chains of Love" and "A Little Respect"—and continues to record and tour.

CLARKE: Alison sent me an email saying, "Do you want to do this reunion thing to celebrate 25 years since the Yazoo releases?" I said, "No, not really." I was really busy at the time. Then the next year Andy said he'd like to take a break and maybe do a solo record. So I thought I could do the Yazoo thing, maybe do a few dates. The next thing you know, management is piling on all these shows.

MOYET: When we did the reunion, I was much calmer and more easy to get along with, and he was much more open and lighter. Consequently, we found that we had quite a lot in common in terms of our sense of humor, and we had a lovely, lovely time.

CLARKE: It wasn't until we did the reunion tour that we really got to know each other. We didn't do so much reminiscing as we talked about our kids. She has three, I have one, so she had a bit of advice for me.

MOYET: Looking back to the eighties, there was so much more room for diversity. A freak was more celebrated than it is now. There was less sexism, bizarrely, in the creative arena. Women could present themselves in a male light but not like the way they have to do it now. The way it's done now, it's almost like playing an aggressive sexuality and imagining that gives women parity, when truly all they're doing is playing to a sexual fantasy and they are no more esteemed and stronger—they're just being sex toys. Back then, women could

employ a male aggressiveness that was far more about feminism and their independence. That had actually been achieved by the women's movement, which seems to have been lost in later years. Women seem to have given up. Young women seem to be giving it away. Once upon a time, our attractive girl pop stars were Bananarama, who presented themselves with light independent spirits, but you never felt they were whoring themselves. There are times now when I feel like it's shocking when you see someone with their clothes on. It's shocking when someone's not offering you their arse to imagine yourself penetrating as they sing.

At the end of the fifties, when the British attempted to get to grips with the rock 'n' roll phenomenon, the singer Marty Wilde was at the forefront of the homegrown movement. At the start of the seventies, when the British were enamored with all things Osmond, Wilde's son Ricky was launched as a domestic equivalent to Donny. When the eighties commenced and there were few solo female pop singers, Wilde's daughter Kim took her place in the family business. Signed by pop mogul and grumpy seventies-TV talent-show judge Mickie Most—everything you like or loathe about Simon Cowell originated with him—Kim Wilde saw instant success with her debut single, "Kids in America." More than a decade's worth of hits predominantly written by her father and brother followed, but her success was on a song-by-song basis: Five years elapsed between "Kids" entering the U.S. charts and her version of "You Keep Me Hanging On" climbing to number one. She didn't have a die-hard following, she didn't have a signature sound, but as far as new wave women are concerned, Kim Wilde was one of the first and lasted the longest.

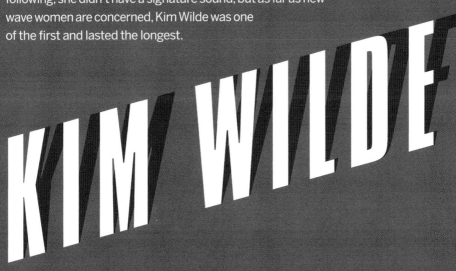

KIM WILDE

JB: Kim Wilde was a sullen, pouting British Bardot with a thin, inexpressive voice and a back catalog that is criminally easy to underestimate. "Kids in America" was as much a rarity upon its release as it is today: a crunchingly simple, super-poppy, three-minute single that sounds on first hearing like you've known it all your life. The Ramones could have done that song, Katy Perry could have done that song—but neither could have done it better than Kim Wilde did. And not just because she did it with an English accent. It was the way she sounded like she was just a little too cool, like she was doing the listener a favor. And she was! Especially in the final bridge, when she gave voice to the deathless couplet "New York to East California / There's a new wave comin' I warn you." The first line is geographically baffling, while the second accurately predicted the turn that American music was about to take.

LM: "Kids in America" is the 1982 version of "Smells like Teen Spirit" and "We Are Young": an adolescent anthem that encapsulated what it was like to be coming of age at a certain time. However, while Kurt Cobain pinpointed the apathy of Generation X, and Fun.'s "Let's set the night on fire" chorus is a sarcastic call-to-arms for overachieving millennials, Wilde's message was earnest and innocent: "Everybody live for the music-go-round." We didn't know about irony back then; we didn't have detachment or distance. We were all about fun (without the period). These days, Ferris Bueller wouldn't be cutting school; he'd be trying to raise seed money for his hot new app.

KIM WILDE: When I was about seven or eight years old, I used to watch *Top of the Pops* on a Thursday night, and that was my world. I remember making a deal with myself that one day I would be on it. Yes, my dad was one of the first rock stars ever [in the U.K.], but I'd already made a firm decision about my life.

My parents were only 20 when they had me. Rules didn't exist that much in our house. We were like kids growing up together, sharing each other's jeans and T-shirts. My dad had the most awesome collection of vinyl, and we had unlimited access to that.

I loved everything that was happening with punk, but I was just as happy listening to Kraftwerk as I was listening to the Sex Pistols, ABBA, and the Clash. I knew that my life was wrapped up with music one way or another, and even though it felt a bit slow to start, especially when I found myself leaving school and going to art college, I had this really strong sense of my own destiny. I'd done some backing vocals on my dad's stuff, and I'd been on the road with him. And I'd done backing vocals on a lot of the Ricky Wilde stuff. But really, deep down, what I wanted to do was get in a band. I remember going to London and seeing a band called the Mo-Dettes. I became a bit friendly with them, and I used to think that seemed the most fun: hanging out with a bunch of girls you love and making pop music.

Ricky had written some songs and had interest from Mickie Most at RAK Records. One day he was meeting with Ricky and I marched into the studio looking like a pop star. I remember making a special effort that day—my hair looked particularly spiky. I was already dying it and cutting it myself at art college. My tutor said it was the most creative thing I'd done while I was there. I went down the King's Road and bought myself some punky new wave trousers and a shirt. Things happened very quickly after that. Mickie asked Ricky who I was and started making noises to him that a couple of producers, Nicky Chinn and Mike Chapman, might do some stuff with me. Ricky thought, *Sod that. If anyone's going to be doing something with Kim, it's going to be me.* He went home that weekend and wrote "Kids in America."

He had the Wasp synthesizer in his bedroom. It was quite a new thing—we're talking about the dark days of technology, pre-Walkman, pre-cellphones. I don't know how he got his hands on this bit of kit, but the pulse inspired "Kids in America." Rick was a big Human League fan. He was the sound maker, and I was the one lending the vocals and the blonde hair.

A lot of people would give me shit for "Kids in America": "What are you singing about—you're not from America." I don't know that it matters that much. I loved the attitude of the song. Do you really always have to directly identify with the lyrics of a song? I didn't think so. I always thought it had something special about it that transcended having it make any sense that a girl from a village in Hertfordshire in the English countryside was singing it. Besides, I liked that it wound people up so much.

It went in the charts on its own steam and the BPI [British Phonographic Institute] or whoever put the charts together pulled it out. They thought it had been hyped [that the record company illegally purchased copies]. There was a lot of hyping that used to go on in those days, and they hadn't put it past Mickie that he might do that to his fledgling artist. So they had to reinstate the song. Mickie would come in every day and tell us the sales figures: 30,000, then

40,000, then 50,000, then 60,000 people were going out every day and buying it. Before we knew it, we sold over a million copies. At the time, I had no way of computing what that actually meant. I had nothing to compare it to, and it was irrelevant to me anyway. I wasn't interested in units and figures and business. All I cared about was the fact that I was going to be on *Top of the Pops* for a few Thursday nights.

When it was a hit in America, they were like, "Why 'East California'? Why not all the way over to the west? Why miss out on that whole section of California that's not mentioned in the song?" And I said, "Well, they already got it. The people from the west side have already got it. We just had to bring it over to the east." I was finding myself trying to come up with any excuse as to why my dad might have written "to East California," and if you ask him, quite disarmingly, he'll just say, "'Cause it sounded better." If I'm honest, I didn't give too much thought to any of the lyrics. I was lost in this fantasy world that my dad had invited me into. I love how

pop music can be completely nonsensical like that.

Musically, I found it really hard to put myself where I thought I should be. I loved too many different kinds of music. I really did struggle, and I think it shows in the early parts of my career. I look a little like I'm not sure where I should be, and it's true: I didn't know. By the time Ricky and my dad had started writing in earnest, I was far, far away. I was 20 years old living in airports all over the world with barely time to think about any aspect of my life other than making sure I didn't miss a flight. I barely saw them except to record. I figured my dad had a songwriting pedigree, so I just let them get on with it. I loved what they were coming up with for me, and even when I wasn't sure, I still went for it wholeheartedly. I played my part, but not in the creative process, putting songs together. It took me quite a few years to start thinking about becoming a songwriter myself.

I was always a bit of a tomgirl at school, a jeans and T-shirts girl. While the others

MIXTAPE: 5 More Songs by British Women
1. "Just What I Always Wanted," Mari Wilson   2. "It's a Mystery," Toyah
3. "Weak in the Presence of Beauty," Alison Moyet   4. "They Don't Know,"
Kirsty MacColl   5. "Eighth Day," Hazel O'Connor

were wearing eyeliner and miniskirts and platforms, I was the girl with the flared jeans and no makeup. As I became more of a woman, I felt more confident and sexy in photographs. They were absolutely tame compared to what's happening now, but that suited me. I liked that I could look pretty in pictures, but my main thing was I loved singing. Image always had a backseat for me, and sometimes I got it really spectacularly right—although most of the time that would be totally by accident—and then a lot of times I'd get it spectacularly wrong. There have been times in my career when I wish I'd been a bit more stylish. I wish I could have pulled it off and had all the top designers clamoring for my attention and begging me to wear their clothes. But they never did, and now I'm really glad I never got consumed by that.

Sometimes a career is driven very much by an artist and their ambitions. A really good example of that is Madonna. We both had a great start, but she had that ambition. I don't think I had that kind of voracious appetite. Had I had that, maybe I could have kept the momentum going a bit more. It was not for want of trying. Rick and Marty were always trying to come up with a hit record—that was the holy grail of each waking day. But all the aspects of creating an image and hype? I didn't have that energy to put into my career. It wasn't coming from me, and as a result, I didn't seem to attract that kind of input from anyone else.

THAT WAS THEN *BUT THIS IS NOW*

Kim Wilde continued to have European hits into the nineties. She ended her recording career to marry actor Hal Fowler and raise a family. She appeared in *Tommy* on the West End stage before going full-force into horticulture and becoming a celebrated TV gardener, presenting makeover shows for the BBC and Channel 4. Wilde then returned to music in 2001, joining various eighties revival tours. In 2003, she recorded the genuinely great "Anyplace Anywhere Anytime," a duet with fellow new waver Nena that went on to be a Top 10 hit across Europe. (Just because we call this one "genuinely great" doesn't mean we don't think similarly highly of other eighties acts' contemporary recordings. We just don't say it.) She is still signed to Sony Germany and continues to tour and record new material.

"Kids in America" resurfaced in 1995 when the Muffs recorded it as the theme to *Clueless*. Subsequently, it's been performed by One Direction on the U.K. *X-Factor* and recorded by acts as diverse as Tiffany, Cascada, Atomic Kitten, and James Last. ("Don't forget Lawnmower

Deth," Wilde says. "They did a death metal version.") The song got a further lease on life in Christmas 2012 when a YouTube clip of a sozzled Wilde wearing reindeer antlers and serenading baffled London subway commuters with a boozy rendition racked up more than 2 million views.

WILDE: My career was tough to deal with at times. It became a roller-coaster ride, and I'd been on the ride for long enough. I'd recorded an album for MCA, and there was not a lot of enthusiasm for it from them or anyone else. So I decided to leap before I was pushed. I found myself getting one of the lead roles in *Tommy*. I thought that was a perfect halfway house between where I'd been and where I needed to go. Also, I couldn't bear the thought of traveling anymore. My whole life had been spent living out of a suitcase. Then I met my husband, Hal, and that was the final nail in the coffin of my career. I really thought I'd never sing "Kids in America" again.

I was 36 and had my spiritual needs. My poor spiritual needs had gone unattended for some time. Falling in love and having children awoke a lot of feelings inside of me, and one of the most powerful was the sense that I needed to get my hands in the earth. It happened at the same time I got pregnant, this great desire to be closer to nature. I spent most of the eighties and nineties plastered in makeup, and I had this real desire to go out and plant roses.

My career began as a video artist, and I was one of the best mimers in the business when I was on TV. But when my career began again, it was focused on live music. I was utterly astonished when I discovered there was still a crowd out there who wanted to watch a middle-aged housewife singing "Kids in America." The feeling was euphoric. I said yes to tours and more tours, and music came back into my life.

The eighties has had a massive revival in the past 20 years—during the nineties, though, it was given short shrift. People quickly forgot the good things. There seemed to be a lot of cynicism, mostly to do with politics and Thatcher, but music got thrown in with it. Greedy and of no substance, shoulder pads, spiky hair—that was eighties music summed up in a few vacuous words. It took a good 20 years for people to go, "You know, those records were great, and that was a fantastic time for pop music."

When I feel really self-conscious about singing "New York to East California," I think of the Police singing "De Do Do Do, De Da Da Da," and then I don't feel so bad. Some records have that special magic about them, and "Kids in America" has it in bucket loads. I'm really proud to be associated with the song, and I've fallen back in love with it after turning my back on it for years. The love affair's back on!

H

JONES

HOWARD

oward Jones was a sensitive singer-songwriter sheep in a new wave wolf's clothing. If he'd sat at his keyboard and sung the same songs in the sixties, the seventies, or even the now-ties, he'd have been equally successful. But he blew up in the eighties, so he jabbed at a synthesizer and had a porcupine for a haircut while a white-faced mime named Jed cavorted around him, bringing the lyrics to life. A native of Southampton, England, Jones was not the only conventional artist to be new-waved up to suit the requirements of the decade; Nik Kershaw and Paul Young were similarly refurbished with gravity-defying 'dos. If Jones enjoyed a longer run of stateside success than many of his countrymen, it was because he gave his listeners more to chew on. He made more than just catchy records—he was a musical Tony Robbins, delivering self-help seminars through song. Howard Jones was just one man, but sometimes one man can make all the difference. (Well, he was actually two men if you count Jed the mime.)

LM: **Top 10 Life Lessons I Learned from Howard Jones:**

1. **Don't try to live your life in one day — don't go speed your time away.**
2. **Don't bite off more than you can chew. (Only so much you can do.)**
3. **Try and enjoy the here and now, the future will take care of itself somehow. The grass is never greener over there.**
4. **You can't change the world singlehandedly. Raise a glass, enjoy the scenery.**
5. **Treat today as if it were the last, the final show, get to 60 and have no regrets.**
6. **Don't be fooled by what you see. Don't be fooled by what you hear.**
7. **Don't crack up. Bend your brain. See both sides. Throw off your mental chains.**
8. **Challenge preconceived ideas. Say good-bye to long-standing fears.**
9. **A thousand skeptic hands won't keep us from the things we plan ...**
   unless we're clinging to the things we prize.
   10. **You can look at the menu, but you just can't eat.**
   (As a vegan, I find this to be particularly true.) **JB:** **Zzzzzzz**

HOWARD JONES: There's a place I used to go when I was in my mid-20s: West Wickham Hill in High Wickham [Southeast England]. It is one of those places that has a fantastic view, and I used to take our dog walking there and reflect on how things were going. It was 1982, and I'd started to get interest from record companies, I was playing big club venues in London, and I got played on the radio in a BBC session. So I was setting out my agenda for my career, and I remember thinking about what I would like to say with my first single. That's where the "New Song" lyrics come from. They were inspired by the fact that I had been working in a cling-film [think Saran Wrap] factory on the shop floor and dreaming of getting my music going. I wanted to put that back into the music and say to people, "If I can do it, so can you—in whatever field you want to work in. Don't accept your second choice or Plan B. Go for what you really want to do and believe that you can do that."

There were a lot of people writing quite doom-laden music and being depressed about the future. That may be how they felt, but I didn't want to align myself with that. It seemed to me that a lot of people were being miserable to be cool. I'm not going to give any names of artists, 'cause I don't do that. And I don't even know if it was just music. It was just a general feeling within people that the future was not going to be good.

Now, if you just go, "Be happy and be positive," and it's done in a shallow way—if you do that without having grappled and fought the battle with yourself—then I don't think it carries any weight. If my music has any effect, it's because it was born from this battle I was having with myself, the general thinking that you have no control over your future. It's not true.

I didn't fit in with the other pop stars at the time, and I think the fans really picked up on that. I was swimming against the tide. I was married—happily. I didn't do drugs. Then, with the fashion stuff, that was all part of the same message: Don't be afraid to not wear T-shirts and jeans the whole time. If you have it in you to express yourself a bit more flamboyantly, then please have the courage and the joy of doing that. No record company ever told me what to wear, say, or do. It's always been difficult to be who you are, but I thought being a pop star is the best way to manifest that.

Having Jed onstage with me, that was another thing that was different. He was part of my act for all of the club dates pre-1983. To have a mime artist who dressed up as loads of characters for different songs—I don't think anybody else was doing that. He wasn't like Bez from Happy Mondays. Ours was more like performance art than a guy just dancing around. It was specific, and the costumes expressed the ideas of the songs.

"New Song" was the first song I ever recorded. It was started at Chipping Norton Recording Studios in Oxfordshire. It didn't turn out as good as it should have, so we went up to Good Earth Studios in London to do some more work on it. It was Tony Visconti's studio; that was where Bowie and T. Rex used to record. I always liked David Bowie, but I really had a problem with his lyrics, because they meant nothing. They were just meaningless. He's definitely a fabulous artist, and the shows I saw him do were some of the best shows ever. I loved pretty much everything about him, but I was like, *What's that mean? What are you saying, David?* Art for art's own sake is just not me. I like being able to relate to what people are saying.

"New Song" is probably my favorite. It is radically different from what you'd hear in most pop songs. The line "Challenging pre-conceived ideas"—you would never

"I realized I needed to work out what I thought about life and the world, how I was going to behave and what philosophy I was going to have. And that was documented in the albums."

hear that in a pop song. That song is packed with stuff like that: "Don't crack up / Bend your brain"—don't be thrown or side-tracked, don't succumb to weakness, be strong. And "See both sides"—that's really important, to see both sides of an argument.

I used to read a lot of books about Eastern philosophy. I really related to Alan Watts's work. He was a Western guy who interpreted Eastern philosophical thinking. From the age of about 21, I realized I needed to work out what I thought about life and the world, how I was going to behave and what philosophy I was going to have. And that was documented in the albums. "What Is Love?" questions the idea that romantic love is the Holy Grail. "Maybe love is letting people be what they want to be"—not putting them in a box and tying them down and making them be what you

want. To really love somebody, you've got to let them express themselves and not try and dominate them and want to make them be like you.

"No One Is to Blame" is a complex song. I was doing promotion in San Francisco with a record company guy, and he said, "Howard, what do you think of all the pretty women here in San Francisco?" I said, "They're great, but I'm happily married to Jan." And he said, "You can look at the menu, but you don't have to eat." That's what sparked the song. What I was trying to do was be honest on behalf of the listener. It was about being attracted to other people and admitting that. You are attracted to maybe half the people you meet, and that isn't a bad thing. You shouldn't blame yourself for that. No one is to blame—this is natural. This is what being a human being is like. So don't think you're the only one. But if you want to consummate that attraction to other people, then you have to be prepared to take what comes with it.

I thought "No One Is to Blame" had potential to be a big radio song. I played it to the head of Elektra Records in his office, on the piano, and I said, "I really think this could be huge," and he said, "No, it's a B-side." It turned out to be the biggest hit I had in America. It's just another example of how you need to stick to your guns and do what you think is right.

THAT WAS THEN
BUT THIS IS NOW

Thirty years after the release of "New Song," the prickly hair may be gone, but Jones continues to tour and inspire his faithful followers. A longtime vegetarian (though now closed, his restaurant Nowhere was a forerunner among Manhattan eateries with meatless menus), he is also a member of the 12-million-strong Buddhist movement Soka Gakkai and oversees one of its choirs, the Glorious Life Chorus, which performs Jones songs in its repertoire. And, true to the title of one of his biggest hits, he still believes that things can only get better.

JONES: I am constantly surprised by the longevity of the music. The great thing for me is that I still feel very happy playing and singing my songs. Imagine if it was a bunch of lyrics that just didn't mean anything, and you had to do it over and over again for years—that would be torture.

I've been married to my wife for 35 years now. We have children, and I've always tried to get the ideas from the songs across to them. I say, "I have tried to train you to stand up to anyone if they're saying something that you don't agree with." And they've become really good at that—so good that they give me a hard time, they challenge me.

At the core, I'm the same person, but I've definitely changed over the years. I'm always trying to become a better human being every day. I've evolved and hopefully have become better at putting those philosophies into practice. It's an ongoing thing until I die.

MIXTAPE: 5 More Positive, Upbeat Songs
1. "Our House," Madness 2. "In a Big Country," Big Country 3. "Happy Birthday," Altered Images 4. "The Safety Dance," Men Without Hats 5. "Right by Your Side," The Eurythmics

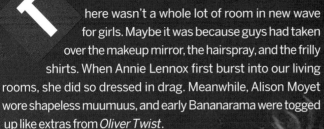

There wasn't a whole lot of room in new wave for girls. Maybe it was because guys had taken over the makeup mirror, the hairspray, and the frilly shirts. When Annie Lennox first burst into our living rooms, she did so dressed in drag. Meanwhile, Alison Moyet wore shapeless muumuus, and early Bananarama were togged up like extras from *Oliver Twist*. In Los Angeles, though, there was no shortage of women who flaunted their femaleness—the Go-Go's, Martha Davis of the Motels, Dale Bozzio of Missing Persons. But Terri Nunn was the fairest of them all. A part-time

"THE METRO"

actress (she'd auditioned to play Princess Leia in *Star Wars*) and one-time Penthouse Pet, Nunn—real name!—was so beautiful that she called to mind Deborah Harry, herself a onetime Playboy Bunny. Nunn planted saucy seeds in the mind of Berlin fanclub member Madonna with songs like the outrageous "Sex (I'm A…)." And yet, it's the haunting synth-made melodies permeating "The Metro" and the Giorgio Moroder gem "Take My Breath Away" we remember them for. Berlin may have hailed from sunny California, but their sound linked them to their namesake city 6,000 miles away.

LM: I loved interviewing Nunn. We gossiped like girlfriends. We talked about how hot Bryan Ferry was, how stunning Debbie Harry (Nunn: "The closer I got, the more gorgeous, and it wasn't the lighting"), how fat Belinda Carlisle was ("She was a house. She would say so herself"). I mean, that's not the kind of stuff you can talk about with Roland Orzabal. I also loved Nunn's unapologetic love of her own music and legacy. Nunn was a hot chick in a cool band during the early eighties, and she knows it. And she had a voice that was almost as distinctive as she was beautiful. She may have started out chirping a silly song about sex, but by "Take My Breath Away," Nunn had matured into having one of the era's sultriest voices.

JB: As greedily (and indiscriminately) as the States gobbled up the latest British new wave export to come down the pike, the reverse was not the case. We treated Blondie, the Ramones, Television, and Talking Heads like deities, but we weren't about to give the phony, plastic, poser likes of Missing Persons, the Motels, the Go-Go's, or Berlin the time of day. We had our own phony, plastic, poser bands, groups like the Regents, Blue Zoo, Fiction Factory, and a plethora of other atrocities we won't sully ourselves by writing about in these pages. (See you in Book Two, guys!) But I'm more mature now. I live in America. I know the generosity of its people. I've traveled the vastness of its highways. Do I still feel the same about American new wave? Kinda. "The Metro" is pretty good, though. Probably because it's so European.

TERRI NUNN: Grace Slick got me into music. That was the call of the wild. I saw her on television and said, "I want to be her!" She was so different from all the other women. They were pretty and sweet and nice, but she was the epitome of both men and women in music, because she stood up with the men and went, "Fuck you!" She was throwing off her top and singing as strong as any of the guys—and just as irreverent and sexy and hot. I wanted the freedom that the guys had.

When I started doing music in the late seventies, it was a completely male-dominated job. Bands like Led Zeppelin and Aerosmith were still ruling the airwaves, and punk had just happened. We opened for Iggy Pop once. I would have loved for us to have had a mosh pit. It always bummed me out because I'd see other bands get mosh pits in the front of the stage and we never had that.

Then the eighties happened. It was an amazing time, one of the best ever in Los Angeles. There were so many clubs to play, like Madame Wong's, Club 88. Any night of the week you'd have the best fucking live music you could possibly want. Punk was still happening: the Cramps, X. But the main thing was power pop, so the Go-Go's and the Plimsouls were initially much more viable than we were. Berlin was "synthesizer music," and people didn't really understand it. We got lumped together with Missing Persons because we were the closest to each other—the girl singer, the synthesizers. But we were very different image-wise. Dale Bozzio was more space-age, very Barbarella, with the plastic things over her tits.

We patterned ourselves after the European bands: Kraftwerk, Ultravox, Roxy Music. Oh, Bryan Ferry—he's a god! We got to open for him once, and I'll never forget it. That glamorous, romantic image: the cool guy with the cigarette and the suit, and all the beautiful women who were dressed up with martinis in their hands. It wasn't like the punk scene or the rock scene; it was classy, very grown-up. And that's really

what I wanted Berlin to be: elegant but sexy. Old Hollywood. The guys in the band wore tuxedoes. I was usually in a dress. No one else was doing that. I wanted kids to look at us and think, *It's really cool to grow up,* instead of *Look at my parents: They gave up on their dreams. Life sucks for them, and that's how I'm going to end up.*

By 1982, KROQ was playing some really weird stuff: Oingo Boingo, Romeo Void, Talking Heads. These were bands that weren't played on any of the rock stations at all, ever. And KROQ was a strong supporter of L.A. bands, which gave us hope that they would play us if we could come up with something that would grab their attention.

So we were like, "Okay, how can we be outrageous? What could be a really bold statement?" And that's how we came up with the idea of our first single, "Sex (I'm A . . .)."

I wrote it about a problem I was having with my boyfriend at the time. Sex wasn't that great. We hit a wall pretty fast, and I wanted to spice it up, but he really didn't. He said, "It's fine if you want to try some new things like role playing, but I'm not a burglar, and I don't want to be a pirate. I'm just a guy, and I like just really boring, normal things, like man on top." So that's what I wrote. I wrote that he's always just a guy: "I'm a man . . . ," "I'm a man . . . ," "I'm a man . . ." But I'm a lot of things! I imagined me dancing around him as all these different characters: "I'm a goddess," "I'm a virgin," "I'm a blue movie" . . . I had never heard something like that talked about in a song, but girls talk about that stuff all the time. Still, I had no idea how the public would respond, and it was pretty drastic. People were either, "You're the devil's children and should not be allowed to live on this planet for saying something like that" or, "Oh my God, this is awesome!" It was never in the middle. I should have had more fun with it, but I was horrified that people were thinking, "You're the girl on the back cover of the single who's wearing nothing except a stole around the important parts, and you have no brain." My mistake was rather than playing with it and laughing, I was like, "Oh, no! I'm a very serious songwriter and singer!" I got defensive. I was 22 years old.

But that song wasn't what Berlin was all about. That was "The Metro." It was '81 when we wrote it, and we were getting better as writers and playing live. When we finished it, we were like, "That's it! That's what we want to sound like!" I've heard that from other bands too, that there's that moment where a sound comes together and defines you. Bam! That's who we are. We had a template.✳

I had never heard anything like it before: deep, dark, romantic, completely unique,

✳RICHARD BLADE, former KROQ DJ and current host of Sirius Satellite Radio's First Wave: Terri and I nearly got married. She likes to tell the story about how I took "Metro" to KROQ and broke it there when they still were on an independent label. I found it at a record shop in Long Beach when I was doing overnights on KNAC and took the single with me to KROQ. [Program director] Rick Carroll called up and said, "What are you playing?" I said, "A song called 'Metro' from Berlin. They're either German or local, I don't really know." And he said, "Leave it in the studio: I want Jed [the Fish] to play it, and Freddy [Snakeskin]. Every three hours, I want it to come up." Terri's producer heard it too and called up and said that the band would love to meet me. I met Terri the next week, and we fell in love instantly and were never apart for a year and a half. "The Metro" was a perfect storm: great female vocals, a catchy chorus, and a story about lost love. It was exotic rather than erotic. It had a driving dance beat that still works to this day. It's about 168 beats per minute! You put that song on, and you cannot sit on your ass.

from the sparsity of the sound and the loneliness of David Diamond's keyboard to the female vocal, the European setting, and the sadness of the lyrics. John Crawford wrote that. He was so incredibly honest about his feelings. It wasn't just about "Let's go get laid and party, woo hoo!" It was "My girlfriend is going to Europe, and I'm probably going to lose her. She's going to meet some great Italian guy, and she's going to dump me." That's what that song's about. The way he talked about his insecurities was completely universal. That was the beauty of our collaboration: His feelings were not male; they were human.

The bridge between "The Metro" and our biggest hit, "Take My Breath Away," was Giorgio Moroder. Getting to work with him was a huge deal for us, because we loved his work with David Bowie, Blondie, Donna Summer. He was so unique that artists went to him to sound like him. When Bowie did "Cat People," that didn't sound like Bowie; it sounded like Bowie on top of a Giorgio Moroder song—and that's what he wanted! So we begged our record label to ask if he would work with us, and he was so huge at that point that we could only afford one song, "No More Words."

It was really just lucky that he was offered to produce and write songs for *Top Gun* while we were working with him. But he didn't come to me first for "Take My Breath Away." He tried out a couple of other, more traditional singers—Martha Davis of the Motels was one—but the producers, including Jerry Bruckheimer, and the director, Tony Scott, didn't like their renditions. So Giorgio came in one day and played "Take My Breath Away" and asked if we'd be interested in doing it. I immediately said yes. Plus, it was the romantic peak of the movie. But John immediately said no. He just thought that great bands didn't do other people's songs, case closed.

While I didn't think it was the greatest song I'd ever heard, I thought it was good. But I never thought it would be a number-

MIXTAPE 5 More Songs from L.A. Women

1. "Destination Unknown," Missing Persons 2. "Johnny, Are You Queer?," Josie Cotton 3. "Only the Lonely," The Motels 4. "This Town," The Go-Go's 5. "Valley Girl," Frank Zappa and Moon Unit Zappa

BERLIN

one hit around the world. The original demo was stilted, rigid. The words sounded syncopated, like they were coming from a Japanese singer: "Watching. Every. Motion. In my. Foolish. Lover's. Game." It was so ... yuck. The words are so romantic and sad and longing. I just wanted to pull the notes out of the structure—"In my fooooolish loooover's gaaaame"—to open it up a bit. So that's how I sang it, and I thought, *Well, if they don't like it, fuck it—who cares? We've*

got Giorgio, we're working on our album. I had nothing to lose to make it mine, so I did. And they loved it.

The song was nominated for an Academy Award, and when it came to performing at the Oscars, that was when I went on my ego trip. They said, "We're going to do a medley, and we want you to sing a verse and a chorus of the song, then we're going to cut to the next song, and they're going to sing a verse and a chorus. . . . That way we can condense everything. And I said to them, "Well, no. If I can't sing the whole song, I'm not doing it," totally expecting them to just be so in love with me that they would go, "Okay!" Well, what they said was, "Oh, well, okay, thank you very much. Click!" And they went and got Lou Rawls. Can you fucking believe that? I watched the awards on television while we were on tour overseas somewhere in Taiwan, and I saw that it won. I look back on that with regret.

While "Take My Breath Away" didn't single-handedly destroy Berlin, it was just one more disagreement between John and me. We were going in different directions on everything. We were the two who were signed by Geffen. We always presented it as a band, but it was really the two of us, and we crumbled. We couldn't agree anymore. By the last tour, we weren't even speaking.

And we were exhausted. That's why record labels want kids, because they want endless energy. They want somebody they can just throw on the road, then put in a studio, then throw back out on the road. It's this endless cycle, and you don't know that you need a life until you fall apart or you become a drug addict. It was five years of that cycle and, holy god, both of us were just tired of everything. We were tired of each other; we were tired of not having a real relationship in our lives. We had no friends, we had nothing except each other and this band, and that

doesn't hug you at night, you know? Getting laid once in a while with people you're not going to see again the next day, that loses it real fast. We were just sick of it all.

THAT WAS THEN BUT THIS IS NOW

 Although 1986's *Count Three and Pray* contained the international smash "Take My Breath Away," the album never gained traction, and Berlin disbanded a year later. Nunn released a solo album, 1991's *Moment of Truth*, before obtaining the rights to the band's name and rebuilding Berlin with an all-new lineup of musicians. Nunn continues to tour and record under the Berlin banner and released the album *Animal* in 2013. She also co-hosts a show on L.A. radio station KCSN with friend and comedienne Wendy Liebman.

NUNN: I'm still fired up about Berlin. This writing partner, Derek Cannavo, and I have that kind of thing like John and I had. Derek and I wrote [*Animal*], and I'm just so excited by EDM music—it's where electronic music has gone. On this album we covered "Somebody to Love," and Grace Slick has heard it! Yes! I played it for her, and she said, "Wow." That was fucking huge for me.

A FLOCK OF

SEAGULLS

"I RAN"

Hip-hop had Vanilla Ice. Hair metal had Quiet Riot. Bloated, inspirational arena rock had Creed. Whatever your taste in music, it will at some point be misrepresented by a monster hit from an artist who makes you cringe and who causes contemporaries to beg, "Please don't judge us by that!" So it was with A Flock of Seagulls. Even in a genre as ridicule-prone as new wave, A Flock of Seagulls made an easy target, thanks to the name, the singer's hair, and the absurd sense of B-movie drama permeating "I Ran." Decades later, though, we remember their name, we certainly remember the hair, and we remember the way Mike Score bleated his way through that "I never thought I'd meet a girl like you-ooo-ooo" lyric. A Flock of Seagulls may have been a punch line, but at least they were an unforgettable one.

JB: As we age, our priorities change. We worry about our bank balances, our aching backs, our prostates. (By we, I mean everyone else. Not me. I'm in tip-top shape. Never better. Well, there's the odd twinge . . .) We place less and less importance on cool—knowing what's cool or being up-to-the-second on cool music. The dwindling importance of cool is a weight off our sagging shoulders. But even in my dotage, when my day consists of when I have to pee and when I don't have to pee, I still wince a little at the thought of A Flock of Seagulls. In my U.K. homeland, they were seen as a joke act, like a band formed by a bunch of oafish characters in a British soap opera. The fact that they were snapped up without a qualm by American audiences almost devalues the success of stratospherically 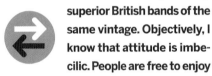 superior British bands of the same vintage. Objectively, I know that attitude is imbecilic. People are free to enjoy whatever they please, and more than that, I'm absolutely able to appreciate that the 12-inch of "Wishing (If I Had a Photograph of You)" is a long, luxurious wallow. But they're still not cool to me. Sorry.

LM: Being one of those qualmless Americans you speak of, I thought they were cool. Prior to the Hairstyle, there was the "I Ran" video, a welcome respite from dull concert-performance clips like Springsteen's unbearable "Rosalita." The latter seemed like it was 20 minutes long, and it was so dingy and seventies-feeling it may as well have been in black and white. But "I Ran"—that was full-on, resplendent Technicolor. The revolving mirrored room with the aluminum foil floor! The alien women with the crazy makeup and dresses made out of Hefty bags! The freaky frontman in the red secretary blouse with the singed blond coif singing about the aurora borealis! I couldn't get away!

MIKE SCORE: In the late seventies, early eighties, I owned a shop in Liverpool called Oz the Magic Hairdresser. We were the punk hairdresser in town—crazy perms, crazy colors. I witnessed the music scene from the outside: I wasn't really a clubgoer. I was 25 and married with a child. But I was involved with people in local bands who would come in and get their hair done: Teardrop Explodes, the Icicle Works. That got me interested. In '78 or '79, Hambi from Hambi and the Dance came into the shop and said they needed a bass player. I was just learning to play, but I told them I was the best bass player in Liverpool, and, probably in their desperation, they believed it. I ended up joining them.

One thing I didn't really like about the after-punk Liverpool scene was that everything was dark. We called it the Raincoat Brigade, because they all wore long coats and hangdog expressions. But they were stylish in their own way. Almost like the hipsters are now. But Hambi were more Talking Heads than Echo and the Bunnymen: not as dark, a bit more fun, and tinged with sixties psychedelia. Then Hambi got a deal with Virgin Records, and they said there were two of us who didn't fit the style of the band, and I was one of them. But they said, "Maybe start your own band and come back to us." I told my brother, Ali, and he goes, "Great, I'll be the drummer!" Frank Maudsley, who worked for me, was like, "Well, let me join too." Synths had just come out, so I said to Frank: "Here, play my bass. I'm going to get a synth." Frank's friend Paul Reynolds slotted in on guitar, and, basically, that became A Flock of Seagulls.

I wanted to call the band Level 7 because I was reading a sci-fi book with that title. It felt really techno and electronic. Then another band came out called Level 42. We were like, "Shit! People will think,

You're just copying Level 42." I'd also read *Jonathan Livingston Seagull*, and it said a lot of things that I was thinking. In the book, the seagulls squabble over food, and one of them realizes he has wings and can fly. He looks at all the other birds flying and says, "They have wings, I have wings. Look how high they're flying. Why aren't I flying that high?" That was the inspiration. I went, "OK, now I want to be a seagull, and my band will be A Flock of Seagulls. We all want to fly that high."

We were never really a part of the Liverpool scene. As I said, Liverpool was into darker bands like Teardrop Explodes and Joy Division. We were more into Devo and the Cars. We'd seen Duran Duran on TV, and they were more in the path that we were going down, except they weren't as electronic as we wanted to be. It sounds big-headed now, but we didn't think Liverpool was ready for what we were doing, though we thought the rest of the world might be. So we made a mutual decision: We're going to London. What we want is to be world-big, not Liverpool-big.

The four of us went and lived in London for two weeks in a van. We went to every gig we could and gave tapes out. One of the guys that got the tape was Tommy Crossan, a soundman for a band called the Yachts. They did a gig in Liverpool, and we opened for them: A Nautical Extravaganza with the Yachts and A Flock of Seagulls. We found Tommy's address and parked outside his door. One morning I said, "Have you listened to the tape?" He said, "No, I haven't." I said, "Well, we're not moving until you listen to it." Tommy ended up co-managing us.

STYLE COUNCIL

"I didn't wash it for a couple weeks at a time because it was just so locked into place—a can of Aquanet every night," Score says. "Once it was up and we had gigs, it never came down. One show, a girl jumped onstage, ran over to me, touched my hair, and fainted. I came offstage that night, and my manager said, 'I think you've got something there!'"

Ninety-nine percent of the record companies rejected us. I don't think it was that we weren't good; it was that they didn't understand what we were doing. One of the labels we were trying to get a deal with was Zoo Records in Liverpool, which had Teardrop and Echo. One day we went up to their offices, and they had a picture on the wall of two people running away from a flying saucer. It was probably from a fifties movie. They said it was going to be the cover of Teardrop Explodes' new album. I mentally put myself in the position of the people running from the flying saucer. Then we went to see the band Fischer-Z, and they had a song called "I Ran." [Editor's note: It was actually called "Wristcutter's Lullaby."] When things are right, they line up. I went, "I ran from the alien girl in the flying saucer who was chasing me," and within a few minutes the whole song came together. "I Ran" wrote itself, as all good songs do.

People used to say to me, "What is the aurora borealis?" and I was like, "How could you not know?" Then, secondly, they would say, "How did you get those words to fit into a song?" You've seen *Close Encounters*. You know when the ship breaks through the clouds and the rainbow-effect thing happens? That's like in the song: "A cloud appears above your head / A beam of light comes shining down on you." When she's coming down on her beam of light, it breaks through the clouds, and there's the aurora borealis.

The concept for our debut album [1982's *A Flock of Seagulls*] is sci-fi too. It's a love album, but it's not about loving the girl around the corner. When you watch *Star Trek*, Captain Kirk always got the green girl, the alien girl. So that was my concept, to be the guy that was in love with the alien, not the girl who works on the checkout at the Publix. Of course, being into sci-fi, we also loved stuff like Ziggy Stardust, "Starman" and "Space Oddity." Bowie's clothes and hairstyle made me realize that if I wanted to be in a band that was going somewhere, I had to have a look.

We were the first band Clive Calder signed to a new label called Jive Records. Clive said to us, "There's a new thing they're putting on in America called Music Television, and they want videos from new bands. Let's make a clip for 'I Ran' and see what happens." We were given a hundred pounds each to get some clothes to wear in the video. The first thing we did was we went to some girls' shops in London. Guys' clothes just weren't up to looking very fashionable or new wave-y. The whole new wave thing was to look pretty. We were like, "Let's grab a few things that make us look different. We don't want to look like we're not happy and not interested. And we don't want to look dark; we want to look bright and sci-fi."

MTV was a little gift from the gods. By the end of that year, "I Ran" had hit the U.S. Top 10, and we'd toured with the Go-Go's and played Madison Square Garden twice. It was meteoric. It was nothing, then everything. By '83, we were supporting the Police on their *Synchronicity* tour, playing to 100,000 people a night.

In the "I Ran" video, I wore my hair curly. After that, I decided to go for a Ziggy Stardust blond, punk look. We were getting ready to do a show, and I'd spiked my hair up. Frank put his hand on top of my head, basically to say, "Let me see in the mirror as well." He collapsed the whole top of my hairdo by putting his hand on it, with the

MIXTAPE: 5 More Songs from the Past About the Future
1. "Together in Electric Dreams," Phil Oakey and Giorgio Moroder
2. "Major Tom," Peter Schilling   3. "Einstein a Go-Go," Landscape
4. "Living by Numbers," New Musik   5. "Living on Video," Trans-X

sides still sticking up—and it stayed like that. Mick Rossi, our manager, was trying to shoo us on stage, so I just went out with it like that. I noticed a few people looking and pointing. When we came off stage, I looked in the mirror, and I remember feeling a bit like, *That looks awesome!*

The next gig, I went for that look and made it even more so. Frank said "God, that's so sci-fi!" So it became my image, to have the aerials at the sides, the wings, and the big thing hiding my face, which I thought was great, because that made me more mysterious. That's how I wore it in the video for "Space Age Love Song." "Space Age" wasn't as big of a hit as "I Ran," but it's definitely one of our best songs—actually, it's a rewrite of a song I wrote called "Nagasaki." It was based on watching a show about the dropping of the atom bomb. My idea was to have beautiful music and horrendous lyrics. Maybe one day I'll redo it with the original lyrics: "A bomber flies, a baby dies, a mother cries. Nagasaki." Now, if you go to "Wishing," I remember when I played it to a friend of mine, she said, "This is going to put you in the top songwriters in the world." It's timeless. Even when I hear it on the radio now, that one stands up to anything. You can put a Beatles song in front of it, you can put a Tears for Fears song in front of it, and it still sounds as good as any of those.

Everybody thought I'd developed this huge ego, because when we did interviews, people wanted to talk to me. Onstage I have a way of controlling the band—I will look at people as if to say, "Start the song now," and sometimes that gets read wrongly. A lot depends on your opinion of the person who's looking at you. I would look at my brother as if to say, "Let's start the song now," and he would never take it as just a look. He would always take it as me trying to control him. As the band gets bigger, you tend to lose that camaraderie. I think that led to the downfall.

THAT WAS THEN BUT THIS IS NOW

By the end of '85, Reynolds, Maudsley, and Ali Score departed the band, leaving Mike Score to employ various musicians so he could continue to tour under the name A Flock of Seagulls. In 2003, all four original members patched things up for VH1's Bands Reunited series, but the re-formation was short-lived. "It wasn't long before all the old problems resurfaced," Score says, referring to the others' desire for democracy and his need to exert control. Soon after, he was again a lone Seagull, but he also began writing and recording his own material, which he describes as "better than any Seagulls stuff." In July 2013, all Score's music equipment and tracks for an upcoming solo record were stolen. Though he now sports a shorn pate, his hairstyle lives on as a go-to joke for bad-eighties style. "I Ran" has been covered by artists including Nickelback and Bowling for Soup, and was featured in a commercial for Cape Cod potato chips, in which the song was performed by a flock of CGI seagulls.

SCORE: When the hairdo became more important than the band, I stopped doing it. People would say, "What happened to your hair?" and I would say, "It might be important to you,

but it's not important to me." For a long time I had it waist-length, snatched back. Then, of course, you start to lose it. I woke up one day and said, "It's all got to go today," and I shaved it off. I looked in the mirror and said, "Now you look better than you did in 1982."

Because of my hair, I'm like a legend of the eighties, right? So I was like, "Why not open a restaurant and have every table have a legend on it?" In 2007, I opened the Legends Cafe in Cocoa Beach, Florida. I had this idea to have a Muhammad Ali table, a Beatles table, a Rolling Stones table, an astronaut table. It had a Mexican bar, Italian dining room, a sushi bar—it was a fusion situation. People loved it, because the girlfriend could have sushi and the guy could have burgers. But I don't think the world that I put it in was ready for it. We had it open for about a year, and because I knew nothing about running restaurants, I ran it into the ground.

Everybody who's had a big hit resents it at some point. You go, "Hey, that song was 25 years ago. Why are you still hanging on to it?" As a listener, you go, "Oh, in '82 I was going out with Billy, and 'I Ran' was on, and we had a great time." I don't play "I Ran" for me anymore; I play it for the people who like it. At least it keeps me being able to be a musician. I'm not digging ditches, and I'm hoping to retire with a small pension.

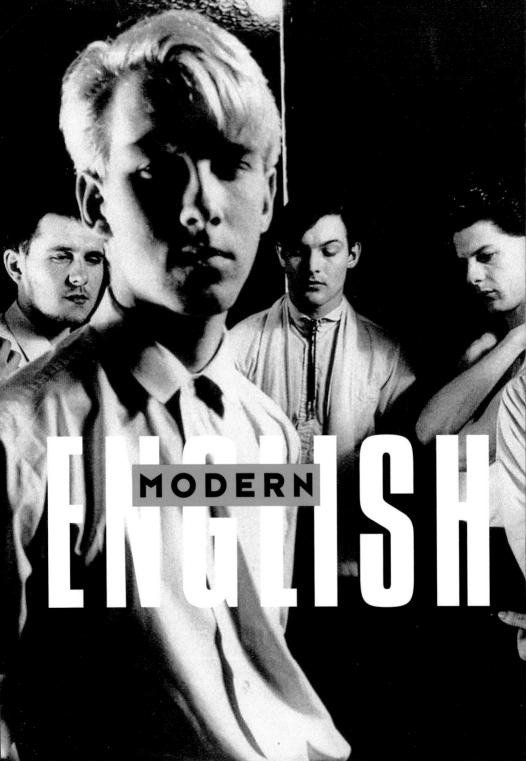

MODERN
ENGLISH

"I MELT WITH YOU"

You know those young-adult novels that today's kids love so much? The ones based in dystopic universes where doomed lovers try to snatch a fleeting moment of romance before dark forces snuff out their young hearts forever? We didn't have those in the eighties, but we did have songs about nuclear paranoia, which served more or less the same purpose. As the arms race intensified, as Reagan and Gorbachev stared each other down, fears grew that these might be our last days. But at least we had a stellar soundtrack to keep up our spirits as we awaited the arrival of rockets from Russia. These were the days of "Atomic" by Blondie, "1999" and "Ronnie, Talk to Russia" by Prince, "Missiles" by the Sound, and "Breathing" by Kate Bush, to name a few. These were also the days of "I Melt with You," which painted perhaps the most idyllic picture of romance in the apocalyptic age. Over the decades, many fresh fears emerged to turn us into twitching, hollow-eyed wrecks, but the jangly headlong rush of "I Melt with You" remains an uplifting reminder that a catchy tune can outlive presidents and their space-defense initiatives.

LM: Whenever I tell people I'm working on a book about the most beloved songs of new wave, they respond with a litany of tracks—"Is this one in it? Is that one in it?" Invariably, "I Melt with You" is one of the first mentioned. Idealist lyrics like "Making love to you was never second best" recall a more innocent time before twerking and choruses like "Tonight I'm fucking you" (thank you, Enrique). And "Never really knowing it was always mesh and lace" is a lyric that could have been written only during the eighties. (When else might someone have attempted to mix two such unlikely fabrics?) At the same time, the music could have been made last week by a U.K. band like White Lies. Ecstasy in the face of Armageddon set to a danceable beat: It's the only way to go.

JB: "I Melt with You" for me falls into the same category as "Under the Milky Way" by the Church: I like it, I sing along to it, it never feels dated, and I'm sufficiently satisfied by it that I never feel the need to listen to another song from their catalog.

ROBBIE GREY: Punk was kind of dying off; it had become very commercialized. A lot of bands who used to play better music started playing three chords just to jump on the band wagon. We just decided to do something a bit more experimental. Other bands, like Joy Division, Wire, they started to do the same thing just to get away from punk's straightforward chord structures.

What we were doing, it felt very modern and very English. It felt special to be British because of the record labels like Factory and 4AD. And I remember when we first went to America, they called it the Second British Invasion. But England was a very bleak place back then. We came from Colchester, in Essex, a small town about an hour from London. They talk about a recession, but there is nothing like England in the late seventies and early eighties. There were times when people were only working three days [a week] because there was no money. There'd be no power—you'd be at home with candles. I used to go watch bands just to steal a microphone if I could get close to one.

So that's what the feel of England was, and I write about things I know. On the first album, [1981's] *Mesh and Lace*, "Black Houses" is all about the nuclear threat and all the nuclear pamphlets that were around at the time. You know, "In case of nuclear attack, paint your windows black and get under the table." [When "I Melt with You" was first released as a single in 1982] I don't think many people realized it was about a couple making love as the bomb dropped. As they make love, they become one and melt together. I remember writing the lyrics in my room in Shepherd's Bush in London in about two minutes. I was stoned. I remember kneeling down on the floor and writing on a scrap of paper these first lines: "Moving forward using all my breath"—so easy to say but so much content—and then: "Making love to you was never second best." They coupled together really nicely. And then, the bridge: "The future's open wide," [because] you've got a lot of negative stuff with the idea of the nuclear bomb.

"I Melt with You" was a love song, but it was also about the good and bad in people. "Mesh and lace" was the hard and soft. I liked the idea of having these different images in a pop song. The last thing we wanted was to write a song where boy meets girl, they go to the cinema and make love, and that's the end of it.

The music was put together in a rehearsal room in London. We just put pieces of music together, almost like classical music. We'd say, "Let's try that piece and that piece together." That's why [1982's *After the Snow*] is such an imaginative and special album. We really do have to doff our cap to Hugh Jones, the producer. He stopped me shouting. I used to just get on the microphone and just shout my words 'cause I wanted to tell people what I felt. He was the one who said, "Hold on a minute, Robbie. You can still tell people how you're feeling, but you can just say it." And "Melt" is the first song I did it on. That's why it's got that very close, not-very-well-sung feel to it on the verses. Let me be straight about this: When we were in the studio, the band had never written a pop song. We were looking at this creation that was coming out of the speakers and thinking, *Oh my god, this is*

MIXTAPE: 5 More Songs About Nuclear Bombs
1. "99 Luftballons," Nena 2. "Two Tribes," Frankie Goes to Hollywood
3. "Dancing with Tears in My Eyes," Ultravox 4. "The Last Film I Ever Saw," Kissing the Pink 5. "Red Skies," The Fixx

different! You know, the whole song just glides. If you took my vocals off, I think it sounds a bit like the Byrds.

Someone picked up an import from England and started playing it on mainstream radio in America, and it just went like wildfire. We used to play to 200 people in art college; the next thing we knew, we were in Daytona Beach playing to 5,000 people who know all the words to "I Melt with You." When we showed up at spring break, we had never played outside before, and we were so scared of losing all our atmosphere without a roof and walls. The promoter said, "You can play to 10,000 people out here or you can go inside and play to 5,000." We said we would go inside instead. That night, all the water was running off the walls, it was so hot. We were wearing coats coming off the plane in Florida—we didn't even know it was going to be hot, that's how clued up we were. And I'll never forget coming off the stage and saying to my manager: "That's it!

"**They talk about a recession, but there is nothing like England in the late seventies and early eighties.... I used to go watch bands just to steal a microphone if I could get close to one.**"

That's what it's all about!" I'd imagine if you spoke to most of the [British] bands from that period who went to America, [they'd say] they were blown away by the difference of audience reaction. European audiences were very thoughtful, very interested in the music—they wanted to see our artistic side. Whereas, when we got to America, people just wanted to have a good time.

THAT WAS THEN *BUT THIS IS NOW*

Fondly remembered as the song that accompanied the closing credits of *Valley Girl,* "I Melt with You" has never really left the airwaves. In 1990, when Modern English rerecorded "I Melt with You" for *Pillow Lips,* their debut with TVT Records, the song made a reappearance on the Billboard Hot 100. Then, in 2010, the group recorded yet another version to be the title track of the male midlife-crisis drama starring Jeremy Piven and Rob Lowe. The band still tours and wouldn't think of leaving their most popular song off the playlist.

GREY: "I Melt with You," for me, was a bit of a burden for a few years early on. We were so big a band from about 1983 to about 1986—we were as big as U2—and we used to get a bit pissed off because everyone wanted to hear "I Melt with You." But not anymore—it pays all our bills. One of the biggest money moments of our career was when Burger King used it. We got $90,000 for that. To be honest with you, Burger King was a strange one. I think they just used [the humming part] to symbolize a [tasty] burger. We said no to a few things.

One was a motorized bunny rabbit that was gonna sing "I Melt with You." We just wanted to say no to something.

I suppose "I Melt with You" can sometimes be a pain in the ass 'cause you want people to listen to your other music, but we don't complain about it. When you're onstage and you see people and they're full of ecstasy when you're playing it, it's fantastic. People say, "The first time I made love was to that song." Or "Thanks very much. I managed to get a load of women thanks to you and that song."

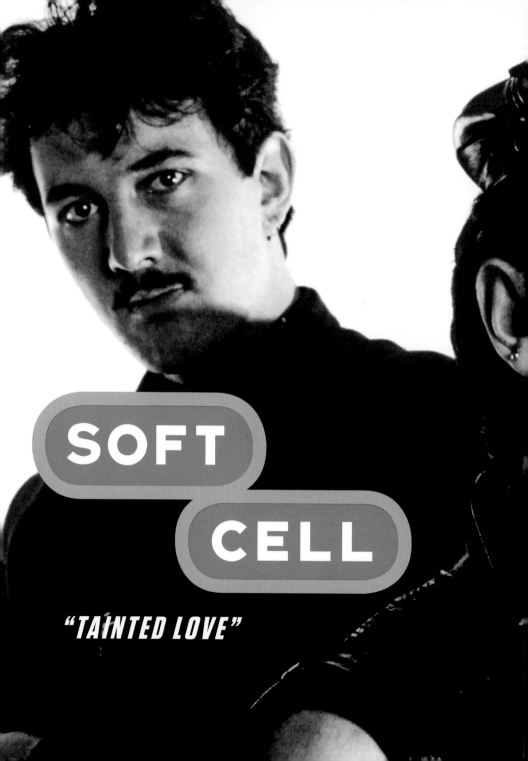

For Soft Cell, the synth duo of Marc Almond and David Ball, their greatest hit was both an albatross and an anomaly. Although they would rack up a total of 10 chart hits in their native U.K. by 1984, around the world Soft Cell is synonymous with a single song: "Tainted Love." An electronic cover of an obscure sixties soul record, the track was not only an international number one but also a Guinness Book of World Records–breaking, 43-week fixture on the Billboard singles chart. "Tainted Love" was impassioned and melodramatic, and featured a deliciously overwrought vocal from Almond, but it was nothing like the rest of their debut album, 1981's *Non-Stop Erotic Cabaret.* That revealed Soft Cell in their true colors—and they were sort of milky white with a hint of faded yellow. Small wonder *Non-Stop Erotic Cabaret* was so fixated on smut, ugliness, and decay. Almond and Ball came of age in a country where the daily tabloids feature bare breasts on one page and editorials preaching morality on the next, and the prominent television personalities were flabby, grotesque middle-age comics who pawed and leered at younger women paid to tolerate them. While their New Romantic colleagues were painting neon pictures of divine decadence and parties that never ended, Soft Cell were forever stuck out on the street, drunk, depressed, and wearing the wrong clothes.

JB: The difference between pop music now and in the eighties is the difference between stage school and art school. It's the difference between wanting to be successful and wanting to be different. Soft Cell were a total art school band. They were pretentious, they were show-offs, and they wanted to shock. There may have been nothing remotely controversial about "Tainted Love," but the first time Almond minced on to *Top of the Pops* and gave a camp, eye-rolling, lips-pursed performance of his big hit, he single-handedly extended Britain's generation gap by a good 18 months. Middle-aged dads raised on rock erupted in fury at the sight of him. No other band before, or since, was that commercially astute and that enthusiastic about wallowing in the tawdry. When today's concerned parents wring their hands about the likes of Miley Cyrus prematurely sexualizing their precious offspring, I think back to 1981. In the U.K., Soft Cell were on every kiddie TV show, every preteen wall, and every radio station, and for a lot of that audience, "Tainted Love" was the gateway drug that led to them hearing Almond singing about seedy films and sex dwarves.

LM: The banned video for "Sex Dwarf" makes "Girls on Film" look like something you'd see on the Disney Channel! There are bare breasts, raw meat, chainsaws and, true to the song's title, a little person outfitted in S&M gear. I know because I just YouTubed it. And that was the first time I'd ever seen a Soft Cell music video. Although "Tainted Love" ruled American radio alongside the Human League's "Don't You Want Me," it did it without the aid of accompanying visuals. Still, "Tainted Love" exhibited more than enough new wave–ness to seize my attention: a sinister, synthesized melody on top of an I-dare-you-not-to-dance beat, and pained, angry lyrics sung in an English accent by a sensitive man who'd been wounded by a careless lover. Now if I could only erase the picture of that miniature gimp from my brain!

MARC ALMOND: "Memorabilia" [produced by Mute Records' Daniel Miller and released in 1978] had been a big dance club hit, and a buzz was starting to happen about us. We'd gone through our cold, robotic, electronic music phase; we'd done our songs about consumerism and suburban nightmares. We wanted to bring a lot more passion to electronic music, a lot more soulfulness, and to bring a punk ethic back where it would be wilder. We thought, *What's the most un-electronic-band thing we can do? How about a soul song?*

Dave was a fan of northern soul music, which was very rare, collectible soul in the North of England in the late sixties. It was very much of the Tamla Motown era—black music for a white audience. People were in competition to get these very rare, obscure records, of which only a handful of copies had been produced. But because these records were very rough and ready, there was a real punky-poppiness to them. We said, "Wouldn't it be great if Soft Cell, for an encore, did a northern soul song?" It was so out there as an idea.

Dave played me a song by Gloria Jones, and another version of it by Ruth Swann. It was called "Tainted Love." I'd been a huge Marc Bolan fan, an obsessed T. Rex fan—I still am—and of course, Bolan was married to Gloria Jones, and she sang backing vocals on all the T. Rex records. So here was a Gloria Jones song, and there was just something immediately infectious about this record. We played it as our encore for a while, and it went down so well that our own tracks became much catchier and more danceable as a result. Myth has it that we based it on the Gloria Jones version, but if you listen to Ruth Swann's, it's much more in keeping with the Soft Cell version. We just gave it our sound: a cold, electronic sound with a passionate vocal.

We recorded all our singles at the time as 12-inch records. We didn't record them as three-minute singles and add to them; we recorded them as 12-inchers and edited them down. We were in the studio messing around with different ideas and came up with segueing into this breathy, sleazy version of "Where Did Our Love Go?" with a breakdown in the middle. We'd hear it in clubs, and it drove people crazy. It was a life-changer for us.

I'd met David Ball in 1978 when I was doing a fine arts course at Leeds Polytechnic. You're given the facilities and told to create your own art, and at the end of the year, you have to present a show. I tried painting and sculpture but was never very good, so I gravitated toward performance art. I made Super 8 films, and that's what led me to working with David.

I was very influenced by trash culture: Warhol and Lindsay Kemp, decadent theatrical stuff but with a punk bias. I did quite a bit of performance art that usually involved films, and I wanted experimentally different soundtracks, so I brought in different musicians to create them. Dave had a synthesizer—which was still an exotic instrument at the time—and we had a lot of musical likes in common. So I said, "Would you do some electronic music to one of my performances?" Dave was writing these songs about consumerism—they were like shopping adverts, great little two-minute pop songs. He said, "If you do the vocals for my songs, I'll do the music for you."

We were quite avant-garde at first. Our early concerts were in the art college and Leeds punk clubs. We got a small following, as well as some quite adverse reactions. We showed films as a backdrop behind us, as did groups like the Human League at the time. Some of them were quite upsetting to people. They weren't pornographic, but they were typical art-student: nudity and cutting up bits of meat. They were very visceral. We were arty and pretentious, but as we went on, the song side developed more, and I started writing lyrics.

We wanted to show the glamour in mundanity. We wanted to sing about things like bedsitters [efficiency apartments] and going shopping and collecting trash and souvenirs. Our songs were about going to supermarkets but imbued with a sense of escaping to a nightlife. When I wrote "Memorabilia," I was DJing at the time, and I was listening to this James Brown record that had this funky repetitive riff. I thought,

Let's turn that funk riff into an electronic riff. Then I wrote a list of things that I liked collecting and sang them the way I used to sing, in a very bored and flat kind of way. It was very punk. The first Siouxsie and the Banshees album, *The Scream*, made a real impression on me. I loved the way they turned these suburban things into nightmares—that was a great influence on the early Soft Cell stuff.

We were signed [to Sire Records] as part of a package deal. [Soft Cell manager] Stevo was really keen on another group called B-Movie, who were much more like a Duran Duran. They were very good, but they weren't Duran Duran. Stevo said, "If you sign B-Movie, you have to sign Soft Cell." We were given an advance of 1,000 pounds and told to spend it on new equipment.

Then suddenly, "Tainted Love" got played on the radio and went up and up the chart, and B-Movie became forgotten. But they still thought we were a strange novelty act. They were panicking that we were so art student–y and unpredictable and had this

MIXTAPE: **5 More Sleazy Songs About Sex**
1. "Relax," Frankie Goes to Hollywood 2. "Can't You See," Vicious Pink
3. "No GDM," Gina X 4. "Turning Japanese," The Vapors
5. "The Dominatrix Sleeps Tonight," Dominatrix

punk ethic. They thought we were going to mess the whole thing up. I remember, before going on *Top of the Pops*, I was trying to see how many of these funny bracelets I could get on my arm. I thought it was a great look. The record company was freaking out: "You can't go on like that! Please, please don't!" That made me more determined to go against them. They tried to bring in choreographers to tell me how to move. From the get-go, we were off-kilter with them.

After "Tainted Love" went to number one [in the U.K.], all hell let loose. I was still living in a shared student squat in Leeds, but one day I was on the outside of television looking in on *Top of the Pops*, the next I was on the inside looking out. I think the record company wanted us to do endless northern soul songs all sounding like "Tainted Love," but Dave and I had ideas of developing and doing something that was a bit more lasting. "Tainted Love" was a double-edged sword: It was great to have the success, but it brought this teenybop attention that we didn't feel very comfortable with. We started to get very, very young fans, yet we were quite strong in our performances—we were aggressive and confrontational. It became a strange situation where we were thrown into this no-man's land between pop and experimental electronic music.

We realized that we could try and put some subversion into pop—depressing lyrics with an upbeat sound so you could dance through your tears. Like "Bedsitter": You're dancing because it's Saturday night, and you're forgetting your mundane life of living in a bedsitter. That became the ethos of what we were about on the first album, *Non-Stop Erotic Cabaret*. Living in sleazy, eighties Britain, repressed people leading secret lives, frustrated living in bedsits—it was the total antithesis of what Duran Duran were doing, which was singing about this glamorous life, and living in Rio, and sailing in ships on beautiful seas. We didn't see life like that. We were in the backstreets. We were very much children of the seventies; we still had that seventies-going-into-the-eighties culture. We'd lived through power cuts and grim times and glam rock. When we went to New York [to record *Non-Stop Erotic Cabaret*], we were drawn to the dark underbelly, and that started to influence our sound and our ethos. It became a real war between us and the record company. They wanted us to be these clean-living guys, and we wanted to see how much we could get away with in our lyrics and our videos. It was

like, "Let's see how extreme I can be or how camp I can be."

Dave and I have always been very different people, and our relationship had become quite distant when we were doing *Non-Stop Erotic Cabaret*. We brought very different influences to Soft Cell. Dave brought experimental electronic music. He loved things like Devo, Throbbing Gristle, Cabaret Voltaire. I brought things like glam rock and Jacques Brel and T. Rex, and chansons, ballads, blues, and a sense of theater. While doing *Non-Stop Erotic Cabaret*, we were thrust together, put in the same hotel rooms. When we moved to New York, Dave found his own place to stay and his own circle of friends, I found my own circle, and we started to drift. Drugs played a part. We'd both become very, very heavily into the New York drugs scene, which was fun, then the London drugs scene, which was much darker for us. It became very destructive.

THAT WAS THEN BUT THIS IS NOW

 Soft Cell made two more albums, 1983's *The Art of Falling Apart* and 1984's challenging *This Last Night in Sodom*. As a solo artist, Marc Almond has amassed a considerable catalog in a dizzying variety of styles, from

cabaret to Russian folk songs to rock and electronica dance music. His hits include "Something's Gotten Hold of My Heart," "Tears Run Rings," "Jacky," and "The Days of Pearly Spencer." Ball formed the Grid in 1988. They saw their biggest success with 1994's *Evolver* album, which included the hits "Texas Cowboys" and "Swamp Thing." Soft Cell re-formed in 2002 for the album *Cruelty Without Beauty*. Their version of "Tainted Love" has been covered by, among others, Marilyn Manson, the Pussycat Dolls, and Paul Young. Rihanna's "S.O.S." was built on a sample of the song.

ALMOND: When we did *The Art of Falling Apart*, we knew Soft Cell was falling apart, and we didn't know how much longer we could hold it together. We put a lot of that anger and frustration into that album, which was a hard, visceral record, and that reflected in our live performances, where we'd throw equipment all over the stage. It was the gradual destruction of the band.

We pulled out our final anger with *This Last Night in Sodom*, which is one of my favorite records. We recorded it in mono just to be bloody-minded, and it brought Soft Cell back to an electronic-punk feel. Then Dave decided he wanted to do studio stuff, and I wanted to do my stuff—I'd already branched out into Marc and the Mambas. There was no animosity. It was just drift. Me and Dave were still friends, but we thought, *We can't go on like this*, so we split in 1984. We did our final tour of America after we'd split because we were contracted to. We'd so had enough of the whole thing that we refused to play "Tainted Love."

After 17 years, Dave had done some mixes for me, we'd been in touch again, and it felt like the right time to do something again. We wrote some songs, and we thought about calling it another name. But Marc Almond and Dave Ball—everybody's going to call it Soft Cell. So, Soft Cell it was.

It's a great feeling for us that people have covered the Soft Cell version [of "Tainted Love"]. If you have a big record like that, it takes over your life for a while. You have to turn your back on it because it becomes bigger than you. You have to move aside from it for a time. But you fall back in love with it, and you have to embrace it, because people will always associate you with it. You can't fight it, so you have to learn to love it as a record, and I do. I have this real love affair with it now. If my life's a show, then "Tainted Love" would be my theme tune. I can't deny people it; it's the thing that got me on *Top of the Pops* and on people's minds. When I'm onstage, I give people my new stuff and they're very patient. Then I have to give them a reward and say, "Thanks for listening to my new songs, now here's 'Tainted Love.'"

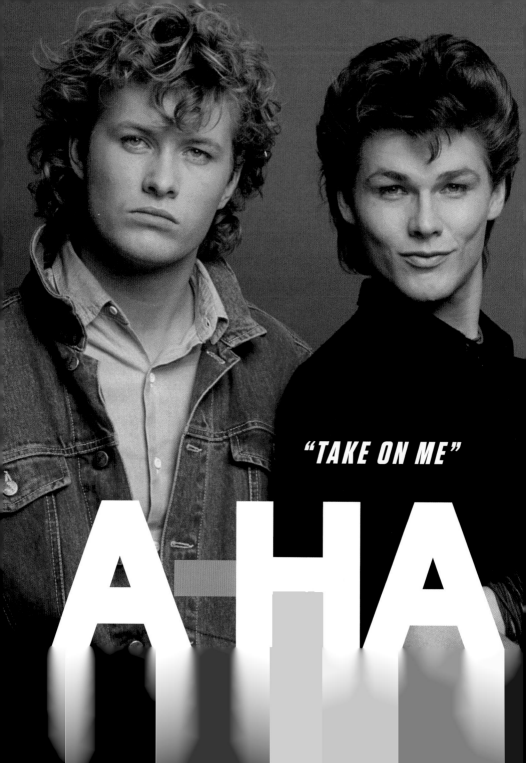

"TAKE ON ME"

A-HA

Bert Kaempfert, ABBA, Blue Swede, Silver Convention, and the Singing Nun enjoyed sporadic hits, but a European artist's presence on the U.S. charts was rare until the early eighties. Suddenly, horizons broadened, language barriers were breached, and America opened her arms to her fellow man from across the Atlantic. More Germans, Austrians, Belgians, Swedes, Welsh, Irish, Scots, and even Englishmen invaded and colonized radio (and MTV) airwaves in numbers not seen since the sixties. Also aboard the boat were a trio of Norwegians, though their country had no prior history of exporting contemporary pop music. But the combination of Steve Barron's eyeball-grabbing video, Morten Harket's cheekbones and quiff, and the bracing burst of menthol freshness that was "Take On Me" made A-ha impossible to resist. Decades after its release, the song is still irrepressible, still instantly recognizable...and Norway has still made no other significant impact on the international pop marketplace.

LM: From that indelible riff that forces you to play air synthesizer to Harket's soaring final falsetto—"in a, in a daaaaaaaaaaay!"—"Take On Me" is a relentlessly catchy pop tune, albeit one with a split personality. There are days when it's the perfect grab-your-gals-and-get-drunk-on-the-dance-floor tune; on others, it's the ideal sit-by-the-window-while-it's-raining-and-sigh selection. As a lover of *Hunting High and Low*, the 1985 A-ha album that evokes the atmospheric and ethereal beauty of Roxy Music (Harket's elegant and unusual voice calls to mind an *Avalon*-era Ferry), I'm able to appreciate the deeper, more wistful side of "Take On Me." Plus, it's a beckoning door beyond which lies darker, more pensive material like the title track and, despite its title, "The Sun Always Shines on TV," two gems that are as seductive and affective as any of my new wave faves and as ageless as Harket's boyish countenance.

JB: Judd Apatow is so open-minded, adventurous, and youthful in his attitude to comedy yet so dull and conservative when it comes to music. In one of the many Apatow family arguments restaged by Paul Rudd and Leslie Mann in *This Is 40*, he harangues her for what he deemed her simple-minded taste in music. The offending tune playing in her car that signaled his tantrum? "Take On Me." Rudd's archive-label exec deems it a brainless jingle and vastly inferior to the Pixies, which he castigated her for not being well-rounded enough to appreciate. I think Apatow was pretty evenhanded parceling out the blame and the flaws to that movie couple, but where "Take On Me" is concerned, he was totally taking sides. Clearly, the guy hates pop. But in terms of its vocals, its lyrics, and its arrangement, "Take On Me" is far from a dumb-ass formulaic pop record.

MAGNE "MAGS" FURUHOLMEN: "Take On Me" was a song I lived with for almost 10 years before it became a hit. I wrote the hook in '77, when I was 15 years old. [A-ha co-founder Pål Waaktaar and I] started when we were 12 or 13. We were called Bridges at the time. We were heavily immersed in the Doors. We didn't really go for the poppy side of the sixties. We sort of liked the Beatles, but it was *The White Album* and the more experimental stuff that was the focus. When the riff for "Take On Me" came about, it was like a guilty pleasure—there was a little bit of shame attached to it. Päl thought it was way too commercial for us. I remember arguing that it was really catchy. We used to call it "The Juicy Fruit Song" because it reminded us of the Juicy Fruit commercials in the seventies.

It was left by the wayside for a long time. Then, when we recruited Morten around '82, he said, "This is a really big hit song!" We had the verse and the riff but a very flat chorus. After we started working with Morten, his incredible range really influenced the chorus—we wanted to see just how [high] he could go. His voice was very elastic and very powerful in all registers, and that influenced our writing greatly.

"Take On Me" stands out from the rest of our catalog. It stood out through all of its history, even as it changed from being sixties psychedelic retro-pop to eighties synth-pop with a vengeance. One of the allures is it brings people in who wouldn't normally go for the upbeat, happy, pop stuff because it has that melancholy streak. The verse and the riff are in a minor key. It's not a happy song—it's quite sad if you listen to it. I never considered it to be a dance track, even though, ironically, the riff is used in "Feel This Moment" with Pitbull and Christina Aguilera. We used to joke about A-ha being ideal for wooden-legged dancers because there was never any groovy approach.

If you grow up in Norway, melancholy is nothing to do with being sad; melancholy is a sense of yearning, a longing, and, probably historically, a transport away from hardship. It has manifested itself in folk music and in art. Think about Edvard Munch and his very expressionist, intense dark landscapes. Think about the musical works of Edvard Grieg: very declarational, very big emotions, very melancholy in essence. The same goes for literature. Knut Hamsun's *Victoria* and *Hunger* were as influential to us as pop music was. Our way into music came about through that blend of Beatles energy with Doors melancholy, and the way we sounded came from the time we spent in England, but the core, the foundation of the writing, comes from the Norwegian culture. Päl's parents would take him to the opera. My grandfather was a musician.

When I was about 14, we [were featured] in a little article in my local newspaper, and when they asked, "What are you going to do when you grow up?" we said, "We're gonna go to England, become huge pop stars, and be bigger than the Beatles." There is [something] very beautiful about kids from this suburb in Norway thinking they're gonna be the first out of the country that hadn't produced any international pop stars. But my father was a musician, so I got a sense that it was possible. Sadly, he died young. When I was six, he passed away on his way to his first gig abroad through a plane accident, which, incidentally, Morten saw as a child. First time I met Morten, we ended up walking three hours through the forest because we'd missed the night bus. Once we'd exhausted our music knowledge, we started talking about our families. I told him my father died in 1969, that he fell down outside of Oslo. He said his family was on a bridge and saw that plane go down. It was weird to realize he had been witnessing my father's death 10 years before we met. I remember walking away from that meeting thinking either he's a pathological liar or it was just the strangest coincidence that we had this kind of connection straight off the bat.

When we came to England as A-ha in '82, there were multiple radio stations playing all this new music: Depeche Mode, Yazoo, ABC, Kid Creole and the Coconuts, Blancmange, Thompson Twins. Our synth sound happened partly by necessity. Before we left Norway, we used to have bass and drums and someone else playing a second guitar, but when we came to the U.K., it was just me, Päl, and Morten, so we had to find a new way of making music. Soft Cell's "Tainted Love" was the first song that made us realize, "We can make music with a lot of emotional impact by using synths."

"Take On Me" has been recorded twice. The first version, we were in with a big producer, Tony Mansfield [Aztec Camera, Naked Eyes, the Damned], and we would listen to everything he said. Gradually we became disenchanted. One of the songs that suffered the most was "Take On Me." It didn't sound like the hit we thought it should sound like. The chorus didn't sound soaring. There was very little emotion; it was too mechanical-sounding. But the record company had the belief that it was a strong contender, so it was released as a first single. We made a video for this version. [One of our managers] was afraid that three Norwegian guys with very dubious fashion sense would come off as gay. His cure was to rent strippers for the video.

We don't like this video, we don't like

MIXTAPE: 5 More Songs by English-as-a-Second-Language New Wavers
1. "Rock Me Amadeus," Falco 2. "The Great Commandment," Camouflage 3. "Big in Japan," Alphaville 4. "Firecracker," Yellow Magic Orchestra 5. "Da Da Da," Trio

that version of the song, but we went with it. It was played on BBC Radio a couple of times, but nothing really happened. We convinced our manager to give us a chance to rerecord "Take On Me" with another producer. Alan Tarney had been suggested earlier in the game, but we had not been too keen. But we saved the day with that second recording. I took this new version up to Baker Street where the American Warner Bros. office was and said, "This is how we should sound," and [they] loved it. Then we were allowed to rerecord "The Sun Always Shines on TV" and the single for "Hunting High and Low" with real strings. We recorded the next couple of albums with Alan Tarney.

Of course, if you say "Take On Me" to anyone, they probably immediately think of the other video. The thing that makes it so special is the hand-drawn aspect. Steve Barron made 20,000 drawings—it was, like, 5 drawings per second. It took three months of postproduction just making the animated sequences. Steve came up with this love-affair story line, the idea of [Morten] coming in and out of an animated world and the real world. At the end, when he's looking about in the hallway and meeting [the video's leading lady] in the real world— that was stolen from *Altered States*, the film by Ken Russell. It was a perfect setup, especially with someone as good looking as Morten. This is what triggered the whole idolization thing, which threw us a bit at the time. But in hindsight, it's easy to see why this real world–versus–cartoon world love affair between an idealized superhero-type figure and the innocent English girl would trigger what it did.

THAT WAS THEN *BUT THIS IS NOW*

 "Take On Me" scooped up six 1986 MTV Video Music Awards and helped earn A-ha a Grammy nod for Best New Artist. However, its follow-up, "The Sun Always Shines on TV," was only a modest hit stateside, and the band's U.S. career pretty much ended there. But that was only the beginning of A-ha's success around the world. They released a total of 39 singles—including the James Bond theme "The Living Daylights"—and nine studio albums, the last being 2009's U.K. top-five *Foot of the Mountain*. The band split after their final live performance, which was at a 2011 national memorial service in Oslo dedicated to the 77 people massacred that year by an antigovernment terrorist. Harket has released five solo albums and continues to tour on his own. He and Furuholmen still live

in Norway, where all three members were honored with knighthoods in 2012. Waaktaar, a painter, moved to Manhattan and changed his first name to Paul and hyphenated his last to Waaktaar-Savoy to include his wife's, as is Norwegian custom. Once a tight-knit trio, the former bandmates now barely speak, but "Take On Me" lives on: There have been ska, punk, and boy-band versions, as well as Italian progressive power metal, Latvian instrumental cello-rock, and Trinidadian soca renditions.

FURUHOLMEN: I'm totally at peace with "Take On Me," but I know there are other people in our group who would rather not talk about that song. At one point we all had a kind of strained relationship to it, but that happens to anyone who has massive success with one song. As much as we don't like to hear it, in America that is our one big hit. You feel for all the songs that you bled for, and the ones that didn't get attention. It's like you have two kids, and someone always talks about how great that one kid is. Although we've had our times of feeling confined by this idea that it was so defining for us, we just have to accept it and embrace it.

We've had our breaks before. In the nineties we disbanded, although it wasn't for-mally done. This time it was, and it would take a hell of a lot for me to go back. We exhausted a few lifetimes together. We don't really stay in touch, although I did spend two hours with Morten a week ago—we hadn't sat down for two hours since 2010. We happened to be in the same hotel in Oslo. He keeps it alive. He's been out there touring—he's been playing "Take On Me" without me and Paul. He can do that. He's the only one [of us whom] people would come and see perform those songs.

There are some bands who continue on just to keep making money. Every year they'll do the summer tour. They don't talk to each other backstage, they sneak in separate sides of the room. I'm not against people doing that. But the three of us have, subsequent to ending the band, given our-selves the opportunity to look at A-ha from the outside, and I'm quite proud of that. It's like a marriage: When you're in it, you tend to take things for granted. It feels like we could have made it work better if we had been a little less careless. But I'd rather look at all the great things that did happen. I'm totally satisfied with what A-ha achieved. I celebrate the idea of what we made together, resting secure in the knowledge that it couldn't have happened without all three of us.

anchester's music scene has long been dominated by oddballs, eccentrics, misanthropes, depressives, villains, and grotesques. The Buzzcocks, Magazine, the Fall, John Cooper Clarke, the Smiths, A Certain Ratio, Stone Roses, Happy Mondays, Oasis. What a parade of impenetrable accents, incompetent dental work, unruly eyebrows, surly attitudes, and black, black hearts. But no Manchester band better embodied their rain-spattered, concrete environment than Joy Division. The year 1979 was a banner one for bleak, nightmarish post-punk classics, like Gang of Four's *Entertainment*, Public Image Ltd.'s *Metal Box*, and the Cure's *Three Imaginary Boys*. These records were made to be moped to in the confines of a predominantly (but not exclusively) adolescent male suburban bedroom. That same year, Joy Division's debut, *Unknown Pleasures*, dealt with similar themes—the ever-popular alienation and despair—but it did so in a transcendent fashion. The combination of Ian Curtis's disembodied growl, Peter Hook's brutally melodic bass, the band's machinelike precision, and producer Martin Hannett's desire to make a record that sounded both spacious and terrifying turned *Unknown Pleasures* into a ghost train ride to hell. "Love Will Tear Us Apart" offered a glimpse of a group capable of forging an emotional connection with a larger audience. But by then, Joy Division were already frozen in time.

"LOVE WILL TEAR US APART"

DIVISION

JB: You know why I liked Joy Division? Because other people did. No point in lying about it: I was a sheep. If I read about a band in the *NME*, and John Peel was playing them, and their records were stocked in one of Glasgow's indie-friendly stores, I would buy them and take them home and play them continuously until either I genuinely liked them or a post-punk version of Stockholm syndrome set in. The 1979 version of me was devoid of a mind of my own—to the degree that I purchased an olive-green thrift-store raincoat that flapped down around my ankles because that was the requisite uniform to properly appreciate the existential anguish of Joy Division. (Having said that, the skies of Glasgow are gray and overcast approximately 11 months out of the year, so that raincoat turned out to be a smart and practical investment.) You know why I eventually came around to liking Joy Division? Because they sounded like disco. They sounded like the Teutonic disco records I bought along with the post-punk indies: Silver Convention, Donna Summer, Munich Machine—stuff I didn't need to make an effort to enjoy. Joy Division's music was gruesome, claustrophobic, unpleasant disco, but it had a pulse that I recognized, and that caused me to respond.

LM: As embarrassing as it is to admit, the first time I heard "Love Will Tear Us Apart" was Paul Young's 1984 cover. I liked his version then, as I still do now. But I can understand the horror with which it was received by Joy Division's army of gloomy fans, not to mention the surviving members. The band, their legend, and that song are precious and seem to remain unexploited, no matter how many T-shirts they sell at Hot Topic. It wasn't until I heard the original that I understood how desperately sad a song it is. This isn't my favorite Joy Division song—that would be the even more haunting "Atmosphere"—but I get why "Love Will Tear Us Apart" universally tops so many best-songs-of-all-time lists. It's a living document that details the hopelessness Curtis felt in his dead-end marriage before he took his own life. "Love Will Tear Us Apart" marked a real turning point for Joy Division…and we'll never know what could have come next.

BERNARD SUMNER: Ian almost died making that song. It was the story of his demise. "Love Will Tear Us Apart" was kind of Romeo and Juliet for real, put down in lyrics. I think the reason for that being a hit [in the U.K.]— apart from the melody, which is brilliant—is that it was such a romantic story. You can't get more real; you can't get more surreal.

PETER HOOK: I would not want someone to write a song about me like that. The lyrics are so poignant and so hurt, it really is shocking. And I never realized for years. When Ian used to sing it, it looked to me like he was having a great time; when Bernard was singing it [years later, with New Order], same. Then, when I came to sing it [with Peter Hook and the Light], I thought, *Oh my god, these lyrics are really dark.* It's a very sad love song—it's an anti-love song—but it sounds like a joyous love song. And I suppose that's its secret. If your heart's broken, you need to fight your way through it.

Ian always had a bag of lyrics with him, scraps of papers with ideas written on them. As we were playing, he'd just delve into this bag and pull something out, mumble it—at least, that's what it sounded like to us—and then he'd elaborate, and it built up from there. The next minute, you had a song. The great thing about Ian was that you didn't really need to hear what he was saying; you

could just look at what he was doing and know that he meant it. That fire, that passion in his body language and his delivery, let you know that everything was okay.

On more than one occasion, Tony Wilson asked Ian to refer to Frank Sinatra. [Before recording "Love Will Tear Us Apart," Tony] gave [Ian] a double LP [of Sinatra's] and said, "Listen to this." It's plainly ridiculous at first sight, but now that I'm a fan of Frank Sinatra—as these things happen as you get older—I can see what Tony meant. He was referring to Sinatra's soul and passion and the delivery. But I think Ian had that anyway, unless maybe he did get it from Frank.

The lyrics always came afterwards. The music always came first, and Ian was very, very involved in orchestrating the music and telling us what sounded good. He didn't tell us what to play; he just told us that what we were playing was great. "Love Will Tear Us Apart" is very simply written. It took us something like three hours from start to finish. Ian went away, thought about the vocal, came back the next day, and we had the song. It came very, very naturally, very easy.

You didn't write songs with a view to recording them in those days. You only wrote songs with a view to playing them [live at a gig]. The first chance you got to play it, you would play it, and judging the audience's

reaction was quite a delight, really, because it was the best way to tell if you're going in the right direction. And they loved ["Love Will Tear Us Apart"]. It's very up-tempo. It's very, very in-your-face—you could say it has like a punk ethic to it. It went down great every time we played it. "Atmosphere" is also a favorite with many Joy Division fans. The reason it's not my favorite song is it's always associated with funerals. Every funeral I go to, they play bloody "Atmosphere." The most popular song at weddings is "Angels" by Robbie Williams, and the most popular song at funerals is "Atmosphere." When I went to [Factory Records boss] Tony Wilson's funeral and they put "Atmosphere" on at the end, I wished we had written fuckin' "Angels."

The thing with Joy Division's music is that each member was playing like a separate line. We hardly ever played together; we all played separately. But when you put it together, it was like the ingredients in a cake. When you eat the ingredients separately, they don't taste very nice, but when you mix them together, they taste wonderful—if you do it right, of course. And in Joy Division, you got that right very easily. Once we got to New Order, we had three of the ingredients, but there was always an ingredient missing.

The only problem with Joy Division was Ian's illness. If Ian hadn't been ill, he'd probably still be here today. The degenerative effects of the drugs he was taking for the illness heightened his depression and made him unable to cope with all of the other things in his life, I think.

But the thing is, I was dealing with Ian on a day-to-day basis, and even though he wasn't well, he looked like he was coping. I know it doesn't seem like that now, and that's one thing I realized when I'd written [the memoir *Unknown Pleasures*]: It really was plainly obvious that he wasn't coping. But the problem was that whenever you asked him, he always told you he was okay, and in your heart, that's what you wanted. You wanted this guy, whom you loved and cherished and revered, to tell you everything was okay. You'd ask him, and he'd say, "Yes, Hooky, everything is fine. Don't worry. Let's carry on." And you'd go, "Phew. Thank God

for that." I've seen friends of mine who've been ill succumb to it and just go into a pit, and it's very, very difficult. But with Ian, it was never like that. He fought it so well, and his whole reason for living seemed to be to make sure you heard what you wanted to hear.

Most of the time that you spent with Ian, though, was relaxed, and we used to have a lot of laughs. It was just us in the back of a van, playing great music. And just when you're getting to the point when it could have been poisoned [by success], it stopped. There weren't wild parties; there weren't drugs, particularly; there were no girls. I wasn't drinking that much, because we had no money—we couldn't afford it!

[After Ian died], we couldn't replace him. That would have been absolutely 100 percent impossible. There was no chance, and we all knew that. We knew that immediately. It's not like when INXS got that guy [J.D. Fortune] in. We could have gotten someone who sounded like Ian, but it wouldn't have been the same.

MIXTAPE: 5 More Songs from the Cold, Dark, Rain-Soaked Streets of Manchester 1. "Hand in Glove," The Smiths 2. "Homosapien," Pete Shelley 3. "Time Goes by So Slow," The Distractions 4. "A Song from Under the Floorboards," Magazine 5. "Beasley Street," John Cooper Clarke

SUMNER: We were New Order for 10 years before we played any Joy Division songs [in concert]. We didn't want people to say, "Oh, they've only made it because of Ian's death—that's propelled them along, and they're living off their heritage." We wanted to make it on our terms, so we spent 10 years doing that. Then one night, I think it might have been Irvine Meadows in California, it was Ian's birthday—not the anniversary of his death, which I don't think is something to celebrate—and we decided to play "Love Will Tear Us Apart" and another Joy Division song. People were like, "Are these new songs?" They didn't get much of a response. When we play them now, people go wild.

THAT WAS THEN
BUT THIS IS NOW

"Love Will Tear Us Apart" was a posthumous U.K. hit. The surviving members of Joy Division went on to form New Order (see page 46). Aside from their not-insignificant contribution to Manchester's musical heritage, the band poured a ton of money into the city's legendary nightspot, the Haçienda. While the club was the epicenter of the city's vibrant rave culture, its financial mismanagement drove the band to the brink of bankruptcy.

Tony Wilson's easy-come, easy-go approach to the finances of Factory Records drove them the rest of the way there. Joy Division's story, as well as the rise and fall of Factory and the Haçienda, were wittily chronicled in Michael Winterbottom's 2002 film, *24 Hour Party People*. Curtis's biography was handled in more somber fashion in Anton Corbijn's 2007 film, *Control*. Peter Hook published a memoir of his Joy Division years, *Unknown Pleasures*, in 2012.

HOOK: Paul Young's was the most famous [cover of "Love Will Tear Us Apart"], and at the time, I hated it.＊But then, we made more money off of that rendition than we ever did as Joy Division. It's quite painful, isn't it? It was smoochy, and it was everything we didn't want to be—cabaret.

SUMNER: New Order was a more commercial success than Joy Division, but Joy Division just keeps selling and selling. It's kind of a self-propelling brand. I hate to use the word "brand," because Joy Division was not a commercial product, but it's kind of a self-regenerating brand. A friend brought his daughter around to my house; she was like 13 or 14, and she had an iPod. I said, "Oh, what are you listening to?"—expecting her to say "Justin Bieber" or something. No: "It's this band called Joy Division." I didn't tell her I was in Joy Division, but her father told her, and next time she came around, she was like, "Can I have your autograph?"

HOOK: Joy Division were an absolutely unique group. We stayed independent, on an independent record label; we didn't go to London like everybody else—we stayed in the place that made us and stayed true to it. We actually entertained a whole fucking city at our own expense for 16 years. I think that is changing the world of musical and world culture.

We wrote fucking great music. The chemistry between the individuals [in the band] was absolutely fantastic, and the individual playing styles of each one of us has been much emulated. Some groups will be like, "I really like Stephen Morris's rhythms," or "I really like Bernard's melody lines and his lead guitar style," or "I really like Peter Hook's melodic bass playing." That actually is very unusual in a group, and everybody tries to emulate that. I hear U2 rip off Joy Division even now. If you look at bands like White Lies or the Editors, some of them take the fixation a little too far. I don't think they capture the naturalness, the relaxed fitting-together that Joy Division had. They have a very manufactured sound; it doesn't sound very

natural. One of the most natural-sounding bands I've heard that sound like Joy Division is the Chameleons.

When you're writing music, it's like you have nothing but this blank canvas. You use the influence and the inspiration to create something. That's what people do with Joy Division. They love the songs. They love the story of the band. The tragic ending is very rock 'n' roll, very alluring, very romantic—that "live fast, die young" story. It's like the perfect ending to your life to go out in a blaze of glory, blowing up on stage at Glastonbury in front of 125,000 people. Rock 'n' roll, man!

✳ **PAUL YOUNG:** Somebody said, "Why don't we find a new song and throw it back into the soul idiom?" Which ended up being "Love Will Tear Us Apart." We asked ourselves: How would Levi Stubbs sing "Love Will Tear Us Apart"? Normally people are like, "You can't do that." But there's me on the first album saying, "I'm going to do a punk song and imagine the Four Tops doing it."

You could say that Morrissey and Marr were a Mancunian Morrison and Manzarek. Only, instead of demanding the world worship him as a snakeskin-clad shaman, Morrissey sang from the perspective of an invisible outsider, forever ignored and underestimated, and he did it while brandishing a bunch of gladioli and sporting National Health Service specs and a hearing aid. The world worshipped him anyway. The Smiths were the first serious, critically revered, independent act with a giddy, overemotional following forever on the verge of hysteria. The Smiths made big boys cry like little girls, and they made big girls wish the men in their lives were more like Morrissey. He was wittier. He felt more. He suffered more. He understood more. The Smiths

THE SMITHS

may never have reached the same arena-filling heights as the Cure and Depeche Mode,

"HOW SOON IS NOW?"

but they earned their place in the Mount Rushmore of modern rock, and it was "How Soon Is Now" that put them there. If the decade has three great doomed love songs—"Love Will Tear Us Apart" and "The Killing Moon" being the other two—"How Soon Is Now?" is the most isolated, the most hopeless, the most alone. But while Morrissey sounds resigned to his loveless destiny, Johnny Marr's music has never been this big, rich, and deep. "Epic" is an overused word—especially in this book—but "How Soon Is Now?" is an epic of adolescent angst: It takes a handful of hurt feelings and makes them into a masterpiece.

LM: The Smiths didn't have a lot of the things I looked for in a band: escapist music videos, male members with makeup, at least one keyboard player. And their name was the most ordinary moniker a group could possibly have. But the Smiths were like no one I'd heard before—or since. Almost immediately upon hearing "There Is a Light That Never Goes Out," they launched straight into my top-five favorite bands and never left. I didn't have to apologize for liking them. And being a Smiths fan reflected well on your movie taste and your literary quotient. Yes, Morrissey was divisive (some might say whiny), but no one ever captured loneliness, insecurity, and fumbling immature awkwardness like he did. No one ever sang my life like he did. I had no idea what a vegetarian even was before I heard "Meat Is Murder"—Morrissey's done more for animal rights in the past 30 years than anyone on the planet! And you know what the best thing he ever did was? Not get back together with the Smiths. Court cases and ill feelings notwithstanding, I'm happy I don't have to see them tainting that immortal legacy. Because no financially motivated reunion of the four now-50-something Smiths could ever equal the show in my head.

JB: Not a fan.

JOHNNY MARR: I think "How Soon Is Now?" is unusual because it sounds really, really good in a club when you're fucked up—and that's okay. "Please, Please, Please Let Me Get What I Want" is a really loved song also, and "There Is a Light That Never Goes Out" has a different kind of love for it. But "How Soon Is Now?" sounds really good in American clubs, and it was made late at night with a kind of swampy, sexy vibe going on. I don't think I've ever said "vibe" and "sexy" in the same sentence—the song must have something good going for it if it makes me use those words!

It was written over a three-day period. On the Friday, I sat down around noonish with my little Portastudio and wrote "William, It Was Really Nothing" and recorded it on a little four-track for the A-side of the next single. Because that was such a fast, short, upbeat song, I wanted the B-side to be different, so I wrote "Please, Please, Please Let Me Get What I Want" on Saturday in a different time signature—in a waltz time as a contrast. I was kind of happied out after writing "William."

On Sunday night I kicked back and treated myself to writing something completely different from both those songs. I had a short, upbeat one and a short, sad one, so I decided to write a long, swampy one with a groove. I always wrote songs in batches of three and usually still do.

MORRISSEY: The song was recorded in North London, in the old Decca studios. It established a certain turning point for the band, even though we were still oddly associated with timidity. I think the lyrics embarrassed the other Smiths, and the producer [John Porter] said nothing, and greater emphasis was placed on the guitars. I'd reached the point where I had to register whatever it was I felt, and Angie Marr [Johnny's wife] was the first person who complimented me on the lyric.

ANDY ROURKE: I've never been embarrassed by his lyrics. They were truthful and down to the bone. I was embarrassed to show my dad the first Smiths 45, "Hand In Glove," because it had a guy's naked butt on the cover.

MARR: I was really excited when I first heard the lyrics to "How Soon Is Now?" But I always was really excited when I first heard the lyrics of all the songs. I expected that the lyrics would be fantastic for every song that we wrote, and they always were.

ROURKE: Usually we would do a very basic run-through in the recording studio, then Morrissey would take a cassette tape and go off to his room or house or wherever and work on [the lyrics] for a day or two. We'd finish the songs, and then he would come in and do his thing over the top. We didn't know what the hell Morrissey was going to sing. It was always a great moment, waiting to see what he would come up with.

MARR: We made the record until dawn. I got a taxi home from Finsbury Park in London to Queensgate and got into bed around 8 or 9 a.m. Then I woke up, and it was dark the next evening, and I realized that we had done something that was really different. I remember thinking, *Did that really happen?* We just caught it in a sort of 24-hour kind of time capsule when we recorded it. The demo was what it was, but things happened in the recording session that really took it up several degrees. It was a real team effort.

MORRISSEY: When the final mix was finished, I took a tape of the song by taxi to Rough Trade Records, played it to Geoff Travis [the head of the label], and when it finished, he said, "What is Johnny doing?

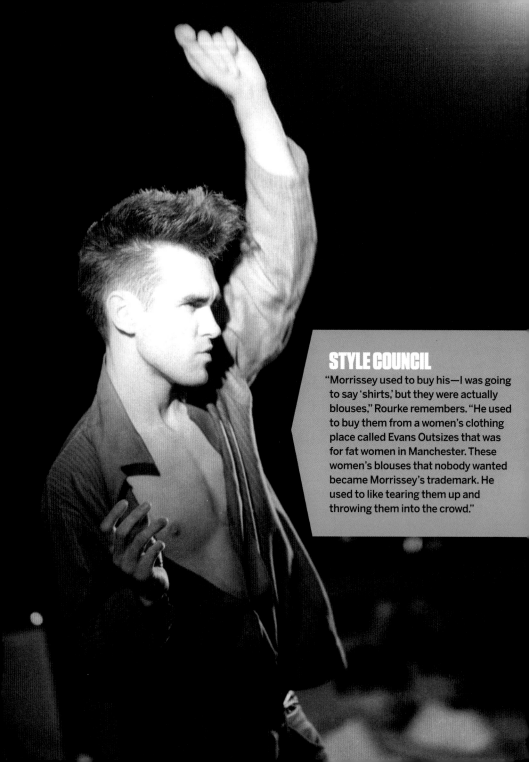

STYLE COUNCIL

"Morrissey used to buy his—I was going to say 'shirts,' but they were actually blouses," Rourke remembers. "He used to buy them from a women's clothing place called Evans Outsizes that was for fat women in Manchester. These women's blouses that nobody wanted became Morrissey's trademark. He used to like tearing them up and throwing them into the crowd."

That's just noise!," and the song became a B-side [to "William, It Really Was Nothing"]. Meanwhile, in the U.S., Sire released it as a single, but couldn't get it on the Top 100 even though it had great radio play [on modern rock stations] and we were selling out large arenas. Also, Sire couldn't secure the Smiths a television spot anywhere! We were paralyzed by the dumbness of the times. So we did our best to change them.

MARR: We formed the group as a positive thing to represent our generation who weren't mainstream. A lot is made of the difference between us and bands like Duran Duran and Spandau Ballet and Culture Club. It's right to point out those differences between those mainstream groups and groups like the Smiths and New Order, who were just a different kind of people full-stop. We were independent groups from the start—the others were very much major-label groups. Pretty much everyone you see on the Band Aid record, almost all of those people, with the exception of Paul

Weller, represented straight, mainstream aspirations. Those bands just aspired to be big, big pop stars. Without having to discuss it, we knew we were all alternatives, and we didn't even consider that we were all on the same page. When I say "we," I'm talking about not just the four individual members of the Smiths; I'm talking about people like Bernard Sumner and Billy Bragg too. You were either on the side of the Cure and Depeche and the Smiths, or you were on the side of the more mainstream acts.

It just so happened that some of the alternative acts got very popular. Depeche Mode got to be a very, very big, well-known group playing stadiums in America. That's the great thing about pop music: Guys with interesting ideas who might be more subversive or challenging can get into the mainstream. So if the Pet Shop Boys have huge hits across the world, it's a great thing. Because it's people who do have something to say and aren't just there purely for fame but can wrap up great attitudes and interesting politics—conceptual and

 MIXTAPE: 5 Cover Versions of Smiths Songs 1. "Please, Please, Please Let Me Get What I Want," The Dream Academy 2. "Hand in Glove," Sandie Shaw 3. "You Just Haven't Earned It Yet Baby," Kirsty MacColl 4. "Heaven Knows I'm Miserable Now," Act 5. Back to the Old House," Everything But The Girl

"We weren't mainstream people; we didn't like 'jock culture,' sexism, and homophobia."

social politics and ideas—in a mainstream, four-minute song. That infiltrates Middle America and the homes of people who need to wake up a little bit. We weren't mainstream people; we didn't like "jock culture," sexism, and homophobia. We didn't like all that nasty stuff, and that's what we'd like to sing about. And we assumed our audience was made up largely of people like us.

ROURKE: When we appeared on TV, people saw normal people. We didn't wear fucking chains or six-foot hair and shoulder pads. They saw normal, almost vulnerable people, especially Morrissey. It screamed out to vulnerable people that they had an ally, somebody who speaks their language instead of this bullshit, plastic-fame stuff. The first time we went on *Top of the Pops,* we were dressed in Marks and Spencer sweaters and black jeans that our manager made for us. We went to the makeup room, and I think John Taylor was next to me, or somebody from Duran Duran who had these thick fucking shoulder pads, chains,

and hair 70 feet high. The makeup woman said, "So, what are you gonna be wearing for the performance?" I was like, "This is it: I'm wearing it." She was like, "Huh?" She thought I was crazy. A lot of it was down to the fact that we were from Manchester. Someone would punch you in the face—or kick you in the face—if you dressed like that. Our shared Irish heritage also played a part. We were all good Catholic boys, altar boys. Although, I don't think Morrissey was an altar boy. I can't imagine Morrissey in a dress. In a tutu, maybe. . . .

I met Johnny when I was 11. When we first started playing music together, we were listening to the Bothy Band and Fairport Convention—really traditional folk music. I don't know how we ended up sounding like we sounded with the Smiths. We were listening to Richard Thompson, early Fleetwood Mac, David Bowie, Iggy Pop, James Williamson. Johnny loved Rory Gallagher. Speaking for myself, I got really into black funk music—a lot of the Smiths bass lines are very funky. Chic was definitely an influence.

I met Mike [Joyce, drummer] and Morrissey when we did a demo for "Handsome Devil" and "Miserable Lie." Mike was this punk drummer who was kind of brash. Johnny was the studious one who always came up with a plan. Morrissey was different, put it that way. He's a very shy and reserved person, but charming at the same time. Luckily, he became a different person when he went on the stage—he had this alter ego. After "How Soon Is Now?," he took it to a different level and gained a lot of confidence and started going crazy onstage and doing all this crazy dancing and rolling around on the floor.

THAT WAS THEN *BUT THIS IS NOW*

 The Smiths have only grown in popularity since Marr's sudden departure in 1987, a move that led to the dissolution of the group and may have taken decades for Morrissey to get over (if he's indeed over it). He has since released nine albums as a solo artist and continues to draw arena-size crowds; he keeps the legend of the Smiths alive by including "How Soon Is Now?" and other classics in his concert set list. So does Marr, who—following a long and fruitful post-Smiths career playing with Electronic, The The, Modest Mouse, the Healers, and others—saw a brief reunion with Rourke during a 2013 tour stop while promoting his solo debut. To date, Morrissey (whose autobiography, *Autobiography*, was published in the U.K. in 2013) and Marr have never performed together again.

MORRISSEY: I've never felt fully present in my own life. I've always felt like a ghost drifting through. I'm not actually flesh. So autobiography is a therapeutic act of self-loyalty, even if, like me, you end up with chapters of self-disgust rather than reams of narcissism.

ROURKE: Last time Johnny was here [in New York City], he came around my house for a cup of tea, and he was on the sofa for seven hours. We were just reminiscing like a couple of old guys. There's never any animosity or anything like that. I still speak with Mike too. I think he still drums occasionally. It's a shame that I don't speak to Morrissey anymore, but I don't think anybody really does. That's his choice.

MORRISSEY: A lot of people are homesick for the Smiths, and not because everyone else is abysmal, but because the songs of the Smiths are so good. With most bands, if they have two decent songs, they end up with five-star reviews. There are so many easy victories these days for other bands, but the Smiths were never promoted and almost never received radio play, and this mystery has protected them in the long run. But a re-formation will never take place because re-formations can only work if the same spirit that made the band form in the first place still exists. But it doesn't.

TEARS **FOR** **FEARS**

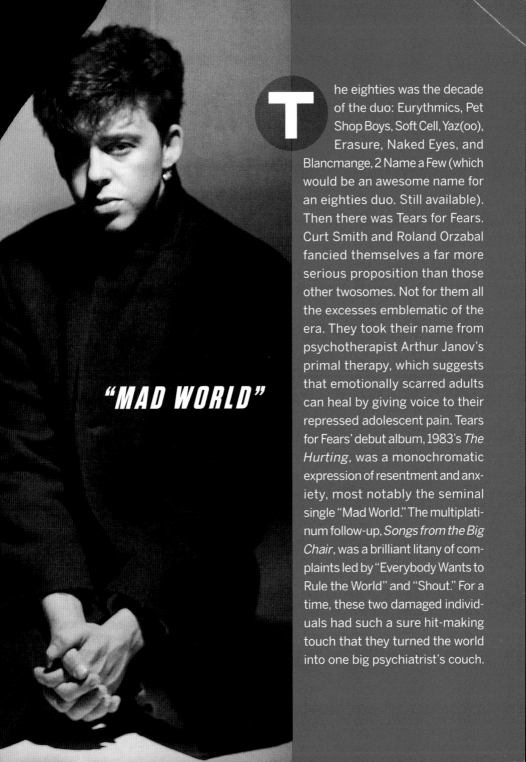

"MAD WORLD"

The eighties was the decade of the duo: Eurythmics, Pet Shop Boys, Soft Cell, Yaz(oo), Erasure, Naked Eyes, and Blancmange, 2 Name a Few (which would be an awesome name for an eighties duo. Still available). Then there was Tears for Fears. Curt Smith and Roland Orzabal fancied themselves a far more serious proposition than those other twosomes. Not for them all the excesses emblematic of the era. They took their name from psychotherapist Arthur Janov's primal therapy, which suggests that emotionally scarred adults can heal by giving voice to their repressed adolescent pain. Tears for Fears' debut album, 1983's *The Hurting*, was a monochromatic expression of resentment and anxiety, most notably the seminal single "Mad World." The multiplatinum follow-up, *Songs from the Big Chair*, was a brilliant litany of complaints led by "Everybody Wants to Rule the World" and "Shout." For a time, these two damaged individuals had such a sure hit-making touch that they turned the world into one big psychiatrist's couch.

JB: Neil Tennant once described the Pet Shop Boys as "the Smiths you can dance to." Tears for Fears were the Smiths with all traces of irony, humor, and self-awareness stripped out. TFF were unhappy, sullen, alone, and neglected. Devotees of primal therapy they may have been, but Tears for Fears did not express their inner agony in an endless, ragged whine. Rather, they made their misery as seductively melodic as possible. Morrissey and Tennant were capable of writing a lyric like "The dreams in which I'm dying are the best I've ever had," but they would have brought a degree of mockery to the delivery of such a line. Tears for Fears found nothing to laugh at. But at the same time, they took care to ensure that such sentiments were delivered in as sumptuous a setting as technologically possible.

The Hurting and *Songs from the Big Chair* are incredibly accomplished records that manage to be both instantly memorable and endlessly replayable. Their best songs seeped into the culture and have lasted a lifetime. And that's any unhappy adolescent's best revenge.

LM: Overexposure to Tears for Fears during their *Big Chair* period—"Shout" was easily the most played-out song of my teen years—caused me to unfairly dismiss their entire discography for at least a decade. It wasn't until the stripped-down Gary Jules version of "Mad World" in the early 2000s that I was finally able to see TFF for what they really are: timeless songwriters. "Mad World" is a classic, dark, brooding slice of self-pity, the kind of song I cried over as an insecure, open wound of a teen, and the kind of song I cry over now when, amazingly, I'm still an insecure open wound of a teen.

CURT SMITH: I was born in the southwest of England: Bath, Somerset. There wasn't really a Bath scene. There was one place to play; it was called Moles. We relied less on fashion, unlike Manchester, Liverpool, or London. There was no competition between bands in Bath. We were kind of it. To this day, I think I'm the most famous person born there. Roland was born in Portsmouth, but he moved to Bath with his mother when he was about 11, after his parents split up. He lived where I lived, in a council estate called Snow Hill.

ROLAND ORZABAL: What did I think of Curt right at the beginning? Well, he was dark-skinned. I thought he was from Eastern Europe or something. He was a friend of a friend who I was staying with, so we went along to see if Curt would come out. But he wasn't allowed out because he'd done something bad or wrong. So my first impression wasn't particularly good. I mean, we got on very well, but I think Curt was a bit of a petty criminal.

The guy I was staying with, I had a band with him. I was the guitarist, he was the bass player, we had a drummer. We were no good. But I heard Curt singing along to a record in his bedroom, which was "Last Days of May" by Blue Öyster Cult, and I thought, *We should try him as a singer*. And we did.

SMITH: When we were 18, mod music was happening—Madness, the Specials. We had this band, a five-piece called Graduate. We wore the eyeliner and the suits. We signed our first record deal when we were 18, with no success other than in Spain, where Graduate had a number-one hit: "Elvis Should Play Ska." We toured Europe in two vans—we were humping the gear and everything. But Roland and I, we were interested in honing our recording skills, making good records. When we left Graduate, we were 19, and there were three pivotal records that really influenced the way we were going to move forward: Peter Gabriel's third album, *Remain in Light* by Talking Heads, and *Scary Monsters* by David Bowie. And Gary Numan was a big influence in the sense that you could actually make records without a band.

We did a demo of a couple of songs, "Suffer the Children" and "Pale Shelter," and started doing the rounds of record companies. Only one wanted us: a guy called Dave Bates, who signed us to Phonogram for a two-single deal. We released both songs as singles. Neither was a hit. The industry in those days—it's not like it is now, where if both flop, you're finished. Dave had heard all the other songs we'd written and convinced the record company to let us make an album. We did the majority of *The Hurting* at Abbey Road, but it took us a year to make, with many fights with the record company about their money we were spending.

Once we'd finished, we got to "Mad World." No one thinks it's quirky now, because it's part of history, but it was very quirky then. There was a plan on the part of the record company: We had to build up our credibility and become hip, and "Mad World" was picked to do that, to get us some press. No one ever expected it to become a hit. They believed there were other songs on the album that would be bigger, like "Pale Shelter" and "Change."

ORZABAL: "Mad World" was a shock. It was supposed to be the B-side of "Pale Shelter." But when I played it to Dave Bates, he said, "That's a single." Thank God.

I never particularly liked "Mad World" very much. But that's why I mucked about with it so much in the studio—programmed it up, spent a long time getting it into the state that it ended up in on *The Hurting.* I couldn't sing it. I still can't sing it—it just doesn't work. I did a quick double track and hated it. I said to Curt, "You sing it." And it was much, much better. He's got a soft resonance to his voice. "Mad World" is, I think, the best vocal he's ever done. It was recorded brilliantly, and it's just incredibly haunting.

In the early days, I'd just write the songs, and if I couldn't think of some lyrics, I'd ask Curt to do them. When we started off, it was very much Curt as frontman and me as studio boffin. It was like that until

"Shout." Because it was such a big hit, when we got to America, people saw us more as co-frontmen. Certainly, in the early days in England, Curt was the pop star, and I was in the background.

SMITH: The recording of "Mad World" took a while, but writing it took an afternoon. We were sitting on the second floor of the Bath flat that Roland used to live in, looking down on people dressed in suits going to work, coming back from work, thinking, *What a mundane life these people must live.* Although since then, I've longed for that.

ORZABAL: That's what kicked the lyric off. I wrote "Mad World" on an acoustic guitar, and I think one of the songs on the radio was "Girls on Film" by Duran Duran. I was thinking, *How did I get from the celebratory glam sound of Duran Duran to this really sort of introspective song?* Although we were trying to look like pop stars, our lyrics were far more melancholic and, some might say, depressing. The line "The

MIXTAPE: 5 More Sad, Sniveling Slices of Self-Pity
1. "There Is a Light That Never Goes Out," The Smiths   2. "10:15 Saturday Night," The Cure   3. "Heaven (I Want You)," Camouflage
4. "Victims," Culture Club   5. "Voices Carry," 'Til Tuesday

dreams in which I'm dying are the best I've ever had," that comes from Janov and his primal scream theory. I remember reading once that your most powerful dreams—in essence, the ones that are life-threatening dreams—are the ones that release the most tension. And I found that myself, when I was 18, 19. Certainly I had some pretty vivid dreams, and I always woke up feeling rather refreshed.

Janov's theories go along with the tabula rasa theory—that we're born, then life etches our character through experiences, good and bad. So that's what Curt and I believed at the time. We both felt that the child was sacred, especially the child that was suffering, hence the curled-up little child on the front of *The Hurting*.

I think that we couldn't really help but be a little deeper than what was going on [in music at the time]. Journalists didn't like it; we were called "po-faced." We had people like Gary Kemp saying, "They're too young to be writing about what they're writing." But [Kemp's and Spandau Ballet's] London scene, with all the glamour and glitz, was not something that allowed for that kind of introspection.

SMITH: After the [1983] release of *The Hurting*, we toured the world for a year. That widens your musical horizons and changes you. The only place I'd been out-

> **"We were 20 when that song came out, so we had a lot of screaming girls, but we also had a lot of shoegazers. Half the audience wouldn't make eye contact; the other half were trying to rip our shirts off."**

side England prior to us having a band was Spain: a holiday in Torremolinos, full of bad English people. We were 20 when that song came out, so we had a lot of screaming girls, but we also had a lot of shoegazers. Half the audience wouldn't make eye contact; the other half were trying to rip our shirts off.

The Hurting was big everywhere apart from America. When we came back to England, we felt like we wanted to make something bigger. We'd grown up a lot and weren't just concentrating on primal theory. The last thing we wanted to do was *The Hurting, Part 2*. We started listening to different stuff, thanks to our producer, Chris Hughes. We were introduced to people like Steely Dan and Lynyrd Skynyrd. We listened to a lot more Frank Zappa. But it wasn't a conscious decision to sound American. The only conscious part was that we never wanted to make the same album twice.

ORZABAL: Everything changed between *The Hurting* and *Songs from the Big Chair*. It was an incredibly difficult album to make. We were working every day, seven days a week, mainly at Abbey Road's Penthouse studio. We would be working until two in the morning. We would be doing vocals over and over and over again. These are the days before Auto-Tune. I remember Curt being in tears in the toilet. There was this new kind of ambition around the band. It was like, "No, you're not going to be introspective anymore." And there was a push for, as Dave calls it, the drive-time single.✱

SMITH: "Everybody Wants to Rule the World" was the last song we did. We needed one more track for the album. We said, "What would go really well with this album is a song that's lighter and has more of a shuffle beat that moves away from the intensity of the rest of the album."

ORZABAL: I had a song, which was originally called "Everybody Wants to Go to War"—not quite so catchy. It didn't fit with the fragile, insular music that we'd done before, so I was a little bit suspicious. But when we came to record it, we did a bit of improvising—myself, Chris [Hughes], and Curt—and it became so simple.

At the time, there were songs coming out—"Two Tribes," Frankie Goes to Hollywood; I think they did a cover of [Edwin Starr's] "War." It was the era of the Cold War, when it was pretty much at its peak, and everyone was worried about the nuclear threat and the possible nuclear exchange

---

✱ **DAVE BATES:** "Everybody Wants to Rule the World" was not originally on *Songs from the Big Chair*. We had "Mother's Talk," "Shout," "Head Over Heels," "I Believe." We were getting close to finishing the album, and it was already great, but we missed what I called the American drive-time single. I explained to them what the American drive-time single was—sun roof off, driving through the desert or driving home during rush hour with a tune coming out the radio and your arm stuck out the window—and Roland replied, "I know the kind of thing you need," and he played this riff. I went, "That's it! That's the one!" And he said, "Well, I ain't doing it." What Roland didn't realize was Dave Bascombe, the engineer, recorded him playing that riff. When Roland went home, [producer] Chris Hughes, [keyboard player] Ian Stanley, and Bascombe put a loop together using that riff; they put the drumbeat together and keyboards over it. When Roland came back, we said, "Check this out." We pressed the button, and there was the basis of a song. Roland could see the possibilities of it. In the end, "Everybody Wants to Rule the World" went on the album.

"Everybody Wants to Rule the World" was about me putting pressure on them to be the biggest group in the world, and the whole idea of world domination and them becoming huge. I believe "Shout" is also about me, because I used to shout a lot. I don't care. It's fine. I just wanted them to be incredibly successful.

between Russia and America. At the same time, the band was starting to become more global in our outlook.

The lyrics were written the day before. We were in Germany mixing the record, and I had to stay in the hotel room and quickly come up with the lyrics for Curt to sing the next day. The only line of any significance is "So glad they had to fade it." That was a reference to a conversation with Dave Bates in his A&R office. It was about the "Shout" edit for radio, that they didn't like playing anything eight minutes long, because they had to pay more money for it. We were arguing with him, and Dave decided to reduce the song by five seconds.

SMITH: Five seconds. You're really telling me it won't be a hit unless we take five seconds off? It was that stupid. We said, "Why can't the radio stations just fade it earlier?" It was a whole power play. That's what A&R men do: They feel like they have to stick their two cents in, otherwise they're not doing their jobs.

We became insular after *Songs from the Big Chair*. It was so huge everywhere, and when we were on the road, we were getting a bit cocky. We realized, in retrospect, the downside of having that much success, which is you're then surrounded by yes men who are making a living off you and coaxing you into doing it again without consideration for the music, just purely to capitalize on the money they've already made.

ORZABAL: Our manager went bankrupt during the *Seeds of Love* tour. We were no longer a unit. Also, the relationship with Bates became strained. And then there was a change of personalities at the U.S. record company [Mercury Records]. Our success in America has an awful lot to do with Dave Bates and his relationship with the U.S. company, and with a change of personnel, it was no longer there for *Seeds of Love*.

We spent too long touring *Songs from the Big Chair*. In hindsight, we should have done a short tour and pretty much gone straight back in the studio. I think we would've been happier. I think it would have been far more successful. There was such a loathing of going out into the world and doing the same songs over and over again. We never changed a set on the *Big Chair* tour.

Personally, I wanted to reinvent Tears for Fears after *Big Chair*, hence coming back with a completely different sound— *Seeds of Love* sounding like the Beatles. I had absolutely no sense—no commercial sense and no business sense—and no one was really arguing with me. So we drifted for four years making *Seeds of Love*. I think everyone expected *Seeds of Love* to be as big as *Big Chair*.

SMITH: During the making of *Seeds of Love*, I was going through a divorce from my first wife, who I'd been with for seven years. We were separated, and I was left with the realization that I got no support from anyone around me. It became very obvious their prime concern was to get me back in the studio to finish this album as opposed to my personal sanity. I had no normal life, and I got no support from anyone. Including Roland. The downside of a duo is you've only got each other to argue with, and we butted heads quite often.

ORZABAL: I'm not sure if I would agree. Moody silences were more the case than butting heads.

SMITH: We'd been in bands together since we were 13; now we were 27. The chemistry between Roland and myself had changed over the years. We were definitely kindred spirits, but bar our humor and our musical taste, we're now very different people. We needed a break from each other. I realized life is too damn short: *I can't do this anymore.* I had to leave the band.

ORZABAL: When you get to the age of 28, 29, lots of things change, especially as you start thinking about kids. I had a very close relationship with Curt, and it was almost as if that had to go before I had kids.

SMITH: I told Roland before we went on tour that I was leaving at the end, which in retrospect was a mistake. It didn't make for a particularly enjoyable tour, and we had nine months of it. Our relationship was horrible. We were hardly even talking. Front of the bus was Roland, back of the bus was me and the rest of the band. I did say goodbye when it was over, but it was an awkward one. The last show we did was Knebworth in 1990: big show in front of 120,000 people. We flew in a helicopter back to London, and literally the next day, me and my now-wife went to Antigua on holiday and never looked back.

THAT WAS THEN BUT THIS IS NOW

Tears for Fears are survived by their back catalog, particularly "Everybody Wants to Rule the World"—now a go-to track on classic rock and adult-contemporary radio as well as all-eighties stations—and "Mad World." The latter was rejuvenated by Gary Jules's mournful voice-and-piano rendition, which was recorded for Richard Kelly's 2001 *Donnie Darko.* The movie's leisurely gestating cult status helped the song become a hit in 2003, when it saw the year out as the U.K.'s most depressing Christmas number one

of all time. "Mad World" continues to be covered, most memorably by Adam Lambert on *American Idol* and most recently by Susan Boyle. The Jules version has become a definitive soundtrack staple; whenever a crime show needs a bleak song to accompany the aftermath of a killing spree, "Mad World" is never far away. In 2004, Smith and Orzabal reunited for an album of new material, *Everybody Loves a Happy Ending*, which has led to semi-regular Tears for Fears world tours and, according to Orzabal, another album of new material coming soon.

> **"I had no normal life, and I got no support from anyone. Including Roland. The downside of a duo is you've only got each other to argue with, and we butted heads quite often."**

SMITH: We didn't talk to each other for 10 years. I moved to L.A. Eventually his manager called me out of the blue and asked if I'd be interested in doing another record with Roland. My initial reaction was "No way! Life's too good!" But then I talked to my wife, and I thought, *That's kind of unfair. It's been 10 years. I don't even know what he's like anymore.* It's unfair to judge someone on the person you left 10 years before. I'm not the person I was 10 years before.

ORZABAL: Well, we didn't have a manager at the time. It was a case of Curt had sent me a fax—I had to do something for him that involved a notary in Bath, some sort of business thing—and he thanked me and said, "Now you have my number; call me at some point." So I called him. Once we spoke and I heard his mid-Atlantic accent, I realized that things had completely changed. We were a lot more grown up. But we've been back together for longer than we've been apart.

SMITH: We met up in Bath. It wasn't weird at all. I mean, it was weird for the first 10 minutes, but after that, it was fine. I was just about to have my first kid, and it became obvious that he'd mellowed considerably. In the first three albums there was definitely ego involved: You're vying for your position and making sure you have 50 percent of the say. But it's the balance of the two of us that brings out the sound that is Tears for Fears.

ORZABAL: When we started playing together [again], we played one show, and Curt said, "Right, let's switch positions on stage." I had

always been on the left, and he always on the right, and we switched over. It was like him saying, "This isn't going to be like it was."

Does the title *Everybody Loves a Happy Ending* refer to our reunion? Yes, because it was a happy ending. Of all of the albums we've made together, I'd say *Happy Ending* is the only one that we really enjoyed [making]. We just had a blast. We'd grown up, no pressure from a manager, no pressure from a record company, no expectations, and just getting back together purely for the sake of seeing what we can do and to enhance your history.

SMITH: "Mad World" and "Everybody Wants to Rule the World" have lasted because of the emotion. You see that in Gary Jules's version of "Mad World" and in Adam Lambert's. He sold it, and Gary did as well. It's one of those lyrics you can get your teeth into. Although sometimes those songs are hard for us to do live because we're not miserable adolescents anymore. We're cranky old men.

ORZABAL: In some ways, "Mad World" has been more successful as a cover version, especially the Michael Andrews–Gary Jules rerecord, which was never how I saw the song. I always saw it as an upbeat song. When they slowed it right down and made it heart-wrenching, the lyrics all of a sudden popped out at me, and I realized for the first time that they were pretty good lyrics. The first time I heard it, my friend had brought a copy of the *Donnie Darko* soundtrack from America and played it in the kitchen. My son at the time was six years old, and he started singing along to the lyrics: "Children waiting for the day they feel good / Happy birthday, happy birthday." And it was like, *Oh my God!* Suddenly I knew what it was like to be a father instead of a child. When Curt and I first started, we had embraced Arthur Janov and primal scream therapy; our idea was to get rich, get famous, and get therapy. Having both come from difficult childhoods, it was very easy for us to sing from what I now call the woe-is-me area. Parents were to blame, the establishment was to blame, children were innocent. Of course, I don't believe that now.

I went through primal therapy in my mid- to late 20s, and when my first child was born, he came out, and it was like everything that I had believed was clearly not true. Because here was someone with a soul, with a character, already, at day one. So I don't believe those things anymore. I don't believe the child is a victim. I think the character of the child is predetermined.

SMITH: We toured South America last year, two weeks in Brazil. Our audience was from 18 years old up to 45. The younger demographic, it's all people discovering *The Hurting* now and relating to it because it's what they're going through. It means the same to those 18-year-olds as it did to us when we wrote it. I hear people saying, "Music's not what it used to be," and I'm like, "Yeah, it is. Don't you remember back then?" The majority of the stuff we listened to sucked. What you take with you is the really good stuff. But there was a ton of shit in the eighties. For every one of us, there was a Flock of Seagulls. ✱

✱ **MIKE SCORE, A FLOCK OF SEAGULLS:** The one word that springs to mind is jealousy. Maybe they didn't see a band like us coming up beside them? Tears for Fears I don't think wrote great songs; they were helped along by a brilliant producer, Chris Hughes. He took the little things that they had and turned them into absolute works of art, little bits of genius. Kind of like the Beatles wrote incredible songs, but I don't think the Beatles would've been anything like they were if it hadn't been for George Martin. I'm not going to slag Tears for Fears. *Songs from the Big Chair* was one of the best albums I'd ever heard. *The Hurting* was good too, but it just showed you where they could be. The thing is, where did they go after that, you know? I think they went kind of downhill. Like I said, I don't want to slag them, because I really did enjoy their stuff, but Curt Smith may be living in a little fantasyland that Tears for Fears was something spectacular.

"IF YOU LEAVE"

ORCHESTRAL MANOEUVRES IN THE DARK

Were they the coolest band in Liverpool? Perhaps not. Did audiences adopt their dress sense? No. Did they surpass their peers in terms of pretension, artiness, and absurdity? Again, no. But Orchestral Manoeuvres in the Dark—who began life making chilly, remote, yearning music—ultimately racked up more hits than anyone else in their competitive city. Long before Andy McCluskey and Paul Humphreys found American success soundtracking *Pretty in Pink*'s climactic prom scene, they were European chart fixtures with songs about telegraphs, telescopes, and typewriters that sounded like songs about girls. Even when the duo caved and penned an actual love song, the blushing recipient was Joan of Arc.

JB: I don't believe there are Beatles people and Stones people and that the two are mutually exclusive. I do, however, think that there are OMD Phase 1 people and OMD Phase 2 people, and that those two parties have no truck with each other. OMD Phase 1 people came on board when they heard "Electricity" on John Peel. This was a song about electricity, but it was not bloodless or mock-robotic like so many records by bands who overidentified with the android lifestyle. OMD Phase 1 people were further rewarded with signature hits of the caliber of "Messages," "Red Frame White Light" and "Enola Gay." The Phase 1 constituency got a little uncomfortable when the rest of the U.K. muscled in on their territory and helped to make *Architecture and Morality* a blockbuster album. At least it was a weird blockbuster album. All the same, it was a 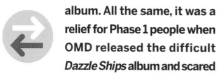 relief for Phase 1 people when OMD released the difficult *Dazzle Ships* album and scared off all the dilettantes. Unfortunately, it scared off so many people that it ignited OMD Phase 2. Which is where I made my excuses and left. OMD Phase 2 wrote solid commercial songs, but I could get solid commercial songs anywhere. Still, even though I was a Phase 1 person, I was also an eighties teen-movie person—an eighties teen-movie person who wrote an eighties teen-movie guidebook called *Pretty in Pink*. So, in the case of "If You Leave," which still packs an enormous amount of emotional impact ("I believed in you, I just didn't believe in me. I love you . . . Always"), I'm an honorary OMD Phase 2 person.

LM: By virtue of my being American, I'm a born OMD Phase 2 person. However, as much as I love "If You Leave"—I, too, am an eighties teen-movie person ("If you don't go to him now, I'm never going to take you to another prom again, you hear me?")—that song was merely the entry point for my OMD obsession. After seeing them open for Power Station, Thompson Twins, Psychedelic Furs, and Depeche Mode, not even McCluskey's onstage jerky jig could prevent me from delving deeper into their back catalog. That's when I became an honorary OMD Phase 1 person. *Architecture and Morality* is so original, so special, so sublime, that if there were no other new wave bands to speak of, the entire genre could still hang its hat solely on that record.

ANDY McCLUSKEY: We'd had "Tesla Girls" in a John Hughes movie [*Weird Science*]. He was a huge Anglophile music lover. He'd had *The Breakfast Club* and "Don't You (Forget About Me)," by Simple Minds, then he approached us and said, "I would like you to write a song for my new film [*Pretty in Pink*]." Our management and record company were over the moon. We went down to Paramount Studios and met him, Molly Ringwald, and Jon Cryer on set. They were kids, and they both said, "I love you." Because even though we hadn't had any hits in America, we had alternative and college radio station play. You could still be alternative in America and sell 100,000 records and be off everyone else's radar. In L.A., KROQ were playing us, but we weren't in the charts. Then John Hughes said, "Here's the script. Write me a song for my big prom-scene ending."

So we did. We came back armed with our two-inch tape of this song we'd written, "Goddess of Love." And John Hughes said, "There's a bit of a problem. Since I last saw you, we finished the movie and did some test screenings, and the teenage girls didn't like the ending." The original ending had Andie and Duckie dancing together. "Goddess of Love" lyrically bore no relationship to the new ending of the movie. He said, "Can you write me another one?" We were about to start a tour with Thompson Twins in two days, but we went into Larrabee Studios in Hollywood. We had nothing—we just knew how the movie ended. We knew that the tempo had to be 120 beats per minute, because they'd filmed the new ending with a song that was 120. Although, when I saw the final version, I thought, *Who the fuck edited this?*, because nobody's dancing to the beat.

We worked till four in the morning, and we banged onto a cassette the rough demo, then called a motorcycle to take it to Paramount. We got a phone call at half-past eight the next morning from our manager saying, "John's already in the office—he's heard the cassette and he loves it. Can you finish it off?" We'd just gone to sleep. It was our day off. But we went back to the studio and finished it; then, after three weeks on tour with the Thompson Twins, we came back and mixed it. That's how "If You Leave" was created—completely off the top of our heads in one day in Hollywood. It was bizarre that we managed to pull something like that out of the bag. If I knew how we did it, we would have done it more often.

And there we were flying in on a Pan Am jet from London to come to the premiere of *Pretty in Pink*, and who's on the plane with us? New Order! The guys from Joy Division who we supported during our first-ever gig eight years earlier in [Liverpool club] Eric's! We're all getting out of limos, off our faces, living the Hollywood lifestyle down the red carpet, all the famous people off the telly telling us how much they love our music. In eight years, the crazy journey we'd been on . . .

At the same time I got my first bass guitar, I had my Eureka! moment: I heard "Autobahn" by Kraftwerk on the radio in the summer of '75. That was when I went, *Now this is interesting. And it's different. I'm inspired! I might be able to do something like this!* Then I got their *Radio Activity* album. I bought the vinyl import, and Paul had a stereo because he'd built one. I only had my mother's mono Dansette. *Radio Activity* became our bible. I was 16, he was 15, and we were listening to this record, going, "They've used a Geiger counter, and chopped-up recordings of people speaking, interfering radio noises. We can do that!"

Paul knew a bit about electronics. He used to make things that made noises that didn't even have keyboards attached so we couldn't play melodies. It was just noises and ambient weirdness. Finally we got a cheap Vox Jaguar keyboard and a Selmer Pianotron—I've only ever seen one—from a combination of part-time jobs and a lot of dole money. We wrote songs for almost three years in Paul's mother's back room on Saturday afternoons when she was at work. Our friends thought they were shit. It was

just a little art project of weirdness inspired by German music. We had to invent our own way of doing things that wasn't necessarily conventional. In hindsight, that is what led to people having to invent a way of songwriting that ended up being much more creative than just sitting at a computer trying to copy someone else.

Paul and I had thought we were the only people in England listening to Kraftwerk, Neu!, some other German bands—all the stuff we'd been listening to since 1975. It turns out we weren't. We were in Eric's in 1978, and the DJ played "Warm Leatherette," and we went, "Holy shit! Somebody's been listening to what we've been listening to, and they've made a record, and it sounds great!" We went to have a chat with Roger [Eagle] and Pete [Fulwell], who ran the place. We said, "Hi, we're Andy and Paul. For years we've been writing these songs. . . . Could we play your club with just us and a tape recorder?" And they said, "Sure. We'll book you in for a Thursday night in October." If Eric's hadn't existed, we would never have thought of starting Orchestral Manoeuvres in the Dark.

There was a conscious thing going on. Young people of an artistic nature who gravitated toward the idea of making music as their chosen art form wanted to establish the fact that they were doing something different. Whether you were influenced by punk or art or electronic music, there was this absolute determination you were going to do something different. The name of your band was part of that. We consciously chose a preposterous name. We were only going to do one concert, and because it was a mad idea—a new wave club, two guys, one playing upside-down bass, keyboards, tape recorder—we thought, *We'll give ourselves a weird name so that people will know we're not rock or punk.* My bedroom wall was my notebook, much to my mother's chagrin. There were song titles and poems and all sorts of stuff on there. So we consulted the wall and came up with the most preposterous title we could think of. It was my idea. "Orchestral Manoeuvres in the Dark" was the title of a song we never wrote. There were a lot of other things on that wall, and it certainly could have been very different, because right underneath "Orchestral Manoeuvres in the Dark" was "Margaret Thatcher's Afterbirth."

We were not cool. Paul and I were very much the outsiders. Our hair was longer than most people's in Liverpool. We were from the other side of the river and still lived with our parents; we didn't live in bedsits. We didn't know all the cool people. The Bunnymen and the Teardrops signed to Zoo Records, and they didn't want to sign us. [Zoo Records boss] Dave Balfe to this day says it was the worst mistake he ever made.

> "We were not cool. Paul and I were very much the outsiders. Our hair was longer than most people's in Liverpool. We were from the other side of the river and still lived with our parents."

So we did our one gig at Eric's supporting another band. There were 30 people there, and most of them were our friends and family, and even then the response was [slow hand clap]. Afterwards, Roger and Pete said, "That was interesting. Would you like to do another gig, because the guys that you supported tonight have come over from our friend's place in Manchester." We'd just supported Joy Division. So even though we'd only planned on doing the one gig, we decided to make it two. We went to Manchester and played at the Russell Club, which was called the Factory that night. We supported Cabaret Voltaire and met Tony Wilson, Alan Erasmus, and Peter Saville. We cheekily sent Tony a cassette with two tracks, "Electricity" and "Almost," the next week because he used to present *Granada Reports* and sometimes they had bands on. We said, "Hey, we met you last week. Could we get on the telly?" Cheeky bastards. He was like, "We've come to the end of the season, but we're starting a record label called Factory. Do you want to make a record?" So we went from one gig to a second gig to "Do you want to make a record?"

I didn't know this at the time, but I later found out he left our cassette in his car, and it was his then-wife Lindsay who wanted to know what was on it. He said, "Some fellows from Liverpool. Two Scouse scallywags pretending to be Kraftwerk." She thought it was great and told him to listen to it again. By the time he finally called us, his wife and Peter Saville had talked to him, and he'd gone from not liking it to saying, "You guys

"Were we arrogant? Yeah, we probably were. We were arrogant in the sense that we believed in our art, and we were pleasantly surprised that we were selling lots of it."

are the future of pop music." To which we replied, "Fuck off, we're experimental. Don't call us pop."

Tony said, "We'll do a record. It will basically be your demo, and I'll send it to all the major labels." They made 5,000 copies of "Electricity." We went round to 85 Palatine Road, which was their office—i.e., Alan Erasmus's flat—and we took them all out of the white sleeves and put them all in the black thermograph sleeves that Peter Saville designed. Every single one was handbagged by myself, Paul Humphreys, or our then manager. The only person to play it was John Peel, who played it every night on the week it was released, and 5,000 sold out in a week. One of them landed on the desk of a lady called Carol Wilson, who had just started a label called Dindisc, which was part of Virgin. She contacted us, and we didn't have any more gigs at the time, so she came up to Liverpool. She stayed in Paul's mother's back room, which was appropriate because that's where all the songs were written. She sat on the sofa, and we played her all of our six songs. About three weeks later, we were playing in Blackpool on a Factory night with Joy Division and A Certain Ratio. She turned up late while we were loading our gear into the van, and she said, "Read this on the way home." So we got in the van and got out the torch…and it's a seven-album contract. This was eight months after we'd played our one-off gig.

We were absolutely adamant that we were going to make music, but we were going to avoid what we considered rock clichés. We were not going to write "I love you" or "You love me." If we were going to write relationship songs, they were going to be so shrouded in metaphor as to be almost unfathomable. Obviously, "Electricity" was inspired by Kraftwerk's "Radioactivity," and when I finally confessed to Kraftwerk, they all went, "Ja, ve know." We could only get inspired enough to write music if it was inspiring to us conceptually. It's hard to imagine in this day and age of *X-Factor* and banjo music being the future that some-body would insist on writing songs about airplanes and oil refineries and telephone boxes. This is what we wanted to write about. We wouldn't allow our drummer to use cymbals because they were rock clichés. I tortured myself for months that I'd finally conceded to use the word "love" on our third album, and I just couldn't find another monosyllabic word to replace it.

So "Joan of Arc" became the first song I used the word "love" on. Carol Wilson used to say to us, "Can you tell me whether you want to be ABBA or Stockhausen?" We were like, "Both."

The first album was a load of songs that we wrote from the ages of 16 to 19 that our friends thought were crap and that went gold and had one hit off it, "Messages." Then we have an album [*Organisation*, 1980] that also goes gold, and we have a song that sells 5 million around the world ["Enola Gay"]. The next album [*Architecture and Morality* 1981] sold 3 million. So we just thought, *This is incredible—we have the Midas touch. We do exactly what we want to do by our own rules and nobody at the record company ever second-guesses us.*

Were we arrogant? Yeah, we probably were. We were arrogant in the sense that we believed in our art, and we were pleasantly surprised that we were selling lots of it. Having said that, by this time we'd sold 15 million singles and 4 million albums, and I was still living in the box [storage] room of

MIXTAPE: 5 More John Hughes Soundtrack Songs 1. "Oh Yeah," Yello (*Ferris Bueller's Day Off*) 2. "Eighties," Killing Joke (*Weird Science*) 3. "If You Were Here," Thompson Twins (*Sixteen Candles*) 4. "I Go Crazy," Flesh for Lulu (*Some Kind of Wonderful*) 5. "Catch My Fall," Billy Idol (*Some Kind of Wonderful*)

my mother's house, seven feet by six feet, with all the platinum albums on the wall. I was like, "You know that seven-album deal we signed? Was it really shit?" It was, actually. It was a better deal than some of the bands in the seventies signed, but "Enola Gay" sold 5 million. Now, for argument's sake, let's say each one cost a pound. We were on a 6 percent royalty, so we got six pence. Now, most of them sold in Europe, so, because Virgin were licensing us in Europe, we were on a two-thirds deal, so we had four pence. The producer, Mike Howlett, who just helped us get a nice sound, was on three points, so he got three pence, and we were left with one—out of which we had to pay the recording costs and all of the video costs and any advances we'd had. So that's why I was still living in the box room at my parents' house, driving a second-hand car that had mushrooms growing in the footwell because it was damp.

We actually weren't that bothered by it, because we hadn't gotten into it for the money. This was our art project, and it's why we confidently set out on the ship Dazzle, thinking, "Well, we started with synth garage-punk, we then went kind of gothic and wrote songs about airplanes and atom bombs, then we went all religious with choral music and Edinburgh Tattoo drums. Every time we decide to do something different, we sell even more records." Then somebody at the record company made the catastrophic mistake of saying, "If you just make *Architecture and Morality 2*, you're going to be the next Genesis." Wrong. Thing. To. Say! We went, "Right, we're going in completely the opposite direction." We decided . . . well, when I say "we," . . . I—'cause it took Paul about 25 years to forgive me for *Dazzle Ships*✳—I decided we were going to make lots of recordings of politics and shortwave radios and cold war Radio Prague call signs, and this time, for whatever reason, we left it kind of stripped. It was bare-bones, and it wasn't sugar-coated with the melodies and the choirs. We picked the song "Genetic Engineering" for a single, which probably did freak people out. We went from 3 million sales to 300,000. We lost 90 percent of our audience between two albums.

Consciously or unconsciously, we dialed ourselves back a lot. By this time, we were old men of 24. Paul was married, and we both had houses, and it was our job. We still thought we were going to try and make art, but I think we got a little more

---

✳ **PAUL HUMPHREYS:** I definitely forgive him. I love *Dazzle Ships*. It was a spectacularly successful album in its complete commercial failure. We had to do that album in order to advance ourselves musically. We pushed our boundaries, and even though we reeled ourselves in from those boundaries, we had to go through that process.

conventional in our songwriting. It was the beginning of us following other people's rules in order to sell records.

To a lot of people in America who just have a passing musical interest, "If You Leave" is our only hit. We're like a one-hit wonder. To a lot of people in Europe, it was anathema. They hated it: "Our wonderful alternative electro band has sold out. They've got this cheesy song about teen-age relationships in a teenage movie in Hollywood." It wasn't a hit in most of Europe. It didn't even make the Top 50 in the U.K. American audiences cannot contemplate the fact that when we play Europe, we usually don't even play "If You Leave." Can you imagine us playing in America if we didn't play it? We'd be shot.

THAT WAS THEN *BUT THIS IS NOW*

Paul Humphreys left the group in 1989. Andy McCluskey continued to lead OMD with varying degrees of success until walking away in 1996. He dabbled in manufactured pop, assembling the Liverpudlian girl trio Atomic Kitten and penning their biggest hit, "Whole Again." McCluskey and Humphreys reunited in 2006. They have released two albums, 2010's *History of Modern* and 2013's *English Electric*, and continue to tour the world.

McCLUSKEY: In America, there are three albums they know: our *Best Of,* so at least half a million of them caught up with all of the European hits; *Crush*; and *The Pacific Age*. Now, *The Pacific Age* is our musical nadir. That was the one where we were writing songs because we had to make an album. We were going round and round America in buses for months on end, and the record company said, "It would be great if we had a new album for Christmas." We were on the treadmill. We were going back to an empty well. We were exactly the sort of band we promised we never would be. There were no concepts, no weird ideas, no "Enola Gay" and oil refinery songs and Catholic saints. I was dragging out lyrics that I would have been appalled by 10 years earlier. And yet Americans love *The Pacific Age.* It was almost like we traded our European success for American success. But all of the success we put into breaking America effectively broke us. By the end of the eighties, we just imploded.

Paul and I were always different guys—personally, socially, emotionally, musically—yet we complemented each other. But we had spent 10 years together, and we were sick of each other. The whole vibe had atrophied. We knew that we weren't making good-enough music, but our solutions were different. It just fell apart. The band stopped, and for six months that was it. Then Paul and [drummer] Malcolm Holmes and [keyboard player] Martin Cooper came back to me and said, "There is value in the name OMD. There's three of us and one of you, and we want to continue." I was horrified. I really didn't like what they were doing musically; admittedly, they didn't like what I was doing, either. I went to Virgin Records, and they said, "We own the rights to these records under the name OMD, and we think of you as the frontman. So if there's going to be either/or, how about you be OMD?" For Paul, in particular, that was hard, because people who'd signed him when he was 19 turned round and said to him, "We choose Andy, not you." That must have been galling in the extreme. ✷✷

I released the *Sugar Tax* album in 1991. That sold close to 300,000—as many as *Architecture and Morality*—and almost reestablished us in America. And then I unlearned my own lesson. I disappeared up my own backside again, trying to make an album too quickly. It was starting to be a struggle, because it was the mid-'90s: grunge, Britpop. We could get our heads around the fact that fashion had changed, that electronic music that was supposed to be the future was now the past; what we didn't get was that we were now in the postmodern era where the future sounded like 1969. I was banging my head against a brick wall, so I stopped.

Then we got into the new millennium, and there was a new generation of people who were bored with the resurgence of rock clichés. They rediscovered electronic music, and people started talking to us. Agents started saying, "Hey, would you like to do a tour? I reckon you could sell out." I'd gone grudgingly—I didn't want to retire in 1996. It was like a soccer player who'd got to the age of 36 and had to hang up the boots and get off the field. Then suddenly, at the age of 46, people were like, "Hey, get your boots back on! You can play again!" And I'm like, "Really? On my own team? With the same guys?"

We booked some gigs across Europe in 2007, and they all sold out, so we did 40 more, and then the problem set in. Being

---

✷✷ PAUL HUMPHREYS: We had no money; we didn't have any ideas. I just said, at the end of the eighties, "Look, I'm exhausted. It's not working, I'm not so happy with the records we're making. Let's take three years off." Which was what I wanted to do. But the record company and management were all horrified because they're making money, and they wouldn't let us do it. There were a lot of divisive people around, and they threw a wedge between me and Andy. They said, "If Paul's not going to do it then, Andy, you should continue with the band." And I said, "Andy, if you want to do that, then you do it. I'm stopping." And that's how it happened. Obviously, Virgin were happier to take OMD with Andy as the frontman because it was a lot easier. He was a more recognizable face, which was always fine with me. That's the way it works with bands and frontmen.

OMD and starting out as a conceptual band, we thought, *Is this it? Have we become a tribute band to ourselves? Are we just going to play the old stuff?* Because some of our contemporaries, their management tell them they need to release a new record because they need a name for their new tour, they can't just play the hits again. I'll mention no names, but there are a lot of bands who make records who shouldn't be allowed to—they don't have anything left to say, they're just addicted to the lifestyle, and they can't stop. We promised ourselves we wouldn't do that. So, once again, we had to be

conceited enough to believe that we actually had something to say. Paul and I agreed that we really needed to unlearn the previous 30 years since *Dazzle Ships* and the more conventional songwriting that we'd grown into and go back to songs that didn't have a chorus. We started with a sample of Voyager 1 going through Jupiter and three minutes of synths and me singing about the contrast between perfect clarity and machinery and how imperfect the world is. And then the big drums and the choir come in, and we fade out. That's how we used to write songs, and that's what we used to write songs about.

NO group bore the brunt of bad timing more than Ultravox. In 1977, they were marketed as a punk band, but they were not really a punk band. As much as singer John Foxx sneered and postured, he was a little more cultured and fey than he let on. Plus, they had a violinist! By the time Ultravox released their all-electronic third album, 1978's *Systems of Romance*, the hearts and minds of the U.K. had already been captured by a plethora of synth acts from the North of England who made Ultravox, the quality of their music notwithstanding, seem like yesterday's men. Frustrated, John Foxx departed the group for a semi-successful solo career. Then Ultravox recruited Midge Ure as their new frontman and gave it one last shot. The highly adaptable Ure brought emotion and melodrama to a band lacking in both. If rebooting the Human League brought out their inner ABBA, adding Ure to Ultravox transformed them into something akin to a computer-age Walker Brothers.

"VIENNA"

ULTRAVOX

JB: Midge Ure is the Zelig of British pop. Back in the post-glam seventies, when the Bay City Rollers were in the ascendant, young Glaswegian Ure capitalized on the brief mania for groups of unthreatening Scottish boys with his teenybop band Slik. Signed by the Rollers' producers, Slik dressed like extras in *Happy Days* and had hits with songs that sounded like Gregorian chants mixed with drunken pub sing-alongs. Fate knocked on Ure's door when Malcolm McLaren approached him on the streets of Glasgow about becoming the frontman for an embryonic version of the Sex Pistols. He demurred, but when the insipid Scottish pop bubble burst,

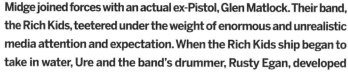 Midge joined forces with an actual ex-Pistol, Glen Matlock. Their band, the Rich Kids, teetered under the weight of enormous and unrealistic media attention and expectation. When the Rich Kids ship began to take in water, Ure and the band's drummer, Rusty Egan, developed an interest in electronic dance music, which led to the formation of Visage. He slotted in a brief stint as Thin Lizzy's live guitarist before becoming the singer of Ultravox—which is the one that stuck. Elsewhere in these pages, I mention telling Human League founder Martyn Ware that his song "Being Boiled" reminded me of "Sympathy for the Devil." When I spoke to Midge Ure, I compared "Vienna" to "A Whiter Shade of Pale." He bought the comparison more than Ware did. Both songs fly in the face of what a hit record is supposed to sound like. Both create their own sense of space and time. Both are disasters to sing at karaoke ("mumblemumblemumble… Pizzicato strings!"). Both are ridiculous. And yet, both songs have lasted a lifetime. And, for a shorter time, "Vienna" gave Midge Ure a steady job.

LM: While many women my age spend endless hours on Facebook posting shirtless photos of Channing Tatum, my idea of the perfect man is Midge Ure. He's romantic and woman-worshipping (see his solo singles "If I Was" and "That Certain Smile"), an unabashed idealist ("Dear God," "Answers to Nothing"); he's cause-minded and humanitarian ("Do They Know It's Christmas?"). Never mind his diminutive stature and the fact that he no longer has hair: Midge owns me the second he begins to serenade me. When he sings, he may as well be ripping his heart from his chest and offering it to you on bended knee. And I'll take it!

MIDGE URE: Slik were about to disappear. We were out scouting for a new record deal and, of course, it wasn't going to happen. I was incredibly fortunate that Glen Matlock, the ex–Sex Pistol, had been talking to Caroline Coon, a writer for *Melody Maker*, who had given Slik a nice bit of coverage, and she suggested that I was the elusive fourth member, the frontman for his group, the Rich Kids.

The band was bigger before they were a band than when they were a band. They were getting front covers even before I joined. I remember reading about them. They were widely anticipated as the saviors of British rock and roll. Glen was incredibly brave asking me to join because it was like tying your hands and your feet and sticking your neck in the noose at the same time because of my background. It stunted the growth of the band instantly. People would look at the covers of magazines and think, *What's this twat doing in a band with a Pistol?* The moment I walked in it put the band back quite considerably, even with Mick Ronson producing the album. Glen was a great songwriter and the sound the band made was pretty vibrant, but it just fell on stony ground. The press called it power pop, which is a dreadful, dreadful term.

[Rich Kids drummer] Rusty Egan was DJing in a little pub called Billy's and he played this stuff he'd been listening to com-ing out of Belgium, Germany, and France—this electronic stuff. I was so excited by the sounds coming out of the speakers that I went out and bought a synthesizer, and that synthesizer well and truly split the band down the middle. I saw the Rich Kids and this synthesizer as a bubbling cauldron: modern technology incorporating all the traditional rock instrumenta-tion. You merge them together and come out with this really powerful sound. Glenn and [guitarist] Steve New just absolutely hated it. When I joined Ultravox, that was the aim, that was the noise I was hearing in my head.

Ultravox, as they were, were still in exis-tence. I saw them go off to America to start their second tour and come back a broken band. John Foxx had quit. Robin Simon had met some girl in America and stayed there. I was putting the finishing touches on the Visage project when Rusty Egan said to Billy Currie, "The guy who should be in Ultravox is standing right here." And that was it: I was a committed member of the band. Although nobody was particularly interested, because they had been and gone by that time. They'd just come off of *Systems of Romance*, which I loved, and then were dropped by the record company. It's very demoralizing, that kind of scenario. They were still incredibly capable guys. They were just a bit lost. Billy was a bit miffed with the direction Dennis [Leigh,

John Foxx's God-given name] was pushing the band in, and Billy didn't feel like he was getting his way, although his talents are all over those records.

The moment we got into the rehearsal room and started making a noise, we turned into a rock band, and I'm not saying that to blow my own trumpet. Something happened, something gelled between the electronics that they had and the guitar playing that I brought to it, and this thing just became incredibly powerful. It went from being a bit lost and despondent to incredibly excited and very, very vibrant.

"Vienna" is pure fantasy. I'd never been there. I didn't know an awful lot about it other than the fact that it had, in its day, been a cultural center. It just seemed to me to be a fairly beautiful, fantastic place to write about, steeped in this mid-European mysticism, this ancient, crumbling facade.

The idea is very basic: Boy meets girl. You're there, and you feel a certain way when you're there, and you vow this wonderful feeling will carry on. But when you come back to your cold, gray miserable life, it just disappears. Like all holidays, you come back home, and it's gone. It was that wrapped up in Billy's fabulous melodies and chord structures.

It started with an idea. I was out to dinner with my old Rich Kids manager and his wife, who was a bit pissed [inebriated].

She said, "You know what you need to do? You need to write a song like that 'Vienna.'" And I was like, "What song 'Vienna'?" She said, "You know, that Fleetwood Mac song: Vieennnnna." She was singing "Rhiannon."

The image of Vienna—the name, the title, singing about the city—that sparked the whole thing. I went into the rehearsal room with Billy later on, and I said, "I've got this thing that I keep singing over and over in my head, "This means nothing to me / Oh, Vienna." And that was the start it. "Vienna" is one classic example of all four members of the band contributing something that's unique to them. "Vienna" wouldn't be "Vienna" without the drumbeat, Warren [Cann] making those ca-cow noises with his syndrums. It wouldn't be "Vienna" without Chris [Cross]'s echoey bass thing, that dug-dugga-dugga. It's certainly not "Vienna" without Billy's piano part and viola solo. And my contribution is the vocal melody and the lyrics. I can't say that every song we ever did together came equally that way, but that one certainly did.

Naïveté is a wonderful, wonderful thing. When you're young, you're doing what you absolutely feel is right. You think you can do anything. The reality is that "Vienna" is an extralong, atmospheric, empty-sounding electronic ballad that speeds up in the middle with a viola solo—and it could have gone absolutely nowhere. Luck played a huge part. The record company saw it as a hit…if we edited it. This was still the time of the three-minute single. We'd already released "Sleepwalk" [highest U.K. chart position: 29] and "Passing Strangers" [highest U.K. chart position: 57]. We were playing Hammersmith Odeon, and the record company were there. The moment we played "Vienna," which was an album track, the place erupted. So there were three-and-half thousand people proving the record company wrong. I'll give Chris Wright, the head of the record company, his due: We'd been arguing about the edit for six months, and he came up to us and said, "Put it out the way it is."

It was an instant hit. It came out in January [1981]. The charts freeze over the Christmas period, so people were desperate to hear something new because they've had enough of Christmas songs. "Vienna" came out and just captured people's imaginations. Professional songwriters would love to know what the right combination is, what's the combination that makes something quality and interesting to a very wide spectrum of people. I think that's what happened here.

"Vienna" was kept off the number-one spot for a couple of weeks by the comedy record, the Joe Dolce thing [the immortal "Shaddup You Face"]. Only in Britain would people buy tripe like that. Then, of course, John Lennon was shot, and ["(Just Like) Starting Over"] went straight to number one. We sat at number two for five weeks. But in the end, "Vienna" outsold both of them.

It doesn't take a genius to look out at an audience and figure out that it's the "Whiter Shade of Pale" of our career. It's something that captures people's imaginations. It still gets played throughout the world today. It still sounds as fresh as it did when we made it. It hasn't really dated. It's got its own kind of peculiar time, kind of like *Blade Runner*— you don't know what century it's set in. It's kind of classical, it's kind of electronic, it's kind of atmospheric. It's just this mishmash of ideas, but it's all Ultravox.

MIXTAPE: 5 More Songs About Cities 1. "Moskow Disco," Telex 2. "Drowning in Berlin," The Mobiles 3. "The Paris Match," Style Council 4. "Get Out of London," Intaferon 5. "Walking in L.A.," Missing Persons

THAT WAS THEN
BUT THIS IS NOW

Midge Ure—sorry, Midge Ure OBE—co-wrote and produced the Band Aid single "Do They Know It's Christmas?" (see page 310) and helped organize the Live Aid concert. His plaintive 1985 solo single "If I Was" went to number one in the U.K. and his album *The Gift* was a number two. Ultravox disbanded in 1987. Ure continued to release solo records with decreasing impact. He got back into the world leader–shaming business when he and Bob Geldof put together 2005's Live 8 concerts. Ultravox re-formed in 2008 and have been sporadically touring and recording since.

URE: I'd been extremely reluctant to reunite in the past. It was a bit like getting back together with your ex from 30 years ago. It happened because somebody said to us, "It's 30 years since you wrote 'Vienna'—don't you think you should go out and celebrate all the work you made together?" And, weirdly, we all felt that it would be fun. It would be interesting to go out one more time and play all those songs. We went back and looked at them and we, not re-created, but we recaptured the essence of what it was we did and that led to the inevitable new album [*Brilliant*, 2012].

I think we probably are an electronic Spinal Tap. There's no escaping that. There's always the danger of becoming a standard caricature of yourselves. People saw Ultravox as a bunch of po-faced scientists as opposed to a bunch of musicians, but we do have a very good sense of humor.

[The eighties] was a different planet. It was a planet where people cared about music. Music was a be-all and end-all to young people. It was our lifeblood. You waited for the next album you were into, you saved up your pennies, and you waved it around proudly when you bought it, and you played it to death. That world doesn't exist anymore. There's only a few old-timers and Luddites who do that these days. There are kids walking around with 20,000 songs on their phones, and they haven't got a clue what any of them are called because they've been downloaded—they've just been passed from person to person. Everyone can afford the same equipment, but not everyone can write a song and make an interesting piece of music. Sometimes when you're limited to very basic tools, you have to be creative; you have to invent rather than just go to a file in your computer and listen to 2,000 bass drum sounds. You have to create your own with your Minimoog and start bouncing it around with echoes to make a pattern. That's how we used to do things in the old days.

"ORIGINAL SIN"

Like their British counterparts, Australia's INXS were as influenced by funk as by punk. Unlike their British counterparts, they weren't afraid of getting their hands dirty. INXS were sweaty, dirty, and sensual, and most of that sweat, dirt, and sensuality emanated from their snake-hipped lead singer. Without Michael Hutchence, INXS would have been a hardworking traditional Australian rock band. Without INXS, Michael Hutchence would have been a tousled, enigmatic singer who fancied himself a bit of an artiste. Together, they were a potent mixture of muscle and mystery, a band of brothers that came from a land Down Under to dish out hit after international hit for more than a decade.

LM: Watching Michael Hutchence was my sexual awakening. He was a pockmarked ruffian with greasy hair, but I couldn't deny the fire he lit inside me as I took in my first INXS concert at Manhattan's Felt Forum. Yet for all that rock-god smolder and swagger, Hutchence had the soul of a poet. My favorite INXS songs reveal a Romeo who yearns for lasting love and a life partner. Some say that this may have been his undoing. Hutchence's death was the first time I'd lost one of my idols.

The day after, I was in Prague, so I thought it apt to visit the Charles Bridge, the setting for the "Never Tear Us Apart" video. There were already a few dozen fans there. That's when I realized he was our generation's Jim Morrison. While interviewing Andrew and Tim Farriss for this chapter, I could tell that they were still dealing with the loss 16 years later. But they weren't melancholy conversations, because we were talking about the part of Hutchence that will never die: his songs.

JB: I started wondering about who INXS's closest modern equivalent might be. A funky rock band proficient at writing pop songs led by a spotlight-hogging singer who makes the ladies itch and drool. The only band anywhere in the vicinity of that description would be Maroon 5. And Maroon 5 don't even measure up to INXS's shoelaces. I listen to "Devil Inside," "What You Need," and "Never Tell Us Apart," and I think, *Boy, could we use a band like that today.*

ANDREW FARRISS: "Original Sin" was a song that Michael and I wrote. Michael had written a lyric about watching white and black kids playing in a schoolyard, and we both knew we didn't want it to be some gratuitous holding-hands, love-song thing. We wanted a song that was funky, which is part of the reason we'd approached Nile Rodgers.

TIM FARRISS: Nile loved the funk in the band, and the fact that we were obviously big fans of his had a lot to do with [his wanting to work with us]. Nile was my hero—that is, Nile Rodgers the producer. I'd heard his stuff with Diana Ross and Michael Jackson, and I was like, "It's the same guitar player. Who is that guy?" Then it blew me away when Bowie used him, and Madonna. I used to drive the rest of the band crazy playing his solo album [1983's *Adventures in the*

Land of the Good Groove] on the tour bus. In fact, we used to sing one of the songs, "Yum-Yum," right before we went onstage every night: "Poontang, poontang, where you want it / Slept all night with my hand on it / Give me some of that yum yum / Before I sleep tonight."

NILE RODGERS: I was in Canada going to check out U2, and INXS were opening. I had never heard a bass drum sound like the bass drum in INXS. I was like "Wow, who is this guy?" I went to their dressing room, and they were huge Nile Rodgers fans. They started singing a song from my solo album in four-part harmony! I was like, "Hey, guys, you want to work together?"

ANDREW FARRISS: [Having Rodgers produce "Original Sin"] really was a big deal, a defining moment. We knew exactly the importance of what that meant, and we put everything we could think of into that recording. We had never been treated with that kind of respect by that level of musician and producer. He was mixing funk up with jazz and blues. In 1983 these guys were the guys—they were top-line, front-end, on-the-radio-all-the-time people and in the consciousness of music, fashion, everything right-there-and-then. So we were no longer skirting the edges of the scene, we were in it. We couldn't believe he'd want to

work with a bunch of young people from Australia. At first people thought we were British because we had funny accents. People would say to us, "Are you guys from Austria?" And then you had Paul Hogan throwing a shrimp on the barbie . . . The funny thing is, we don't call it "shrimp," we call them "prawns."

TIM FARRISS: We were the first young white band to use Nile. I remember seeing John Taylor, and he was saying how much [Duran Duran] would love to work with him: "You used Nile Rodgers, eh? How was he?" I was like, "Awesome, man, but I don't think he likes bass players." I was trying to turn him off to the idea. Sure enough, they ended up using him. That trick didn't work.

ANDREW FARRISS: When we tracked "Original Sin" in the Power Station [in New York City], I remember Kirk [Pengilly, saxophone], Jon [Farriss, drums], and Michael had done some backing vocals, and Nile said, "Yeah, that's pretty cool, but you know what? I think we need a different kind of voice on one section of this." The next minute, Daryl Hall walks through the door, and we're like, "Daryl Hall's in the room?!"

RODGERS: When I walked into the studio, they were intimidated. I said, "I can't make a record with people who are in awe of me." They had already done a vocal arrangement of one of my songs that was a flop. That's some kind of weird hero worship. I picked up the guitar and said, "We're gonna rehearse the song." Then I went out and secretly told the engineer to record the rehearsal. This is a true story: "Original Sin" is a one-take record. After we finished rehearsing, I said, "We're done." They said, "What do you mean?" I was like, "That's it, that's the take."

ANDREW FARRISS: The song caused some difficulty for us—not so much everywhere else in the world, mainly in North America. It was virtually banned from U.S. radio, and the record company freaked out. We'd had quite a lot of success with the first two singles, "The One Thing" and "Don't Change." Then, when we pulled "Original Sin" out, they were like, "You're going to do that?" It just wasn't the kind of song that people would have had on the radio at that particular time. We loved the song. Michael was very proud of his lyrics. We sought our own way of putting an idea of love and peace and humanity into a song. It's not that the lyrics were crazy, but I think once you get close to identifying something or talking about a subject, it's like the elephant in the room: No one wants to get into it, so you just don't go there.

RODGERS: Michael always thanked me, because I'm the one who changed the lyrics to "Original Sin." The lyrics were not [originally] "Dream on black boy / Dream on white girl." They had written "Dream on white boy, dream on white girl, wake up to a brand new day / Dream on black boy, black girl . . ." I felt bad, like I was superimposing too much of my own life. I was raised by interracial parents, and I've always seen the conflict of interracial relationships. I was like, "Guys, wait a minute. If we talk about original sin, we can make this even more taboo by making it an interracial couple?" What's really funny is, I get Daryl Hall to sing, and his manager, who was Tommy Mottola at the time, called me up and said, "Nile, are you trying to get my guy killed? What do you mean by all this 'Dream on black boy, white girl' stuff?" I said, "Well, you know, Tommy, it's a better song like that."

ANDREW FARRISS: "Original Sin" was the most important song at the early part of our career. It helped us to define what we wanted to do musically. We took it much further with [producer] Chris Thomas. We really developed that funk rock. We were always experimenting and chopping and changing with our big melting pot of music influences. It's not that we stopped doing that—it's just that we found something we thought was a magic formula, and it worked.

TIM FARRISS: Michael and Andrew were a great team. They were like chalk and cheese as people, and that is important, because you'd have yin and yang in the room. Andrew would be pensive and withdrawn and very thoughtful, deep-thinking, whereas Michael was more vivacious and very spontaneous. They started out as close friends. Michael was quite the shy person. I think that some people do that because then they're the dark horse or the quiet mouse that roared. Once fame and fortune became involved, Michael would prefer to be sitting at the runway at an Yves Saint Laurent thing surrounded by models, where Andrew would rather be at home on his farm putting in fence posts.

ANDREW FARRISS: Michael and I were unlikely friends. We met in a schoolyard [in Sydney]. He came from Hong Kong, and he didn't know anybody. I think he was feeling very intimidated, and I helped him through that. I was interested in sports, which Michael was never really interested in. He liked motocross and dirt bikes, and poetry, Hermann Hesse and *Siddhartha*. We didn't talk about music much at all when we first met. Then he went to live in Los Angeles for a while. When he came back to Sydney, I realized that his experiences of going to school in Hollywood made him a lot different than a lot of the other young people I was playing with in my high school bands. He'd experienced cultural things that none of us could have dreamed of. He'd already spent some of his childhood growing up in Asia, and that was very unusual. Also, girls were crazy about the guy.

Michael probably wasn't a great singer when he started, and I don't think he was a particularly good stage guy. But he was always a good lyricist, and later on he became a great lyricist and a great live performer and a fantastic singer. Michael wrote the bulk of the lyrics—he usually came up with all the music and feels and grooves, and sometimes melodies. His lyrics changed [over the years]—they became more and more important to him. Michael felt he could actually talk to people through the lyrics and

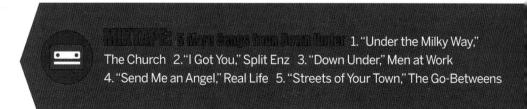

MIXTAPE: 5 More Songs from Down Under 1. "Under the Milky Way," The Church 2. "I Got You," Split Enz 3. "Down Under," Men at Work 4. "Send Me an Angel," Real Life 5. "Streets of Your Town," The Go-Betweens

discuss things without someone judging or misquoting him. One of the most beautiful legacies is a song that millions of people know, because you're like, "Well, there you go. No one's going to screw that up, because they all know the lyrics, and they know exactly what I was thinking."

We liked all kinds of music and, as a young INXS, we used to mix it all in together. In Australia, when we grew up, you wouldn't have different formats of radio stations like you have now. Back then, you would hear every style of music—pop, rock, sometimes even classical—on the same station. So I was a fan of David Bowie, the Sex Pistols, but the other guys in INXS and I, we were also fans of blues-based music, straight rock, and our own Australian pub scene. The scene that we came out of, it's very much a big pub environment where you have large rooms with working-class men smoking cigarettes and just getting drunk all of the time. If you wanted to play music and make it, you'd have to survive in that environment.

For the first album with Chris Thomas, we recorded "What You Need," another big game-changer for INXS. That was our first Top 5 hit in North America and a Top 10 around the world. I remember getting a call at the time from our manager, Chris [Murphy]. He said, "Aren't you excited? We should be opening a bottle of champagne." I said, "Yeah, that's great. Thanks for calling," and put the phone down. I suddenly became really uncomfortable. I thought, *What's wrong with me? I should be thinking, "I'm awesome" or something.* Then it hit me like a freight train: "If we don't do that again, then that's as far as we got." It hit Michael too. We thought, *Holy shit, we're going to have to try and better that somehow. How the hell are we going to do that?!* That's where the next album, *Kick,* came from. We were on a bus in Germany, and we said to the others, "Look, we know everyone's a songwriter. But we really need you guys to seriously consider letting Michael and I run with this next album artistically and creatively. If you just trust Michael and I, we'll give you the album you want." I'll never, ever forget that moment.

TIM FARRISS: We could have made vocal objections, but we didn't. We said, "Cool. Whatever's clever for Trevor."

ANDREW FARRISS: To give Michael and me that nod of approval was very wise of everybody. We just had to write some great songs. *Kick* was a monster album for us. It had four Top 5 hits in the United States and also had another song, "Mystify," which went Top 10 in Europe and other places in the world. There are three brothers in the band—we've had our differences, but as brothers, we sorted all of that shit out when we were young.

THAT WAS THEN *BUT THIS IS NOW*

INXS was one of the biggest bands on the planet through the mid-nineties, ultimately selling more than 40 million records and racking up a total of 61 singles from 12 studio albums. Their driving, guitar-funk sound was buoyed by Hutchence's rock-god persona, which he cultivated via glossy, high-profile romances with Helena Christensen and Kylie Minogue (reportedly the inspiration behind the hit "Suicide Blonde"). Hutchence was dating British TV presenter Paula Yates, the mother of his daughter, Tiger Lily, when he was found dead in his Sydney hotel room in 1997. The coroner concluded that it was a suicide. The surviving members subsequently performed with several singers, including J.D. Fortune, the winner of the ill-fated reality-TV competition *Rock Star: INXS*, before calling it quits during a 2012 concert in Perth, Australia.

TIM FARRISS: The last tour we did was with Matchbox Twenty. We got such respect from those guys—clearly they were influenced by us to a large degree. Rob Thomas✳ worked with us on the [2010] album *Original Sin* that has remakes of a lot of our songs. We had a different song choice picked out for him, but he said, "Sure, I'll do that song if you give me a go at 'Original Sin.'"

ANDREW FARRISS: When I think about many acts, some of whom I really love, I can think of maybe one, two, three songs of theirs that I would know why they would be in people's consciousness or memories. But I think that one of the interesting things with INXS is that we had different songs in different countries that attracted different people, and over a long, long period of time—decades.

TIM FARRISS: [I remember when] Queen took us under their wing. We did the opening for them all over Europe, doing stadium after stadium. I remember sitting in Freddie Mercury's big, palatial hotel suite overlooking Lake Geneva after the Montreux Pop Festival. Freddie was

✳ **ROB THOMAS, Matchbox Twenty**: We got to see them play with Michael once at a radio festival we played together. To see them play is to realize, "Holy shit, this is one of the best pop-rock bands on earth." Years later, Jon Farriss came out to a show in Australia. That led to them asking me to sing on the remake of "Original Sin." I wasn't going to try to "do" Michael. He is impossible to imitate, so you don't even try. Michael is hands down one of the greatest frontmen in music. The style, the voice—all of it. Any way that I was ever influenced by him really comes down to small, pale imitations compared to the real thing. There is a fearlessness about him. Watching him at Wembley Stadium with 70,000 people, he looks as comfortable as if he were in his own living room.

playing some new material that he'd written on this huge stereo, and he and Michael were singing at the top of their voices into each other's faces with their noses literally an inch apart. It was like a sing-off. It was one of those moments where I felt like, "What am I doing here?"

Michael's close friends were of the notoriety hall of fame: Simon [Le Bon]✷✷ and his wife; toward the end, Bono and [his wife] Ali. I think other celebrities could understand Michael, and he felt more comfortable around them than hanging out with people who just wanted to adore you because of who you are, whereas [other] celebrities don't give a shit. They're leading the same life you are.

I took my son to see AC/DC—or Aca-daca, as we call them in Australia. We went back [stage], and we're hanging out with Angus Young, and I said to him, quietly, "How did you guys deal with the loss of Bon? How long does it take you to get over that?" And Angus said, "Oh, about three weeks." I went, "God, it's been six years for us," which it had been at that time.

We were collectively openly discussing [coping with Michael's death] only when people asked, like media. It's been our own journey and one that we had to discover for ourselves without being influenced by too many other people. My wife said, "Maybe you guys, particularly Andrew, should get counseling on how to deal with this." It has affected him in just the way you think it would: floundering, looking for a song…It was very hard for him when we worked with other singers. He couldn't work with [INXS singer from 2000 to 2004] Jon Stevens, so that wasn't going to happen. Even though Jon was a great friend and an amazing singer, he wasn't the frontman Michael was. But then, who is?

ANDREW FARRISS: It was my younger brother, Jon, who was the one who got up on stage [in 2012 to announce that the band was splitting up]. Having been touring for 30-something years on and off, we figured it was about time we did some other things. It doesn't mean we don't want to be INXS; it doesn't mean we may not record together again. We probably will. We just wanted some time out to explore other things. I like the guys in INXS. I know what they've been through, because I went through it too. They're good musicians, and they're good people. If I'm not with them, I miss them.

✷✷ **SIMON LE BON, Duran Duran:** Michael was my best friend. We were two singers who didn't feel that we were in competition with each other. We had a great love of life, and a lot of our passions were very, very similar. [Duran and INXS] were two bands who really embraced that rock star lifestyle. Michael and I just clicked with each other, and we just had a fantastic time together—we really did.

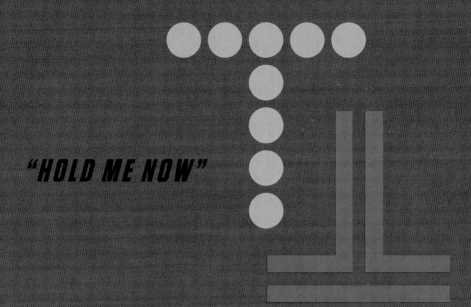

"HOLD ME NOW"

THOMPSON TWINS

At the start of the decade, the Thompson Twins were a seven-strong band of Dickensian scruffs whose heavily percussive shows inevitably ended with drunken British students invading the stage and pounding trashcan lids and empty soup cans not quite in time with the beat. And then suddenly they weren't a seven-piece, and they weren't scruffy. The Thompson Twins evolved quickly and skillfully into a Benetton advert made flesh, an unthreatening three-piece hit machine with big hats and even bigger hair. The Twins' output also evolved: Where once they were rhythm-driven, their greatest hits emphasized their melodic strengths. No one heard "Hold Me Now" and started banging on a trashcan lid.

JB: The Thompson Twins were my hate-watch—my *Newsroom*. Even in that age of artifice, I found them suspect. I didn't buy their skin-shedding. To me they would always be one of these bands that wasn't good enough to be Pigbag. I found Tom Bailey's voice devoid of emotion. Their image turned my stomach. The hair made me heave.

 And as for those songs . . . I still remember every note, every intro, every chorus. I will say this for the Thompson Twins: Their best songs were built to last. Even though I professed to hate them, I still had a tiny place in my tiny heart for "Hold Me Now" that pleaded for the chance to be understood, forgiven, and loved.

LM: One of the most romantic moments in cinematic history has to be when Samantha Baker thanks Jake Ryan for getting her undies back. "Make a wish," he says, the titular sixteen candles ablaze on a birthday cake between them. "It already came true," she answers. *Kiss.* Have to admit, though, I wouldn't love that scene half as much if the Thompson Twins' "If You Were Here" weren't playing in the background. That Tom Bailey knows romance—and he knows women too. That's what I always think when I hear "Hold Me Now." I miss the Thompson Twins. They are one of the few bands in this book who've truly disappeared—no reunion tours or acoustic reimaginings of their greatest hits for them. For that reason, we forget how massive they were. But whenever I hear one of their big, perfectly produced smashes, I'm transported back to a time when they were kings for a day, presiding over a sold-out Madison Square Garden like the Black Eyed Peas of the eighties.

TOM BAILEY: Although we could be accused of being somewhat formulaic, we were trying to express ourselves—in a cartoonish way, maybe, but in a real way. In those days, there was a rule of thumb that to give an album a fair crack at achieving maximum sales you needed four hit singles. You would write songs until you were pretty sure you had four or five that fit the bill, then you could maybe stretch out with some of the other material, make it longer or slower-paced or more experimental. It was a formula in the sense that the industry presented a gateway filter to you: Your songs had to be radio-friendly, they had to be a certain length, they didn't have to have long intros, you had to go out on a chorus—all those standard songwriting things that are nothing more than conventions but you have to learn about them in order to seriously have a go at it.

You know you're writing [songs about] the same subject that's been written about a thousand times before. It's how you stop it from becoming clichéd and try to retain some kind of credibility for the cultural demands of the moment. "Hold Me Now" came partly from a real situation. Alannah [Currie] and I at this time were lovers. We'd gone somewhere to do some writing, and after an argument, we kissed and made up, and that song came out of it. No one sets out to say, "What would we do if we'd fallen out? How would we write a song about making up again?" But it actually happens, so you just latch on to that moment. It's a precious thing that you can write about quite easily, and it's something people want to hear about, even though it is a little sentimental. It's a part of human nature.

There were difficulties being part of a couple and being in the band, and you manage those. But there are also great advantages. Your business doesn't take you away from your home when you're both in it together. We thrived on that for a long, long time. We always had separate hotel rooms, which is something we started doing because we didn't want people to assume we were a couple and we wanted to keep that side of our lives private. So we pretended that we were separate, but then we found that it was a great way of not burn-ing out on each other. So we were together when we were together, but we also built in this time apart. It led to a rather strange way of conducting our relationship. Even subsequently, when we bought a house, we had separate bedrooms because that's the way our relationship had developed. It was quite odd looking back, but it seemed to be very healthy for us at the time.

The band started in Sheffield [in 1977]—it was three school friends: myself and a couple of friends [Pete Dodd and John Podgorski]—then we decided to move to London and try to make it. I'd gotten in touch with an old friend and told him I was moving, and he said, "Well, I'm squatting, and there's a place around the corner." I squatted in South London for years and years. I had … it wasn't exactly the dole but supplementary benefit, which was 16 pounds a week plus 4 for paying my housing co-op fees. I had to be really careful about whether I bought a packet of cigarettes or a bag of chips, and I'd jump over the barriers of the Tube. It was slightly embarrassing because I never quite got round to leaving the squat until our third album.

When you listen to those earliest recordings, you can hear we were a guitar, bass, and drums outfit, and the songs we were keen on were very much in that punk or post-punk vein. I remember being a big

"We wrote almost a manifesto and said, 'Instead of hoping or pretending to be pop stars, we're actually going to be pop stars. We're going to treat it as a serious job.'"

fan of Wreckless Eric, that chugging guitar and relentless spewing of lyrics. I became interested in what was known as world music and, in particular, Indian and African music that had something going for it in terms of everyone getting involved. There was an underground enthusiasm about our first album [1981's *A Product of . . . (Participation)*], which I like, but it sounds small and a little bit fragile compared with how the band sounded onstage, which was raucous and noisy. It got to the stage where we were making instruments out of tin cans, and there were so many lying around that other people joined in. We encouraged that, but it's a funny thing to be famous for. In fact, it became destructive in the sense

that people would show up just to jump on stage. When we became the stripped-down version, the three of us [the recognizable lineup of Bailey, Currie, and Joe Leeway] decided we couldn't do that anymore. It was dangerous.

We were coming to the end of our second album [*Set*, 1982] with Steve Lillywhite. That felt like a big moment for us, with the big-name producer and working in an expensive studio, and it happened so quickly that we hadn't had enough material. I had finally earmarked enough money to buy a synthesizer and a little drum machine. I wrote "In the Name of Love"—every single part including the percussion—lying on my bed with the synthesizer on the mattress next to me. It was the writing on the wall for that version of the band. Instead of seven people writing it, only one person had written it and it was very much the fruit of technology. They all got to play a little bit on it, but they were basically playing the things I told them to play.

I got a phone call: ["In the Name of Love" is] number one in the Billboard dance chart." I said, "What does that mean?" My interpretation was kind of naive and British, which was that it was like the dance chart in the back of *Smash Hits*. But people said it was a really massive thing. The searchlight of interest had wandered around various departments of music, and suddenly everyone was very interested in knowing what was going on in nightclubs.

We toured that album in Europe and the U.K. quite successfully in terms of getting bigger audiences, but I don't think the band really knew what to do next. By that stage, Joe, Alannah, and myself were living in squats on the same street. When everyone else went home, the three of us would carry on scheming and coming up with ideas. We had become a central core of activity. The original band ground to a halt, and it left the three of us to pick up the new direction. The new version had a very strange division of labor: I did all the music, Joe designed the live show, and Alannah wrote lyrics, but her main job was looking after the visual side: videos, photographs, that kind of stuff.

I remember someone in the Human League saying they woke up one day and it was okay to be a pop musician. "Pop" had been a dirty word for so long during the punk era, then someone said, "It's okay, you can have intentions to be popular. You can make music that's not for enthusiasts only." We decided that we must have a solid idea. We wrote almost a manifesto and said, "Instead of hoping or pretending to be pop stars, we're actually going to be pop stars. We're going to treat it as a serious job. If we haven't had a major hit in the next 12 months and been on *Top of the Pops*, then we've failed in our intentions and can go back to being experimental musicians." It seemed like an interesting thing to do—not because we were hell-bent on being famous, but it seemed like the serious way of approaching that task. It was the template for everything we subsequently did over the next three albums.

In terms of MTV, "Lies" was the first hit. I think MTV were just looking for something wacky and British, and they picked half a dozen things and put them into rotation. "Lies" failed in the U.K., but "Love on Your Side" became a bona fide *Top of the Pops* hit, and one of the promotions guys said something like, "Enjoy the next couple of weeks because it only ever happens once"—that kind of giddy ride to the upper

MIXTAPE: 5 More Songs by Three-Piece Groups
1. "Smalltown Boy," Bronski Beat 2. "Tunnel of Love," Fun Boy Three 3. "Robert De Niro's Waiting," Bananarama 4. "Life in a Northern Town," The Dream Academy 5. "Sonic Boom Boy," Westworld

atmosphere. At the time, I had no idea what he was talking about; for me, it was just more of the same. But in retrospect, it's something you never really recover from—suddenly aspects of normal life are taken away from you.

For me, the era that I look on fondly as a golden age of synth pop started with the Human League and ended with Frankie Goes to Hollywood. Something happened there with the celebrity hype machine. It had become so powerful and so effective and so silly. I remember Frankie Goes to Hollywood releasing a different mix of their record every week, and it was just to keep their chart position. I thought, *Wow, has it really come to this?* Also at that time, videos had become the most effective way of selling music, and I realized I spent more time and more money on videos than I did on music. I didn't want to do that anymore. I spent half my time hanging around video and photographic studios spending a fortune on looking good.

That was around the time of Live Aid. I was in New York recording [1985's *Here's to Future Days*] with Nile Rodgers, and we took a break from the session to drive to Philadelphia to do Live Aid, which is how come the band we played with was members of Chic, Madonna, and Steve Stevens from Billy Idol's band—all people who were hanging around Nile's empire, which was very exciting. I thought that was an amazing event but also completely overblown, and I didn't feel that we had a successful performance. I met Joan Baez, who had been a massive influence on me as a kid, so that was my biggest thrill of the night. Nile was under strict orders not to go drinking after the gig, because that had been a problem. Can you believe we went back to the hotel after the show and played Scrabble? We didn't even stay for the rest of the night. Maybe our enthusiasm for the big time was waning.✱

✱**NILE RODGERS:** Tom Bailey was right. You could watch history change in front of your face from the post-punk, club-kids, gothy thing to more glam, like Madonna. Everybody talks about the Queen–David Bowie performance in the U.K., but I was at JFK Stadium in Philadelphia, and there was nothing more rousing than when Madonna said, "I ain't taking off shit today." The set was almost irrelevant. I'm sitting here with the biggest record of my career [*Like a Virgin*], a 20-million seller, and this woman walks on stage and delivers that line, and you could see that the crowd was loving this new type of vulnerable, highly sexual thing. It was no longer about being dark and mysterious; it was about being upfront and open and "Fuck you!" Madonna was bringing in more of the R&B dance groove that has really never left our spirits, but in America we didn't want to admit it because of the whole "Disco Sucks" thing. The eighties music is still rooted in groove R&B music, and that stuff had never gone away. When you think about records like "Relax" or ABC's "The Look of Love," you can see these guys are heavily influenced by American R&B.

THAT WAS THEN
BUT THIS IS NOW

Following the departure of Joe Leeway in 1986, Tom Bailey and Alannah Currie (who married in 1999) carried on as a duo. In 1993, they changed their name to Babble, releasing two albums. Bailey—now divorced from Currie—continues to arrange and record music under the name International Observer. Currie upholsters furniture using the carcasses of animals who died naturally or were run over by unobservant drivers. Leeway works in hypnotherapy.

BAILEY: I've no particular interest in being the Thompson Twins again. People are calling me all the time and trying to get me to do it and arguing about the benefits—how much I'd enjoy it and what a thrill it would be and how the fans are dying to see me—and I just don't get it. I have to find some personal trick, some strategy for enjoying it. Otherwise I'd just feel, *Why am I here? Why am I doing this?* It has the risk of being embarrassing for me.

Essentially, what it comes down to is money and to see if bands re-form after they've split up under acrimonious circumstances, whether there might be a strange, experimental thrill to see whether it can be put back together again. But when someone like, say, Culture Club, re-forms to go on tour, it's because they actually want to do it. I do quite a lot of work with Indian musicians, and one day I said to an agent, "I've got this great idea. I'll go back and perform Thompson Twins songs but, get this, we're going to be sitting cross-legged, and I'll have a sitar and a tabla playing with me, and it'll be fantastic." The agent said, "No, you won't." He said those things are about people who want to relive the past, not to be challenged with some new creative endeavor.

I don't see much of Joe because he's in California. Alannah, I see from time to time, partly because we have a couple of kids together, so we have an interest in looking after them. But we once said, "Should we do it?" And within 10 minutes we were arguing about which songs we should do and what we should be wearing, and I thought, *Oh my God, it's too much stress.* But when Alannah's out of money, she'll be on the phone wanting to do it.

"DON'T YOU (FORGET ABOUT ME)"

SIMPLE MINDS

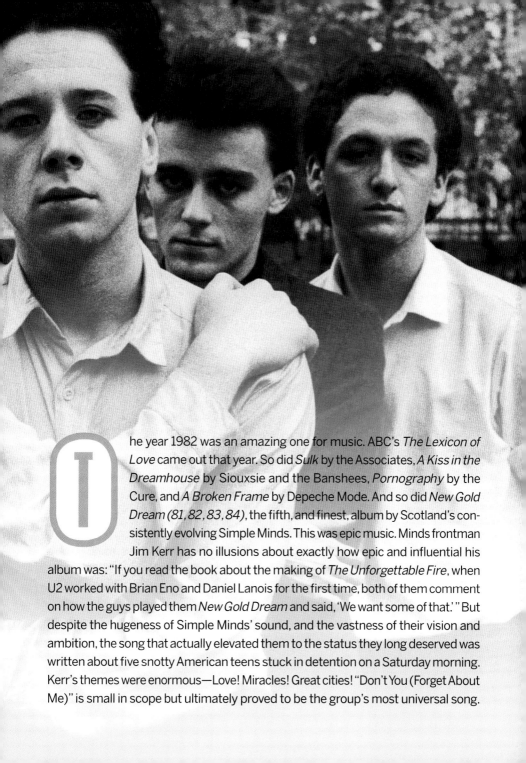

he year 1982 was an amazing one for music. ABC's *The Lexicon of Love* came out that year. So did *Sulk* by the Associates, *A Kiss in the Dreamhouse* by Siouxsie and the Banshees, *Pornography* by the Cure, and *A Broken Frame* by Depeche Mode. And so did *New Gold Dream (81, 82, 83, 84)*, the fifth, and finest, album by Scotland's consistently evolving Simple Minds. This was epic music. Minds frontman Jim Kerr has no illusions about exactly how epic and influential his album was: "If you read the book about the making of *The Unforgettable Fire*, when U2 worked with Brian Eno and Daniel Lanois for the first time, both of them comment on how the guys played them *New Gold Dream* and said, 'We want some of that.'" But despite the hugeness of Simple Minds' sound, and the vastness of their vision and ambition, the song that actually elevated them to the status they long deserved was written about five snotty American teens stuck in detention on a Saturday morning. Kerr's themes were enormous—Love! Miracles! Great cities! "Don't You (Forget About Me)" is small in scope but ultimately proved to be the group's most universal song.

JB: You know that Morrissey song, "We Hate It When Our Friends Become Successful"? And that line, "And if they're Northern, that makes it even worse"? Multiply that by a million and that's how natives of Glasgow feel about anyone from their hometown achieving even the slightest degree of success. Anything that makes us think they're better than us. We're bloody-minded that way. I certainly was when I first encountered Simple Minds. Didn't they used to be tragic local punk band Johnny and the Self Abusers who played in the pub down the road from me? And suddenly they were pretending to be this pale, enigmatic, icy synth outfit? Pull the other one! I—and it must be said, most of Glasgow and the other bits of Britain not worth mentioning—afforded Simple Minds zero attention and respect until their second outing. While 1979's *Real to Real Cacophony* may have one of the all-time groaners for a title, something had happened to this band between albums. Something that made even the most resentful and pigheaded of Glaswegians—i.e., all of us—grudgingly admiring. Somehow, the group had managed to outgrow the suffocating Bowie-isms

 that made their first album, *Life in a Day*, so easy to mock. Somehow, they'd grown muscles of their own. The next album, 1980's *Empires and Dance*—the one with "I Travel" and "Celebrate" on it—was even stronger. But Simple Minds were never cool, not like the fey, jangly bands from the West End of Glasgow who recorded for Postcard Records. So I still acted like I found them nonsensical (though, to be honest, Jim Kerr's drunk-actor-playing-Hamlet frontman persona didn't make it that difficult). Then they recorded the theme to *The Breakfast Club*, which was, at the time, my favorite film by my favorite writer-director, and that was all very confusing. But, with hindsight and maturity, I can now say, hand-on-heart, that the incarnation of Simple Minds who were active from 1979 to 1985 were the best band to ever come out of Glasgow. But that doesn't entitle them to think they're any better than the rest of us.

LM: Ally Sheedy was wrong: I grew up but my heart didn't die. I'm not even that big of a *Breakfast Club* fan (I'm more of a *Pretty in Pink* girl), but whenever I hear the first few seconds of "Don't You (Forget About Me)," I'm back in high school and waiting for my life to start.

JIM KERR: Being in any working-class city in the U.K. [in the seventies] and being a male in any working-class city, there wasn't much going on. We were brought up with both the church of football and the church of *Top of the Pops*. Of course, being in Glasgow, *Top of the Pops* seemed a universe away, nothing that any of us could touch let alone enter until the punk movement came along. For me, punk's most potent thing was not the music especially, but the DIY manifesto that you could beg, borrow, or steal a guitar and make a noise. Whether you were any good or not was subjective, but it put an end to the notion that you had to be able to play like Rick Wakeman or Eric Clapton or go to a music conservatory in Vienna.

Johnny and the Self Abusers were the much-maligned precursors to Simple Minds; on the other hand, some people would say we've been downhill ever since. Had that not been the catalyst it was, we'd still be sitting in the pub saying, "One day we're going to do this," which was what had been happening until then. Music was very centralized in London, so the Scottish bands would all go there, saving up whatever they could before, staying in a squat, endure a miserable existence for a few months, and then split up. We were the only band that started playing in Glasgow pubs, doing our own material and having queues around the block, albeit it was free

to get in. There was such a thirst for the whole punk/new wave thing that led us to think, "You can do that from up here." You could get a review in the *NME* or *Sounds* or *Melody Maker*, all those bibles. You could get a buzz going from your hometown without having to move to London. In fact, the A&R men, for the first time ever, were starting to get on the plane and come up and see you in your natural environment. It laid the ground for scenes to develop where it wouldn't have been possible before.

Within the first few minutes of the first-ever Johnny and the Self Abusers gig, both Charlie Burchill, my songwriting partner in Simple Minds, and myself looked at each other and thought, *Hang on, wouldn't it be great if we could* *really do this?* Even though no one could play or hear a note, it was just white noise, people were jumping up and down. We thought, *There can't be anything better than this, so we'd better try to work out how we can make this work in the long term and take it around the world.* After six months, we began to be serious about it, which is when we stopped Johnny and the Self Abusers. Two days after that, we were writing songs—some of which were featured in Simple Minds' debut album— but certainly the seeds had been sown with that first-ever gig.

> **"Sonically, the heartbeat behind 'Don't You (Forget About Me)' is total Simple Minds. It will never be ours, but, in a good way, the song belongs to everybody now. It belongs to that generation."**

The success, especially in Europe, of *New Gold Dream* had taken us into these much bigger venues. We were playing arenas for the first time. They put us out in front of crowds at festivals of 60,000 to 70,000. It definitely wasn't overnight but [headlining our own shows] went from playing to 3,000 to playing to 12,000 within a year. At times we were probably trying too hard, but there was the thing of trying to reach the back of the hall, trying to master an audience. For instance, when we played some of these festivals, there would be much bigger acts than us at the time: Elvis Costello, Van Morrison. Very good artists, but they weren't cutting the mustard. It wasn't happening. The music was going up in the air—they weren't involving the audience. I don't know if it even dawned on them. But we wanted everyone to get involved, and I think that showed. A huge thing happened with the band when we got a drummer like Mel Gaynor, who is as heavy as John Bonham or Keith Moon. The fact that we'd got this guy who could not only groove but rock—we were like kids with a new train set. We wanted to use it every song, so we lost a lot of subtlety, but we were excited with the noise that was coming out.

New Gold Dream and *Sparkle in the Rain* had got a lot of college radio action, and that was great, but no money was spent on them, which was frustrating because some of our contemporaries were starting to break through. Money we were making elsewhere

MIXTAPE: 5 More Songs from Scotland 1. "Party Fears Two," The Associates   2. "Don't Talk to Me About Love," Altered Images 3. "Forest Fire," Lloyd Cole and the Commotions   4. "Candy Skin," Fire Engines   5. "Oblivious," Aztec Camera

we were putting into tours of America, and we were continually losing it. We were starting to feel gypped, to say the least.

The whole thing with "Don't You" was a bit of a comedy of errors. We had an A&R guy at the time called Jordan Harris, who said, after *New Gold Dream* and *Sparkle*, it was good news, bad news. He said, "We should have got behind these records. Too late now. But there's a buzz growing on a daily basis." We were about a year away from a new record. He said it would be great to have something meanwhile to feed the machine and keep the momentum going. We didn't have anything ready, and he said, "Well, actually, there is something happening that would be great for you." [Simple Minds' label] A&M were starting to do movies. He introduced *The Breakfast Club* to us, then he slipped in the notion that there was a song that would be right for us to do. We said, "Wait a minute, we don't do anyone else's songs." He said, "Don't worry, this'll work because it really sounds like a Simple Minds song." Well, that made it worse because we thought, *We're Simple Minds!*

It turns out that we'd played L.A. a few months earlier and [composer-producer] Keith Forsey had come backstage and given Mick MacNeil, our keyboard player, a cassette of the song. Mick had played it, didn't think much of it, and forgot to tell us. But Keith had been waiting to hear

from us. Finally, Jordan, who was a smooth operator and a lovely man, managed to get us to consider the track. As far as the demo went, Keith sang on it, and it sounded like Richard Butler—like a Psychedelic Furs thing. I could see them doing it, but I couldn't see Simple Minds ever, and it wasn't the kind of lyric I would write. So we, as it's well known, knocked it back a number of times. People have said it was offered to Bryan Ferry, but I asked Bryan and he said he never got approached with it, so I don't know if that's true.

What turned it around wasn't the fact that we woke up and smelled the coffee. The thing that did it was Keith came over to London off his own back. He knew we weren't doing it, he got in touch and said,

"It sounded like a Psychedelic Furs thing. I could see them doing it, but I couldn't see Simple Minds ever, and it wasn't the kind of lyric I would write."

"I'm a big fan of the band anyway; maybe we could work together in the future. I hear you're in London, can I come and hang out for a couple of days?" Lo and behold, we liked Keith more than his song. You know when you like someone, it's like, "He's our new pal." We thought he was great, and at the right moment, he said, "Why don't we nip in and do this thing and get the record company off your back? If it doesn't work, it doesn't work. If it does work, who knows? "It was literally a few hours in a drafty studio in Wembley, and the rest is history.✱

As soon as that song starts, it's Simple Minds. We put our heart and soul into it. A lot of people could have done that song. Richard Butler could have done it. But he couldn't have done it like that. It wouldn't have jumped out the radio at you like that did, and it wouldn't have had you jumping out of your seat at the end. Sonically, the heartbeat behind it is total Simple Minds. It will never be ours, but, in a good way, the song belongs to everybody now. It belongs to that generation and it's a pleasure to play it, and every night we play it with full gusto.

We never just go through the motions, because it's a song from a movie that means a lot to a fair amount of people and you want to respect that.

Sometimes I get in a cab and the driver will say, "Where do I know you from?" I usually say *Crimewatch* [the U.K.'s version of *America's Most Wanted*]. Or they'll say, "Are you in a band? Is it Simply Red?" And if I say it's Simple Minds, they'll say, "I love that song." And people ask if it gets on my nerves that it's always that song. If we'd been a one-hit wonder, then maybe it would—and they might say, in the States, that is the case. Well, you know, we've sold gazillions of records and we've played to gazillions of people. You don't have to love all the albums. It's an honor to us if you even like one of them. People fell in love to that song; they got married to it. The song never strangled us. Jimmy Iovine, who produced *Once Upon a Time*, said, "Look, this thing's a monster! You'd better have something to follow it up." Well, "Alive and Kicking" got to number two in the Billboard charts. It was held off by Michael Jackson. We did all right.

✱ **DEREK FORBES, original Simple Minds bassist:** "Don't You" wasn't on *Once Upon a Time* because Jim was reluctant to do it. He felt detached. He treated it more like an advert. But I know that he grew to like it. The start with all the Hey-hey-heys, the bit that people love, and all the la-la-las at the end, were down to Jim, and that was genius. That's what helped make it as big as it still is today.

THAT WAS THEN BUT THIS IS NOW

Simple Minds was a fixture on the global stadium circuit well into the nineties. Latter-day albums like 1989's *Street Fighting Years* and 1991's *Real Life* were as colossal and pompous as the band's earlier work, but a certain spark was missing. As seriously as Kerr took himself, his romantic life made him a U.K. tabloid fixture—especially after his marriage to Chrissie Hynde ended and he took up with pouty blonde starlet Patsy Kensit. Still, Simple Minds remains an internationally popular live act. The band, which now consists of the original core duo of Kerr and guitarist Charlie Burchill, currently plays shows that give equal weight to the hidden gems from their early days and to the anthems from their heyday.

KERR: By the early eighties, it was not only cool to be in the *NME*; you wanted to be in *Smash Hits* as well, because the Associates were, Echo and the Bunnymen were, and Orange Juice were, and ABC were, and the Human League were. There was just a lot of shiny new pop that had an edge to it but was still very much pop in the melodic sense. For a long period, the eighties were much maligned. Whenever anyone talked about the eighties,

it's usually for a crappy pop show you get at two in the morning, Oh this is the eighties! And it'll be Bananarama, and it'll be Doctor and the Medics, and it'll be A Flock of Seagulls or whoever had the most outrageous hair. I'm not saying that wasn't a part of it, but it wasn't the eighties.

The Associates, ABC—they were actually staying at the same down-market hotel in London we used to stay in. As they were doing their records, we were doing ours, so there was definitely a feeling, a collectiveness. At night you would meet up, "We're number 30 this week!" "We're number 15!" Depeche Mode would come in—even though they were from Basildon, they'd hang in the bar because the Bunnymen would be there, Teardrop Explodes, the Human League. There was a whole feeling of new pop, and whenever people ask me about it now, I think all those people were mates and not one of those bands sounded like each other. There wasn't a collective sound like there was a sound of the sixties, but there was an amazing imagination. That was a very potent collection of kids—and we were kids at the time—and I still listen to a lot of that music to this day.

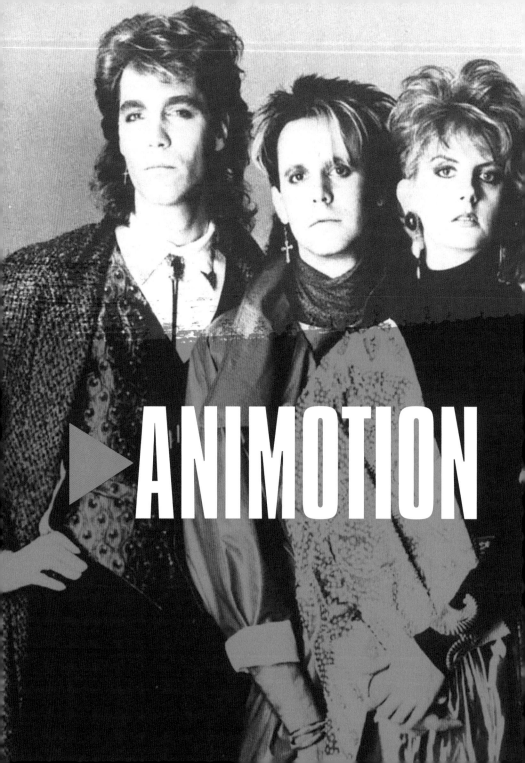

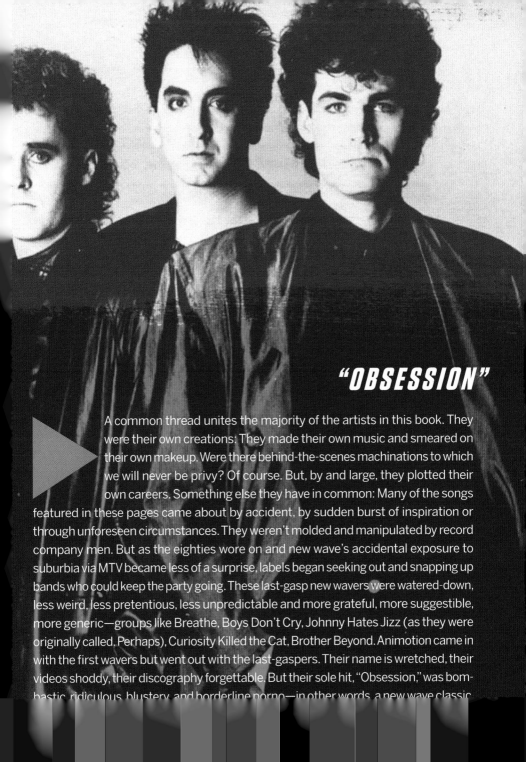

"OBSESSION"

A common thread unites the majority of the artists in this book. They were their own creations: They made their own music and smeared on their own makeup. Were there behind-the-scenes machinations to which we will never be privy? Of course. But, by and large, they plotted their own careers. Something else they have in common: Many of the songs featured in these pages came about by accident, by sudden burst of inspiration or through unforeseen circumstances. They weren't molded and manipulated by record company men. But as the eighties wore on and new wave's accidental exposure to suburbia via MTV became less of a surprise, labels began seeking out and snapping up bands who could keep the party going. These last-gasp new wavers were watered-down, less weird, less pretentious, less unpredictable and more grateful, more suggestible, more generic—groups like Breathe, Boys Don't Cry, Johnny Hates Jizz (as they were originally called. Perhaps), Curiosity Killed the Cat, Brother Beyond. Animotion came in with the first wavers but went out with the last-gaspers. Their name is wretched, their videos shoddy, their discography forgettable. But their sole hit, "Obsession," was bombastic, ridiculous, blustery, and borderline porno—in other words, a new wave classic.

JB: Though I have traveled this great nation far and wide, though I have ventured to strange and exotic territories, one thing never changes: There's always a strip joint near the airport playing "Obsession." And when it comes on, the girl on the pole wakes from her torpor, just a little, and even I am sufficiently moved to fork over a few crumpled-up bills. What does bad-eighties-movie sex sound like? Erotic thriller sex? It sounds like "Obsession." Holly Knight co-wrote my all-time favorite American new wave pop song, "New Romance" by Spider (also performed by Lisa Hartman's singer character Ciji on *Knots Landing*!). But "Obsession" is her Hall of Famer—and, also, her Hall of Shamer.

LM: As a fan of the Power Station, I thought it'd be interesting to talk to Knight's "Obsession" co-writer, Michael Des Barres. And he was as funny and creepy and dirty as I'd hoped he would be. I thought, *Case closed. We have our chapter.* Then I thought, *Shouldn't I be talking to the group that had the hit?* For me, Animotion were an afterthought. They were no more and no less than a vehicle for a hit song. Nothing wrong or shameful about that. But, as it turns out, there *was* something wrong and shameful about the Animotion story. It is a tale of heartache, backstabbing, disloyalty, and despair—almost as melodramatic as obsession itself.

MICHAEL DES BARRES: Every era produces classic songs that people lost their virginity to. I wrote one that stuck in people's heads because the idea of it is, "Who do you want me to be to make you sleep with me?" Which is: "I'll be anything you want—just fuck me," which is a big human notion.

I wrote the words to that song in L.A. six months into '81. It's tied in with my sobriety. The word that was being bandied around in these 12-step rooms was "obsession." At the same time, there's a movie I saw that made an enormous impression on me: *The Collector*. The brief narrative is a young, working-class boy cannot find a girlfriend. He wins the pools, which is the lottery in England, and buys a country house, where he collects butterflies. Then he decides to collect a lover. He kidnaps a girl, takes her back to the house, and keeps her in the cellar.

Mike Chapman introduced me to Holly Knight, [who] had written "Better Be Good to Me" and "Love Is a Battlefield." She said, "What have you got?" and I said, "You're like a butterfly, a wild butterfly / I will collect you and capture you." She had no idea what I was talking about, but she could write a hook. I knew it was a duet. The song came, and it came really fast—which is not an expression I particularly like. I sang it in one take, she sang it in one take, Chapman mixed it in an hour, and it made millions for all of us.

[It was] in a [1983] movie called *A Night in Heaven*. It starred an eighties guy called Christopher Atkins, who played a male stripper. Some A&R dude heard it and decided to recut it with a band called Animotion.

BILL WADHAMS: Halfway through the [recording of our debut] album, "Obsession" comes in, and it was nothing like the rest of the album. Everything else was written by me, and the sound I was going for was similar to early Police. Andy Summers came from a classical guitar background and so did I. One of my favorite bands was Steely Dan. Our A&R man at Polygram Records, Russ Regan, said, "I think you guys could be a Fleetwood Mac for the eighties." Then our producer [John Ryan] went to London, and when he came back, he said, "Have you heard of Frankie Goes to Hollywood? Have you heard this song, 'Relax'? Well, I've got this song called 'Obsession,' which I think could be a hit for you guys." He played me Holly and Michael's version over the phone. The

male part is spoken. I said, "That's kind of interesting, but could I sing it?"

ASTRID PLANE: When I heard "Obsession," it knocked me over the head as a huge hit. I got a tingle up my spine, and I just knew we needed to record it. Though it wasn't the direction that Bill was writing his songs in, I felt it would be well received, and I thought it was the direction we should be going in.

WADHAMS: Our guitarist and keyboard player put a huge stamp on that song. We had just brought in a keyboard player named Greg Smith—Greg did the demos for the *Thriller* album—and he put in a whistling flute sound that wasn't on [the original]. Then guitarist Don Kirkpatrick came in, and he was just absolutely blazing. He was just warming up his guitar, [but] the producer said, "That's it. Done. Print it." It was just one take from beginning to end.

PLANE: The song was kind of spooky—that obsessive, driving thing that wouldn't give up. My only reservation, and it sounds so silly now, was that lyric, "Who do you want me to be to make you sleep with me?" My fear was that it wouldn't be played on the radio because of it being too racy. Being that the lyric could have been interpreted as very dark, we decided we wanted a more

"**But by the time we got into the teens and still had a bullet, the phone was ringing off the hook. I said, 'At this point, I don't care who wrote it. We're about to go on the ride of our life.'**"

██████████

fun, kooky, colorful video. We got access to one of the Hollywood movie-costume places, and they gave me Cleopatra's headpiece that Elizabeth Taylor had worn.

WADHAMS: [Astrid] was the girlfriend of the bass player [Charles Ottavio], and I was about to get married to someone else. But various directors submitted their video treatments, and almost all of them said, "Bill and Astrid meet and they're obsessed with each other." I didn't want that. I didn't want my first song released and put on MTV to be "I love Astrid," because I loved someone else. It's not just that it creates some problem at home; it's not how I want to represent myself in this band. I wanted to be my own person, more like Fleetwood Mac.

Stevie Nicks and Lindsey Buckingham… well, they were a pair, but by the time they really hit, they were already broken up. They're not really singing love songs to each other.

Then one director said, "Let's make it like a Fellini movie. We're going to take the line 'Who do you want me to be' and we're going to bring in all these random characters." They went down to Hollywood Costume Supply and started picking out Antony and Cleopatra, a samurai warrior, a spaceman. After the thing was shot, my youngest brother said to me, "I just saw the video, and I can't tell whether it's really cool or really stupid."

In the video I'm in a suit, and she's got wild makeup and her hair is sticking off to the side. Stylistically, she was much more of a Cyndi Lauper, wild, wacky thing, and I wanted to be more Mr. Cool, like Bryan Ferry, Sting, Robert Palmer. Even through our first or second tour, we had a difficult time, [Astrid] and I. We were not at ease with each other.

PLANE: We were these two very strong personalities with very different ideas about what should be happening. To me, there's nothing more boring than a guy standing there playing guitar looking at his shoes. I want to see stuff happening. I feel like I had a better sense of the big picture, like what is interesting for the audience to see. They want to see us interacting, and Bill wasn't used to that. But over time, we got more comfortable. And, strangely, that tension between us actually seemed to work onstage.

WADHAMS: It wasn't until years later that I realized that that was kind of cool, that we were coming from two different places and there was a tension between us that created a bit of mystery.

PLANE: There were a lot of politics going on as far as the timing of the release of the record. We wanted it to come out, and the record company was stalling, saying, "It's right before Christmas. We really ought to wait until the new year." Living in L.A. and having other friends in bands that had been signed and then shelved, I had this fear that they would just forget about it. So we really pushed. There used to be this thing called Battle of the Bands that they did on [L.A.'s] KROQ: They would play two songs, and the public would vote. Well, "Obsession" was

up against "Relax," and we were thinking, *We don't stand a chance*. But actually, "Obsession" did beat "Relax"!

WADHAMS: When it hit the charts, every week it was jumping almost 10 points. At first, I was like, *Shit! I am going to be a part of a hit song, but I didn't write it*. But by the time we got into the teens and still had a bullet, the phone was ringing off the hook. I said, "At this point, I don't care who wrote it. We're about to go on the ride of our life."

PLANE: The fans started going crazy. We played one underage club in L.A., and we were in the dressing room getting ready. My boyfriend at the time, the bass player, had already taken to wearing makeup. He was putting the powder on and the foundation, little bit of blush, eyeliner. Then, all of a sudden, Bill and the guitar player are like, "OK, give us that eyeliner. We want some of that." That was a turning point. We went onstage and the fans were grabbing jewelry off us. One girl shredded the tights off of my legs!

MIXTAPE: **5 More Last-Gasp New Wave Songs** 1. "Shattered Dreams," Johnny Hates Jazz 2. "How Can I Fall," Breathe 3. "(I Just) Died in Your Arms Tonight," Cutting Crew 4. "Your Love," The Outfield 5. "Two of Hearts," Stacey Q

"We went onstage and the fans were grabbing jewelry off us. One girl shredded the tights off of my legs!"

WADHAMS: But Animotion had some inherent problems. You had the Animotion that really was, and the Animotion that was on "Obsession." That song is so different from my writing. Our original drummer didn't play on the track; it was done by Fairlight drums. Our original bass player did not play on "Obsession"; it was done by a session player. It started with firing our original drummer, firing a keyboard player who was a great guy and great keyboard player, but he didn't play on "Obsession." We just wanted Greg, the session guy who'd played with Marvin Gaye, Diana Ross, Michael Jackson, to be in the band.

PLANE: There was also a problem with John Ryan. He did a great job on "Obsession," but his methods were cutthroat as far as getting what he wanted, bringing in outside players and pretty much running the show without asking our input. John would try to drive wedges between all of the band members. He would tell me, "Oh, you don't need Bill. You're the star." As a band, we agreed we weren't going to work with John Ryan again, but when the [recording] started, people started caving.

The other problem was that we hadn't written "Obsession" ourselves. The record company felt it was fair game for every songwriter in town to pitch songs for our [second] record. So here we were, having to compete with all the top songwriters to get songs on our own record.

WADHAMS: Once again, the producer comes in with another Holly Knight song, which was "I Engineer." The record company says, "That's the one we'll put out first, because she's the hit writer." "I Engineer" came out, and it looked like we were on our way to another hit. Then one of the in-house promotion people [at Polygram] said, "Your record's gonna die. We've been given a priority of making this band Level 42 a hit in the U.S." So the second album tanked. Then our A&R man left, and this new guy came in, Bob Skoro. Our first meeting with him, he said, "I don't like your first two albums. I don't like your live performance. I like 'Obsession,' but I don't like anything else." I thought, *We're screwed.*

PLANE: It was still that same old problem of "What musical direction are we gonna go in and who's gonna have a say in it?" The songs that they were going to be putting on our third record, I was horrified. The record we were making didn't represent us, [and the bass player and I] were at very bad relations with Bill.

WADHAMS: We hired new managers, and they said, "We think you should replace Astrid and her boyfriend, the bass player. We think you could get a stronger woman. Polygram London doesn't like Animotion because Astrid upset them when she was there for interviews. They didn't like her character. You guys are never gonna make money as a five-, six-piece band. Cut it down to size, bring in a stronger woman, and the record company will get behind you again." After some deliberation, we met with Astrid and Charles. We said, "The band is breaking up, and we're taking the name."

PLANE: I will never forget it. We've never really talked about it in depth because it was so painful, so awful, so ugly.

WADHAMS: We felt bad about it, but we went back to [our managers] right afterward, practically shaking. We said, "The deed is done." They said, "Cool. Matter of fact, we've already told Polygram that this is happen- ing, and we told them that you guys were going to get someone to replace her—like Cynthia Rhodes." They were managing Richard Marx, and Cynthia Rhodes was Richard Marx's fiancée.

We had another meeting with the record company, and Skoro said, "You gotta go with Cynthia Rhodes. If we put Cynthia Rhodes in front of this band, we can't lose." Immediately, we looked at each other and said, "We're going to be sidemen to Cynthia Rhodes!" I actually liked Cynthia a lot. If we'd been able to choose, we might've chosen Cynthia, but we were sort of forced to choose her.

PLANE: It was a very terrible time. On the one hand, we had our hit, we were famous. But on the other, we had no say in our career, and we were making a record, but it wasn't a record that I wanted to be on. And the way that Bill was being manipulated by the management company, it pierced a big hole in the dream of what it was to be a pop star. You were nothing. You were an item that was going to be on a shelf to be sold, and if they felt like you weren't sales-worthy, then [they'd] toss you in the trash.

WADHAMS: Sadly, we wanted to be the Fleetwood Mac of the eighties, but at a certain point, we realized we were the Monkees.

THAT WAS THEN *BUT THIS IS NOW*

Wadhams left Animotion before the release of their third album. Led by Cynthia Rhodes—a.k.a. Penny from *Dirty Dancing*—Animotion had one more Top 10 hit, 1989's deplorable "Room to Move." In 2001, Wadhams convinced Plane to join him in reviving Animotion for sporadic live dates with eighties package tours and appearances at nightclub nostalgia nights. Wadhams currently makes his living as a graphic artist. Plane, who married and then divorced bassist Charles Ottavio, is a vocal coach. Des Barres achieved notoriety as the villain Murdoc on TV's *MacGyver* and as the Power Station's concert tour and Live Aid fill-in for Robert Palmer. He still receives sizable royalty checks from "Obsession."

WADHAMS: A radio station here in Portland called me and said, "Would you appear at an eighties night at this club? We'll give you a thousand dollars to show up and sign some autographs." I called Astrid and said, "Would you like to fly to Portland and maybe we'll lip-synch 'Obsession'?" We've been playing together ever since.

We wouldn't be able to do this if it weren't for "Obsession." It's like a muscle car that sits in the garage, and everything about it is shiny.

I go on YouTube and see Michael Des Barres performing at SXSW, and he prefaces "Obsession" by saying, "This is a song that I wrote that made me a bloody fortune." The year that "Obsession" [was a hit for Animotion], each member of the band made about $50,000; the next year, just about nothing. Whether it's fair or not, it doesn't matter because I don't know that Michael Des Barres ever sang a song that was an international hit. I wonder whether he would trade having been the singer of the hit song for the money, if he would've been able to walk out on stage, sing "Obsession," and have people go, "That's the voice, that's the hit that we love."

DES BARRES: I've never had to struggle since. When I got the first check, I remember looking at [my ex-wife] Pamela and our baby, and we just sank to our knees. It's put my kid through college, [supported] two wives, and more besides. One song enters the lexicon of American consciousness, and it will take care of you for the rest of your life.

PLANE: We are still in debt to the record company to this day.

BAND AID

On October 24, 1984, the BBC's African correspondent Michael Buerk presented a six o'clock news report on the famines devastating Ethiopia. Bob Geldof, the voluble, charismatic frontman of the Irish post-punk band the Boomtown Rats, was part of the viewing audience. Geldof's recording career was sputtering to a halt, but his new incarnation as a rabble-rousing agent of change was just beginning. Buerk's report motivated Geldof to recruit Ultravox singer Midge Ure to assist in rounding up every available British pop star for the purposes of making a fundraising record to aid Africa. "Do They Know It's Christmas?" quickly grew bigger than the sum of its

"DO THEY KNOW IT'S CHRISTMAS?"

parts—and its parts were pretty huge: Duran Duran, Spandau Ballet, Bono, George Michael, Sting, Boy George, and Paul Weller, to name a very few. It evolved beyond a song and became a means by which the nation could ease its conscience. It also altered the face of what pop music had become. After Band Aid and Live Aid, the world looked and sounded a little different. There was less flaunting of wealth and less overt escapism. There was less exhibitionism, less makeup, and less fun. In retrospect, it seems "Do They Know It's Christmas?" brought down the curtain on the new wave era. It was a wake-up call that the delirious five-year party was drawing to a close.

JB: Here's how completely consumed the U.K. was with the give-till-it-hurts spirit of Band Aid. The week before the release of "Do They Know It's Christmas?," the number-one record in the country was "I Should Have Known Better" by a little Glaswegian guy named Jim Diamond. He'd had a taste of success a couple of years earlier with the group Ph.D., but this was his first solo hit. He was already in his thirties; he didn't fit the pop star mold in either looks or sound. It was obviously a big deal that he'd made it. When he performed his chart-topping hit on *Top of the Pops*, he did so wearing a "Feed the World" T-shirt and imploring the audience at home to put "Do They Know It's Christmas?" in first place the following week. I was a cynical prick in those days, but even I—even I!—reacted in shock and disbelief whenever anyone dismissed Band Aid as a publicity stunt intended to revive Bob Geldof's music career. First of all, it was obvious to anyone with or without ears that nothing was going to revive Geldof's music career. Second, there was something about being part of a mass audience that was galvanized into a community through the power of pop music that was exhilarating, even to the more uncharitably inclined of us. Third, "Do They Know It's Christmas?" is a pretty bleak seasonal charity record. "The clanging chimes of doom"? "A world of dread and fear"? "Tonight, thank God, it's them instead of you"? If Band Aid did, as its last-chapter placing in this book would suggest, signal the end of the era, what better, what colder, what more overdramatic way for new wave to go out?

LM: The morning that "Do They Know It's Christmas?" premiered on the radio, I snuck my Walkman into Mr. D'Angelo's science class. All of my new wave heroes on one record? No way was I going to miss that. A few months later I found myself having arguments with my classmates over which was better, Band Aid or USA for Africa. They argued that America had the bigger stars—Bruce Springsteen, Michael Jackson, Bob Dylan, Cyndi Lauper. I argued that their song had no soul. Even worse, it turned charity into an excuse for patriotism: "Only we Americans are strong enough to save the world." Today, if we are to compare the tracks purely as competing pop songs, the Brits are ultimately triumphant. Even though some of its stars are in need of a little charity themselves (whatever happened to Marilyn?), "Do They Know It's Christmas?" reemerges as a radio favorite each and every December. When was the last time you heard "We Are the World"?

MIDGE URE: I was doing *The Tube* [the TV pop show co-presented by Paula Yates, then Bob Geldof's girlfriend] up in Newcastle when I spoke to Bob and he said, "I've just seen [Buerk's] report." That was the start of it. Then Bob and I met up. He'd written something the Boomtown Rats had turned down—which shows you how good it was. He turned up with this half-baked song and played it at me, and every time he played it, it was different. He had the basic lyrics, except his original version was, "There won't be snow in Ethiopia this Christmas," which, even for him and his rubbish timing, doesn't fit. You can't make that scan.

I knocked together an arrangement of this basic idea, and I spent four days in my studio with my electronics, sampling and lifting. The drum sound at the beginning of that track is lifted from "The Hurting," by Tears for Fears. I lifted it straight off their track and told them about it 10 years later. All the multitracked vocals at the beginning, it's me sampling my voice and doing all the trickery and stuff that you do. Within the week, we had the song written. I played all the instruments of the record in my studio.

We glued it all together, all these bizarre ideas, and we had the "Feed the World" bit at the end. Then, of course, we had one day for everyone to do the song. We had to turn it around stupidly quickly to get it to pressing plants, so that we would have it ready in time for Christmas release. We had 24 hours to record all the vocals, Phil Collins's drum parts, mix the track, and get it next morning to the pressing plants, otherwise we'd miss the deadline.

When I finished the demo, I wasn't convinced it was a good song. I've now got to go in and sell the biggest artists in the world on singing this thing. A couple of them had been over to my studio earlier: Le Bon✱ had heard it, Sting had heard it. They came and sang a couple of bits beforehand. So they had heard the track, but the majority of people who turned up that day hadn't heard a thing. So they walked in expecting to sing on this dreadful piece of crap. Fortunately, it wasn't that bad.

Because of my background—I'd already produced umpteen artists, production was in my blood; I'd dealt with Visage, for God's sake!—I knew most of the

---

✱ **SIMON LE BON, Duran Duran:** My favorite thing was Francis Rossi and Rick Parfitt from Status Quo, who weren't really part of that whole new wave scene at all but were a popular rock band from the 1970s. They couldn't stop giggling. They got fits and giggles on the microphone and really couldn't sing their part. It started to piss off some of the people in the studio, but the rest of us were just falling around laughing.

"Bob wrote the line 'Tonight thank God it's them instead of you,' and Bono had a problem with it: 'Why would you sing that?'"

singers. I knew the Duran✶✶ guys and the Spandau✶✶✶ guys, and they were just as petrified as I was. They're the ones who had to stand up in front of their contemporaries and sing this thing on a Sunday morning. That's not so easy to do. Nobody was feeling the grandiosity of their existence.

We worked blind to give everyone a line each, and Bob and I don't even appear on it. We're on the chorus somewhere. It was really just down to getting people to sing a couple of lines each and see what we had. Paul Young ended up with more lines than anybody because he was hugely popular at the time, and he's just got such a great voice. Whereas with Bono, U2 were still an up-and-coming college band. Bob wrote the line "Tonight thank God it's them instead of you," and Bono had a problem with it: "Why would you sing that? Why would you say that?" Bob quite calmly explained, "It's not them rather than you. It's thank God, it's not you. You don't have to face that. We'll be sitting on Christmas Day with our families and turkeys, and these people haven't got any choice."

Lots of people couldn't make it on the

✶✶ **NICK RHODES, Duran Duran:** We were one of the first people to say yes, which I am proud of. Because I think it helped to say "I've already got Duran Duran" to get other people on board. It was such a bizarre mix to have us, Spandau and Status Quo. You had Boy George and Marilyn, and you had Paul Weller, who I seem to remember arrived on the bus. I remember Simon singing with Sting, and I loved how great their voices sounded together. I thought, *Wow, that sounds great. We should work with him again.* So we invited Sting to work with us on one song on the *Arcadia* album, on "The Promise."

✶✶✶ **TONY HADLEY, Spandau Ballet:** The night before we were in Germany on the piss with Duran, having a real good drink. By the morning, we were all pretty rough. We didn't look great. I remember arriving back at Heathrow, and someone said, "God, there's all the press, there's cameras out there, there's about 400 screaming fans." We were like, "Oh, shit!" All of a sudden we're all in the bathroom trying to make ourselves look presentable—you know, Nick Rhodes putting stacks of makeup on. I think we all put a bit of makeup on that day, actually. So we went to the studio [Sarm West in Notting Hill], and it was a very British affair. It was like, "Cup of tea and a biscuit?" We all crowded into the control room, all the singers, and Geldof said to me, "Go on in, Tony. You go and do the bit first." I went, "What?!" then, "Okay, all right, fine." So everyone's watching me as I go down the stairs into the [recording] area. At one point I was going to sing a higher bit, but I hadn't had much sleep and was a little fragile. Anyway, luckily, two takes and that was it: My bit was done.

day or didn't get it. We were desperate to get Bowie, we'd have loved to get more females, we'd love to have gotten more black artists, and it just didn't go that way. We only had the rest. It wasn't a bad selection we had. Given time, we could have balanced it out a little more.

The moment I heard Bob and Maxwell [Lord Robert Maxwell, owner of the U.K. *Daily Mirror* tabloid] scream at each other down the phone at four o'clock in the morning about who was going to get the rights to the official Band Aid shot of the artists—I think the Mirror Group wanted to sell the poster for their AIDS campaign, and Bob was saying, "Not on your fucking life. We'll take it to the *Sun*"—I knew something big was happening.

When we'd finished the record, it was eight o'clock in the morning. The master went off to the cutting rooms and then straight to the factory, and Bob went to Radio 1 with a cassette. He went on the Simon Bates show and played the cassette, and I heard it getting played over the air as I'm driving back to my little house in Chiswick. I thought, *That's something else. I've never seen anyone do that before.* I went home and had a couple of hours sleep, and when I woke up, all hell had broken loose.

THAT WAS THEN BUT THIS IS NOW

 "Do They Know It's Christmas?" was number one in the U.K. for five weeks. It sold more than 3 million copies. The following year, the Live Aid concerts in Britain and the United States were watched by an estimated 1.9 billion people across the globe, raising more than $283 million. Acts performing on the day included Adam Ant, Style Council, Ultravox, Bryan Ferry, David Bowie, Elvis Costello, U2, Spandau Ballet, Nik Kershaw, Howard Jones, Paul Young, Simple Minds, the Pretenders, the Power Station, the Thompson Twins, Duran Duran, and the Boomtown Rats. It still didn't help Bob Geldof's music career. But it did get him an honorary knighthood and a reputation as a man the very mention of whose name causes governments to quake in fear. His tireless endeavors in the field of activism have been a clear influence on Bono and countless other celebrity philanthropists.

URE: After Band Aid and Live Aid, there was a whole slew of Farm Aid and Ferry Aid that all came out.✱✱✱✱ People suffered from charity fatigue. They just got tired of it. For Band Aid and Live Aid, there was something in the air that was tangible, that was real and honest. It wasn't a cheesy "Aren't we wonderful, hey let's all get together and make the world a better place" song. It was actually quite a harsh, brutal thing. It was a very British thing to do, to come out with a song like that and punch above your weight.

It worked then, but if it's repeated and it's not an original idea, the gloss comes off it. You could see that a couple of years after Band Aid with the Nelson Mandela 70th birthday concert at Wembley. All the artists that we'd tried to get for Live Aid were all queuing up to get on the Mandela thing. It didn't quite sit right. All the record company execs outside sitting in their limos were rubbing their hands because they thought it would sell a gazillion records the way U2 did after Live Aid.

✱✱✱✱ NICK **RHODES:** I don't wish to sound disingenuous, but I think the British one was very heartfelt and naive, and then suddenly America stormed in with "We Are the World." The title alone says something to you. I wouldn't want to belittle anybody's effort. All I'm saying is that the Band Aid thing was put together very quickly. It's got a charm to it. "We Are the World" was this big, lush production. And in many ways it does define the differences between American music and British music at that time.

Is it too cynical now? Is it too easy to put something like that together now? It wouldn't be a couple of huge concerts. It would be a simulcast. It would be a pay-per-view performance. It would be on the Internet. It's a very different world. I don't know if the necessity of something like that would happen now. The necessity for doing something like that exists all the time, but whether there'd be a desire for it, I don't know. People consume music in a very different way. It doesn't seem to be as all-important as it used to be for us. Kids have got computer games and a million other things to keep themselves entertained. We had music and our imaginations, and that was it.

I'm not sure if growing up with new wave was a blessing or a curse. It was a blessing, sure, in that, as a movement, it was new and interesting and relatively erudite and filled with amazing, endearing, and sonically novel music. It was a curse, though, in that it completely screwed up my idea of what men and musicians are supposed to do and be.

See, new wave was gentle. It was introspective and, almost always, fairly yielding and soft. I mean, the toughest that new wave ever really got was Echo and the Bunnymen's "Do It Clean" live, which is still pretty gentle, all things considered. Great, but gentle.

New wave wonderfully and shamelessly (and gently, of course) borrowed (i.e., stole) from its idols and influences. Everyone, almost en masse, loved Kraftwerk and Bowie and Roxy Music. And everyone, almost en masse, shamelessly borrowed from Kraftwerk and Bowie and Roxy Music. Personally, I tried to have it both ways and straddle the early-eighties genre fence, as I was into hardcore punk at the same time I was into new wave. So I'd be listening to Black Flag and Bad Brains and then put on Spandau Ballet and Haircut 100. I loved hardcore, and I still have some facial scars from early-eighties Black Flag shows, but new wave was what spoke to me and my little postadolescent heart. I loved the idea of Circle Jerks' "Wild in the Streets," but Ultravox's "Vienna" was what I listened to over and over again.

New wave was, for me, also about geographic escapism. I lived in the suburbs of Connecticut, and new wave represented Berlin and London and Manchester and Paris and parts of the world that seemed as glamorous and far away from Connecticut as one could possibly get while still remaining on the planet. I'd put OMD's *Architecture and Morality* on my Walkman and drive around Connecticut at night pretending I was in Berlin or Manchester, wearing a black suit and talking about semiotics and synthesizers with anyone associated with Factory Records. Being a broke suburban new wave fan meant making do with whatever I could get my hands on. I couldn't afford records, so I'd tape them from my friends. I couldn't afford new clothes, so I'd try to make oversize suits from the thrift store look like something Midge Ure would wear while wandering around Prague. I couldn't afford real equipment, so I'd play my cheap Casio keyboard, imagining I was Vince Clarke playing synths with Daniel Miller somewhere in London.

One thing new wave wasn't was libidinous. The classic new wave romance songs not only didn't mention sex, they didn't even really allude to anything even remotely sexual. It was as if the new wavers decided that sex and dirty clothes were passé and that their halcyon future and present were going to be populated by sensitive androgynes wearing cool suits. This was confusing to me, as I'd try to date girls (and, later, women) and wonder why I wanted to have sex, when clearly my new wave idols only encouraged me to put on some black trousers, sit with my girlfriend, hold hands, and maybe cry a little while listening to "Charlotte Sometimes."

See, new wave had some clear "pros," like Kraftwerk, Bowie, Roxy, old suits, synthesizers, drum machines, sensitivity, gentle vocals, etc. And some clear "againsts," like work boots, jeans, pub rock, long hair, denim vests, distortion pedals, guitar solos, etc. It took me a few years in the late eighties to realize that not all pub rock made by musicians with long hair was terrible (even though, to be fair, most of it was).

And beyond the eyeliner and nice old suits and gentle lyrics, there was the actual music. Which was, to a suburban Connecticut youth, revolutionary. It was nuanced and textured and sounded like nothing else. My schoolmates were listening to "Lola" by the Kinks, and I was listening to "Joan of Arc" by OMD. My schoolmates were listening to "Sugar Magnolia" by the Dead, and I was listening to "Original Sin" by Theatre of Hate. My schoolmates' music sounded kind of old to me. Midtempo seventies rock music with no subtlety and nuance just couldn't compete, sonically or emotionally, with what was being made by Brits and Europeans with drum machines and synthesizers and analog delays. And new wavers even had the decency to make guitars

409820 HALL Richard "Moby"

not really sound like guitars. It took me a few records to figure out that Gary Numan and Ultravox even had guitar players.

New wave was its own world, with its own influences, its own sonic landscape, its own codes, its own lyrical bailiwick(s), its own aesthetics. And to a teenager growing up in sad and dry suburban Connecticut in the early eighties, new wave represented the most perfect and complete escape I could've ever hoped for. So to everyone in this book who made the records that made adolescence bearable: Thanks.

ACKNOWLEDGMENTS

LM, 1987

JB, 1984

This book simply would not exist without the passion and support of the following: David Cashion, our Abrams editor and fellow new wave obsessive; Tina Wexler and Dan Kirschen, our ICM agents; Meg Handler, our trusty photo editor; Evan Gaffney, our designer; David Blatty, Maya Bradford, Melissa Esner, Claire Bamundo, Jeffrey Yamaguchi, and everyone at Abrams; and Paul Adams, Tracey Davenport, Shirley Halperin, Moby, Patty "Punk Masters" Palazzo, Nick Rhodes, and Rey Roldan.

Thanks also to Gina Achord, Kitty Amsbury, John Ares, Tom Brennan, Zena Burns, James Carrier, Charles Charas, Beatrice Colin, Terry Cooney, Katja Deiters, Amy Galleazzi, Brian Greenspan, Brian Hayes, Jeremy Helligar, Peter Hook, Matt Isom, Katy Krassner, James Masters, Dawn Miller, Thom Monahan, Ken Phillips, Cheryl Plambeck, Julie Pocock, Lisa Revelli, Record Runner, Christopher Sacco, John Taylor, Bryan Thomson-Di Palma, Len Vlahos, Mike Wehrmann, Amy Wolfcale, and Candice Yusim.

Lori would also like to thank: her husband, John, and Baxter and Little Boy; the Majewskis and Cliffords; Susan Vaughan, Rotem Bar, Christina Ferrari, Elizabeth Stone, and Anthony "Pete" Colasurdo; Duran Duran and all her Duranie buds, including the late Patti Neske (née Girvalo) and Greg Stanuszek; and her BFF and curmudgeonly co-writer (I say that with much love), Jonathan Bernstein.

Jonathan would also like to thank the United States Immigration and Naturalization Service.

Finally, thanks to all of our new wave idols (and their many weird and wonderful fans), who so generously gave us their time, their memories and, most of all, their music.

madworldbook.com
facebook/MadWorldBook.com
@MadWorldBook
@LoriMajewski
@JBpeevish